Discovering Islam

DISCOVERING ISLAM

Making Sense of Muslim History and Society

Akbar S. Ahmed

London and New York

First published in 1988 by
Routledge & Kegan Paul Ltd

Reprinted in paperback in 1989, 1990 (twice)
and 1991 by Routledge
11 New Fetter Lane, London EC4P 4EE
29 West 35th Street, New York, NY 10001

Set in Linotron Ehrhardt
by Input Typesetting Ltd, London
and printed in England by Clays Ltd, St Ives plc

Library of Congress Cataloging in Publication Data

Ahmed, Akbar S.
Discovering Islam.
Bibliography: p.
Includes index.
1. Islam—History. 2. Islam—Essence, genius, nature.
3. Islam—20th century. I. Title.
BP52A35 1987 296′.09 87–4967

British Library Cataloguing in Publication Data also available
ISBN 0–415–03930–4

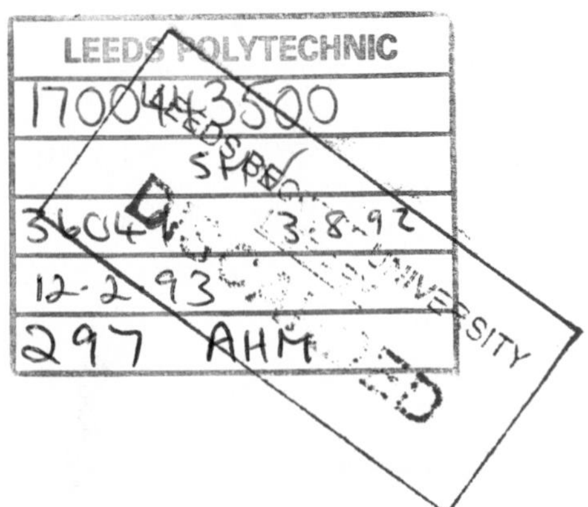

for Umar
with love

Contents

Part Two Contemporary Muslim Society

Preface

In two seminars held in Islamabad in 1985 when presenting some of the ideas in this book I cited the Urdu poet Faiz Ahmed Faiz and the Islamic scholar Maulana Mawdoodi. I was criticized by the distinguished 'rightist' scholars present for the former ('godless communist') and 'leftists' for the latter ('agent of Western imperialism'). Neither side was prepared to conduct a dialogue or attempt to understand the other point of view. Western scholars at the seminar criticized me for being too 'Islamic', some Muslims for not being Islamic enough. As I believe Islam to be the middle path – the Quranic *ummah-i-wast*, the middle nation or, to echo Imam Khomeini, *nah sharq nah gharb*, neither East nor West – and that a Muslim must steer a middle course I was unrepentant. This book will no doubt arouse similar reactions; its middle position will thereby be vindicated.

A literary rather than academic form has been adopted in order to address a wide and general readership. For this purpose footnotes and page references are omitted in the text. The South Asian usage of Arabic (*ul* for *al*, etc.) is an anthropological reflex not meant to offend the punctilious Arabist. The material is largely based on seminars given between 1982 and 1985, and what I learned from discussions with colleagues at various academic centres in Harvard, Princeton, Moscow, Delhi, Jeddah, Tokyo, Istanbul, London, Islamabad and Paris. I would like to acknowledge their hospitality and support.

The writing of the book was actually undertaken in 1985–6 when I was posted in Baluchistan. Although I enjoyed my posting, conditions in the field were not encouraging for academic work. There were no libraries or academic colleagues to consult. In Makran, where I spent most of 1985, mail and telephone connections were erratic. Because Makran was devoid of electricity – and therefore electric typewriters or copy machines – my work was slow; the first draft was flown to Karachi, over an hour's flying time, for photocopying. Furthermore, official duties did not allow a regular schedule for writing or reflection. More than once I left off in mid-sentence to settle tribal disputes, supervise flood relief, and attend to visiting VIPs; and on one occasion, in the summer of 1986, to cross into the Sind in hot pursuit of dacoits to retrieve a Baluch chieftain who had been kidnapped by them.

In a book with so vast a scope and so eternal a theme some repetition of ideas is inevitable. I am guilty of a certain amount of cannibalism. Some of the material has appeared in *Asian Affairs*, London; *The Christian Science Monitor*, USA; *Current Anthropology*, Canada; *Dawn*, Karachi; *The Guardian*, London; *Herald*, Karachi; *Journal of the Institute of Muslim Minority Affairs*, London; *The Muslim*, Islamabad; *Purusartha*, Paris; *The Royal Anthropological Institute News*, London; *The South Syndication Services*, London and *The Times of India*, Delhi. The author gratefully acknowledges the sources.

Warmly acknowledged are Professors Khurshid Ahmad, R. Abdul Wahab Boase, (the late) Ismail al-Faruqi, Ernest Gellner, Ashraf Ghani, Khalid Ishaque, T. N. Madan, Francis Robinson and Anita Weiss for their comments and stimulation during the formulation of this book. My wife provided invaluable assistance in discussing and typing the book; it is as much hers as mine.

The piety, universal tolerance, gentleness and respect for knowledge I saw in my father reflected Islamic virtues; these sustained him in difficult and changing times. The book is dedicated to my son Umar with the hope that his discovery of Islam will be the possession of those very aspects of it which I observed in his grandfather.

Akbar S. Ahmed
Sibi, Baluchistan
January 1987

1

Introduction: discovering Islam

The images of Islam prevalent in the world are of brutality, fanaticism, hatred and disorder: Libyans killing policewomen in London, Palestinians hijacking passenger planes, Iranians seizing foreign embassies and Indonesians blowing up the Borobudur temple in Java. The very names of the Muslim leaders of our times – Khomeini, Gaddafi, Arafat – have become symbols of these images. It is V. S. Naipaul's vision of Islam and Muslims (*Among the Believers: An Islamic Journey*, 1981): 'Rage was what I saw . . . Muslims crazed by their confused faith.'

These images stem partly from a lack of understanding of Islam among non-Muslims and partly from the failure by Muslims to explain themselves. The results are predictable: the hatred feeds on hatred. I saw 'kill a Muslim for Christmas' written in the London underground stations. Following a nuclear holocaust, American science fiction writer Robert Heinlein has the white survivors enslaved, men castrated and baby girls eaten by Black Muslims, neatly fusing religious and racial prejudices (*Farnham's Freehold*, first published in the 1960s). The Muslim leaders, hated and despised, are reduced to Walt Disney villains: 'Kho Maniac, Wacky Kaddafi, Yucky Arafat' ('Garbage pail adults', *MAD*, back cover, September 1986). The repugnance is contagious. Even the staid London *Economist* is not immune and panders to the stereotype: Imam Khomeini was 'Savonarola' and Colonel Gaddafi 'the Devil's godfather' on its covers. The colours, red and black, were striking and indicated hell; both men appeared minatory and forbidding.

For Muslims therefore, it is a good time to pause, to reflect, and to attempt to re-locate the main features of, to re-discover, Islam. We therefore take stock, not because we have arrived at any significant stage of the Islamic journey but because the sheer range of trajectories and approaches, and consequent confusion, obliges us to attempt clarification. The problem is not that there are too few answers but that there are too many.

This book sets out to tackle a number of important questions: how are we to understand, or discover, simply yet intelligently the history of a major world religion and its relationship with its society? What are the keys to Muslim society – those which will allow us to make sense of how Muslims behave, what motivates them, what are their concepts of right and wrong? How are we to explain the turbulence in contemporary Muslim society which has helped to create the negative images of Islam?

We need answers to other related issues in the Islamic world: how are we to make sense in Turkey of the tensions generated by the pull of an Islamic identity on the one hand and a European one on the other? Of the seemingly endless Shia revolution in Iran? Of the ongoing process of Islamization in Pakistan? Are there common themes linking these societies, universal principles that we can discern? Or is each society responding to earlier, atavistic obsessions reflected in the complex relationship of Christian Europe to Turkey, in the history of Shiaism in Iran, and in the relation of Hinduism to South Asian Muslims, the inheritors of Pakistan? Can we make any sense of Muslim history? Or is it all random dates, the rise and fall of despots and dynasties living in marble buildings and gilded harems? Is the past dead, ossified in mechanical ritual and neglected holy texts? Or is it part of our lives?

In attempting to answer these questions I have written this book which developed as a result of travel, talk and reading. Writing the book confronted me with my ignorance, with how little I know; it also stimulated me to learn and listen. The task is daunting. And living in a world of change and crisis I am ill-equipped for it. The book has had to be honest. I am not impressing examiners or pleasing audiences.

For me personally – in an Islamic sense when I have just turned 40, the critical age for Muslims – it is an appropriate time to attempt the exercise. The voyage in search of Islam is a journey into my own past. It is a voyage that opens doors to the past taking me straight to the seventh century. It is also a voyage of self-discovery. The attempt to peer into myself, my culture and my roots was stimulating and gratifying, but also disturbing.

As a Muslim I cannot write this book as a neutral spectator or observer. I am also a participant, an actor in the drama. Muslim triumphs stir me, Muslim failures create despair in me. Like Allama Iqbal I was deeply moved in the long-deserted mosque at Cordova, once a dazzling city of Andalusia, Spain. Still young, an undergraduate in England, I felt a strange nostalgia, a bitter-sweet emotion, as if I had been there before. I failed to understand the inexplicable effect of Andalusia and the fate of its people – the Moors – over my mood. Later, understanding, I would call it the Andalus syndrome, the fear of extinction induced by the fate of the Moors, which would permanently haunt Muslim society (see 'The Andalus syndrome in south India', in chapter 8).

I was able to see some of the majesty of Islam, the greatness of its men and women, and, elsewhere, sense the confusion in contemporary Muslim society, discover the transparent hypocrisy of some of its leaders. The exercise created in me a sense of belonging to a larger whole; it also made me aware of the diverse elements that influence my own life. The book is thus part autobiography, part history, part literature and part science.

The Muslim ideal

In order to help answer the questions posed above I will create a key, a model, an ideal-type. Max Weber's concept of the ideal or pure type is a useful one. But we must bear in mind its limitations. It depicts an average derived over time which reflects combinations, mixtures and modifications. It is only an approximation of, not a substitute for, reality.

With these qualifications, we base our ideal in seventh-century Arabian society. The device will assist in explaining Muslim society and history from the inception of Islam to our times, and over space from one kind of society on one continent to another on a different one. As we apply it we will learn about different places and times.

The two key elements of Islam, supporting and inter-locking, are firmly and unequivocally located in one book and one life (chapter 2). The holy Quran is the single divine Book of the Muslims and the life is that of Muhammad, the Prophet of Islam, which constitutes the *sunna* – his behaviour, practice, sayings and values. Together they form the *Shariah*, the 'path' for Muslims. Further instruction is obtained from the lives of the Prophet's companions. The Prophet's own position is central to Islam. The fundamental Islamic declaration of faith rests in belief in Allah and acceptance of Muhammad as the Prophet.

Together the two, a book and a life – 'we are calling out to you with the Quran in our right hand and the *sunna* in our left' Hassan al-Banna would proclaim in Egypt – define and inspire the Muslim, affecting his life from birth to death. They are the primary sources of Islam. They provide us with a good idea of how a person ought to conduct himself to be called a Muslim. The ideal aims at paradise in the next world and satisfaction, if not success, in this one. We thus have not only a way of looking at the world but of living in it.

My main argument, simply put, runs thus: the ideal is eternal and consistent; Muslim society is neither, as we will see. Islamic history offers abundant evidence that there is a dynamic relationship between society and the striving of holy and learned Muslims for the ideal (chapter 3, 'A theory of Islamic history'). The vision of the ideal, and aspiration to it, provide Muslim society with its dynamics. In the face of powerful rival forces or weak leadership Muslims have slipped from the ideal. Tension, change and challenge are created as people living in an imperfect world strive for it. The ideal allows each individual to possess a charter of action. Its interpretation too is individualistic, providing it with a dynamic and volatile nature. From the Kharijis who assassinated Ali, to the Shias who deified him, to the Wahabis, who desecrated his tomb, it has provided a charter of action (also see 'Mahdism and millenarian movements', in chapter 3). Thus the ideal provides an inbuilt mechanism in Muslim society for constant renewal and revival of faith.

The constant pressures from within to renew, change and reform, across the Muslim world are neither modern nor new; they represent the quest for the ideal in an imperfect world. Islam was always reviving after declining; always being re-discovered after being neglected. As I will illustrate, this revivalism or resurgence is not a twentieth century phenomenon. The sense of déjà-vu which permeates Muslim society is not so much a reliving as the recreating of the past. The more the times change, the more certain features in society remain the same.

The Western perception of the revivalism, rediscovery or resurgence of Islam is faulty, as the West links it with Arab oil, PLO guerillas and Imam Khomeini. This is a mistake. The phenomenon has been in motion since the seventh century, continually emphasizing the drive to return to the Golden Age, the ideal times of the Prophet. Non-Muslims would usefully understand the return in the context of striving for the ideal and its values, not a turning back of the clock to remote, earlier times.

Certain fundamental problems which accompanied Islam's rapid expansion and universal message, particularly the persistence of pre-Islamic social and cultural systems also need consideration. In the following chapters we will see how Islamic notions of society, history and politics were imposed on local structures and organizations, sometimes merging, sometimes clashing with them.

Islam comes with definite, specific ideas and does not encourage duality. We thus see the tension in the villages, away from the centres of Islamic learning, between the Islamic macro world-view and the day-to-day humdrum values dealing with kin and cattle of village society. It is the stress in society between what social scientists call the Great Tradition of a world religion and the Little Tradition of local, regional, village culture. We will define the latter as ethnicity and illustrate through cases how it is an important source of stress in contemporary Muslim society.

'In certain ways Muslims are the same everywhere, and yet their societies are different everywhere,' I wrote in an earlier book (*Religion and Politics in Muslim Society*, 1983). Confronted by the wide range and diversity of Muslim societies, the present generation of write[illegible]ggests their categorization thus: Moroccan Islam (Dale Eickelman, 197[illegible]stani Islam, Malay Islam and so on. 'One is bound to conclude that th[illegible] not one Islam but many Islams' (Edward Mortimer, *Faith and Power:* [illegible]*itics of Islam*, 1982). But the categorization is not new. It is at least as [illegible] as European colonization: for instance,

Indian Islam, by Murray Titus (1930). This is the easy way out. And it not only simplifies grossly, it also distorts. It is no answer.

We will attempt an answer below. For as it is true that in the thought of Muslim scholars and in their texts there is clarity, and a broad consensus regarding the ideal, it is also equally true that the way Muslims order their lives is sometimes far from the ideal. Economic, political and ethnic – social, cultural – pressures act to compromise notions of the ideal, thereby creating ambiguity around it. The demarcation of Muslim societies is therefore not a division between white ideal and black non-ideal but an ongoing relationship between the two marked by areas of grey. Taken together the arguments raised above will assist us in our search for a world-view, an Islamic world-view of society and history.

South Asian perspective

Although I have attempted a universalistic frame of reference a South Asian bias is apparent in the material. The perspective remains tinted by my South Asian location and experience which affect my understanding and interpretation. I maintain that my material can no more be rejected for its South Asian bias than that of Ibn Khaldun for containing a North African one. I do not wish to be apologetic about it.

In some important senses South Asia is one of the most crucial and dynamic areas for Islam. Its population alone is almost 40 per cent of the total Muslim population. The region is placed between the Middle East, Central Asia and South East Asia; it is a filter and store-house of diverse human knowledge.

The role of the South Asian Muslim is a remarkable one in the modern Muslim renaissance. Some of the most renowned and influential Muslim thinkers of the twentieth century – Iqbal, Azad and Mawdoodi – have lived here. The first Nobel Prize winner in Muslim countries comes from Pakistan. So does Faiz Ahmed Faiz, the most celebrated Urdu poet in recent times and winner of the Lenin Peace Prize. Salman Rushdie, another South Asian, is the only Muslim to win the Booker Prize for literature. Seven of the ten authors in the first major book on Islamic social sciences, *Social and Natural Sciences: The Islamic Perspective* (1981), edited by two distinguished Arabs, Ismail al-Faruqi and Abdullah Naseef, are South Asian; so are the leading Islamic economists (see chapter 10). But it is not all brains for South Asian Muslims. They have also made a mark where brawn is required: in cricket the world's fastest bowler is Imran Khan; in squash the world champions are the Khan family; in hockey there is a generation of Pakistani Olympic gold medallists.

The South Asian perspective also explains why the refugees discussed in chapter 9 are Afghans not Palestinians. The Palestinian refugees command wide sympathy and support among South Asian Muslims, but the Afghans are closer to home, their tragedy more recent, their wounds fresher. Also, while

Israel is important, for South Asians it is not the main focus of ideological wrath and strategic interest which it is for Arab Muslims. But the Israeli question is implicit in the discussions of Saladin, who re-took Jerusalem for the Muslims (chapter 3, section 3), the Islamic offensive under King Faisal of Saudi Arabia (chapter 8), and its support by the USA in spite of actions such as the slaughter at Sabra and Shatilla (chapters 10 and 11).

The one constant – a perpetual source of wonder and surprise – is that our perspective and therefore perceptions differ depending on where we stand. Walking in Regent's Park, London, after lunch with the Islamic historian Professor Francis Robinson, I enjoyed the perfect day in June. The sky was a clear blue, the flower beds were ablaze with colour, the fountains sparkled with bubbling water and the birds chirped and darted about with abandon. The smell of roses and fresh-cut grass was almost intoxicating. 'This', I sighed, 'must be what heaven is like.' 'An Islamic vision,' replied Francis. 'I would prefer less green, less water, more brown, more sand, date-palms and above all, warmer weather.'

Marx, Mao and Moon

We in the late twentieth century are confronted with a bewildering legacy of faith, ideology and myth, with a modern apparatus of secularism and disbelief overlaying it. We confront a complex and diverse choice of beliefs and ideologies which compete for and motivate social groups. Karl Marx, Jim Jones, Bhagwan Rajneesh, Mao, Gandhi, and the Reverend Moon – where does one stop? – convey different messages to their followers. Orthodox texts are translated, sometimes mutated beyond recognition, in the context of regional, social and political conditions; Catholic priests lead Marxist peasant revolts in Latin America; communists publicly criticize Marx in China; North Korea is a Marxist show-piece, South Korea a capitalist one; Yemen is divided into Marxist and orthodox Muslim halves. It is not an easy world to understand.

In spite of the work of Karl Marx and Max Weber we are still on the threshold of knowledge about the way societies develop and behave. The relationship of religion and culture with society is still under examination. Europe, and to an extent the USA, developed because religion, the church, was separated from the state, we are informed in learned theses. Japan on the other hand, did so because of its religious culture, its traditional society. India's take-off is inhibited by the density of the spiritual content and values in society; South Korea's progress includes spiritual values. The paradoxes remain unresolved; the experts still search for answers.

It is not easy to find one's bearing in the bewildering range of intellectual positions. And if one is a Muslim it is more confusing. Abdallah Laroui, a Moroccan academic, has described some of the powerful cross-currents in the Muslim world (*The Crisis of the Arab Intellectual*, 1977). Islam's positive views on the widest possible range of subjects do not help. Take the perennial controversy in the social sciences, the 'nature' versus 'nurture' debate, as an example. The former explains human behaviour through innate, inherited characteristics, the latter through acquired ones based on upbringing. Islam is on the side of the latter. How a child is brought up determines how he behaves and thinks in later life. 'Every infant is born in the natural state, it is his parents who make him a Jew or a Christian or a heathen', said the Prophet. It is tempting therefore to see choices, as many do, between black and white, Marx or Muhammad.

God was dead for Marx; for Weber the tension between 'science' and the sphere of 'the holy' was unbridgeable. The Western, industrial world was learning to live without the notion of God. But Nature abhors a vacuum. The void was filled with ideas of fascism, nationalism, socialism and capitalism, all presupposing those of materialism.

We may trace the important conceptual roots of contemporary social theorists – Marx, Weber, Malinowski, Lévi-Strauss – to notions derived from materialism, in particular that of exchange, whether of food, sex, shells or money. These ideas are embedded in the European industrial society within which the social scientists lived. The central notions, indicators of these theories, are reciprocity, transactions, networks, optimization and maximization. Exchange defines and engenders relationships between people who attempt to optimize and maximize. The transactions tend to dehumanize people as they attempt to extract the best possible terms through every means available.

'Alienation' for Marxism, 'repression' for Freudian analysis and 'anomie' for Durkheimian sociology, the pivotal concepts of Western social sciences, may be translated literally: conflict and disorder are suggested. These ideas are only partially, and only in special cases, applicable to non-European traditional societies. For when the Western masters of modern thought ventured to write about African and Asian peoples they often became victims of what they attacked: colonial and racial prejudice. Their work is scattered with common inaccuracies and fallacious myths. If they were not such respectable icons they would have attracted the criticism reserved for Orientalists – those who interest themselves in the Orient, once picturesquely described as East of Suez. But bits and pieces of their philosophy are available in large parts of the Muslim world and although only half-understood, they continue to excite and stimulate.

Islam has much to give to the twentieth century. Perhaps not in terms of politics – there are too many estranged kings and colonels with Muslim names. But, on another level, traditional rural and tribal life reflect continuity and stability in contrast to Islamic politics. The calm and continuity are perhaps best symbolized by the Muslim call to prayer which wafting, sinuously lingering, in mid-air calls people to a life of reflection, goodness and peace.

'Islam', Professor Ernest Gellner wrote, 'did not engender the modern world, but it may yet, of all the faiths, turn out to be the one best adapted to it' (in the foreword to *From Nationalism to Revolutionary Islam*, edited by S. A. Arjomand, 1984). It will only be so if we are able to draw from Islam its core values of peace, truth, knowledge and brotherhood so that they serve humanity. None of the major problems facing human society – poverty, population, pollution, famine and refugees – are specifically Muslim problems. But they form a sad legacy to pass on to the twenty-first century, a poor commentary of our times.

Discovering Islam

Islam in the future will continue to be a dynamic force in Muslim society, checking growth in certain directions, encouraging it in others. Unlike those societies which have relegated religion to the place of worship only, Islam will continue to pervade all aspects of life in Muslim societies: Islam as dress, as food and as behaviour. And there are a great many Muslims about who will be influenced by these ideas.

There are estimated to be over 800 million Muslims. Muslim enthusiasts inflate the figure to one billion, about twenty percent of the world population. Almost one in every four nations in the world – about forty-four – are Muslim. The number tends to fluctuate at the margin as they fuse – Egypt and Syria – or fissure – Pakistan into Bangla Desh. The populations in these nations do not represent the full strength of Muslims. Large Muslim minorities live in non-Muslim nations, notably India, the Soviet Union and China.

While the twentieth century cannot reject Islam – it is here to stay as a force – in turn, Islam must accept the twentieth century. It will not go away, and rejection is the easy way out. Islam must come to terms with the twentieth century; by doing so it will come to terms with itself.

There appears to be uncontrollable emotion in Muslim society which sweeps everything before it, preventing the Islamic resurgence from being harnessed. We Muslims need reason and argument to make sense of the Islamic passion. Mine is the statement of a Muslim concerned about his society yet acutely aware of its tensions and those generated from the world around it. One answer is to lull ourselves into believing that when we look into the mirror we see perfection. Like the Greek god Narcissus we fall in love with ourselves. I call this Narcissistic anthropology. It will lead nowhere.

Being Muslim allows me special insights but also places certain constraints upon me. In any case, as I have suggested elsewhere (Ahmed, 1983; *Toward Islamic Anthropology*, 1986) the role of the neutral social scientist is almost mythical. In most cases he is both actor and observer. To present an accurate, objective view he must learn to balance the two roles.

It is not a good time to look at Muslims. The earlier breadth of vision, tolerance and self-assurance are missing. A new element of hysteria, shrill and discordant, has entered. Khomeini condemns Saddam Hussain as *shaitan*, devil, the USA as the Great Satan; Arabs view Israel in similar terms; others denounce the Arab princes as debauched wastrels; under the Qadi of Madinah a commission found Colonel Gaddafi guilty of apostasy.

The colonial era has left deep scars. Rejecting the West, berating it for the shortcomings of our world, is seductive, an easy way out. We remain transfixed with the image of the aggressor, the predator; it is part of the colonial legacy. But it is time to turn our gaze inwards. We need to look at ourselves realistically, clinically; as we are not as we imagine we are.

Muslim arguments rapidly degenerate into aggressive polemics or apologetics. Most Muslims see such an exercise as an on-going, sometimes virulent, debate with Christianity and Judaism. Spirited defence is provided as to why the Prophet married so many wives, etc. For me such polemics and apologetics are sterile.

Islam's bad press goes beyond the colonial period. It is partly a result of the posture of conflict or confrontation at one stage or another with almost all the world's universal religions. For more than a millennium Islam confronted Judaism, Christianity, Buddhism and Hinduism. Conflict and hatred, but sometimes also synthesis as we will see below, marked the encounters.

This book is meant neither as apologetics nor as an attack but as a statement. Indeed for me personally the encounter with the West – at some of its most attractive places, Cambridge, Harvard, Princeton – has been neither bitter nor barren. The different perspectives have shown me how similar the problems of mankind are, how they lie embedded in the universal civilization of which we are part, and how confronting these problems help one to understand oneself and one's society.

History will be presented here in broad sweeps, in ways which traditional historians may not approve. Society will be generalized about in a manner calculated to cause anguish to traditional anthropologists. Issues will be simplified and broad conclusions drawn. The approach will not be encyclopedic. Our history will be interpretative not narrative. Although the arguments in the book are simplified, the method of the social scientist – reliance on case studies – is employed; and from these cases general principles will be drawn.

The sights, noises and smells of Islam's cities and villages – the full range of a living civilization – are presented in order to help discover Islam. We will not discuss classic architecture, rare calligraphy and ethereal music. Our discovery is rooted in society.

The book consists of an introductory chapter and two parts. Chapter 2 examines the social significance of the life of the Prophet in early Muslim society. It suggests the ideal of Muslim behaviour based on that life and the holy Book. The Arab stage of Muslim history, Umayyads and Abbasids, is then reviewed in the next chapter. This review of early Muslim history will illuminate subsequent social and cultural developments.

Islam carried a message of peace, of universalism, of brotherhood, of the unity of human beings. This is contained in the Quranic verses *la ikra fi ad-din*, 'there shall be no compulsion in religion', and *lakum dinukum wa lyedin*, 'your religion for you and mine for me'. But that is not the full story. Let us not romanticize it; not all Muslims heeded the Quran. The spread of Islam was often accompanied by hatred, oppression and brutality. The legacy of Islamic conquest remains to haunt Muslims in areas where they are no longer in command, as in India. Muslim history and society are not free of ignorance and tyranny. These are Muslim lapses, not Islamic qualities.

Islam also encountered other world religions, caste and race divisions. Its own society was affected. Accretion and synthesis resulted from the encounter. Society was to remain in flux, rejecting and absorbing elements of what would become central obsessions, Christianity for the Ottoman Turks, Hinduism for the Muslims of South Asia. Therefore an attempt is made in chapter 4 to draw universal principles, common themes, from the history and society of the three great Muslim empires, the Ottomans, the Saffavids and the Mughals and identify their central obsessions.

It is easy to be dazzled by the caliphs and sultans of Islam when looking at history. But Muslim history is not all conquest and kings nor anecdotes of lusty emperors and bored empresses. It is also the lives of the saints, mystics and scholars, which forms the subject of chapter 5. The latter, forming a sort of opposition party to the establishment, often speak for the dispossessed in society, the ordinary villager, the remote tribesman. However opposed the two, kings and saints, there are interesting convergences and configurations between them around the notion of the ideal.

Muslim groups living on the periphery of what were once Muslim empires and in isolated groups are discussed in chapter 6. In recent centuries they found themselves in danger of being overwhelmed by larger non-Muslim populations. Their response was either to fight, *jihad*, or migrate, *hijra*. The precedent to migrate under extreme pressure was established by the Prophet's own *hijra* from Makkah to Madinah. An interesting alternative appears to be emerging in the cases of the large Muslim minorities in India, the USSR and China. The adjustment between Muslims and the majority in these nations is a painful and still unfolding story. But what is important is that both majority and minority are learning to live with each other; an alternative to *jihad* and *hijra* is available.

Chapter 7 discusses the impact of the colonial period on Muslim society. Also discussed is the myth of the noble savage created by Europeans around certain Muslim tribesmen, in particular the Berber, Bedouin and Pukhtun.

Part Two concerns contemporary Muslim society and contains various cases.

Although Islam for a Muslim is a neat and tidy way of explaining the world, and the hereafter, satisfactorily, society is not so. It is untidy with many loose ends and rough edges; explanations for its behaviour are often unsatisfactory. Islam and Muslim society do not always fit and the cases will illustrate the levels of conjunction and disjunction between the two. The cases in chapter 8 have been selected to reflect different kinds of society, thereby allowing us to appreciate how Muslims adjust the ideal to their circumstances. Saudi Arabia, in which Muslims dominate, and south India, in which they are an impoverished minority, provide us with two kinds of examples. The cases in the next chapter are chosen to represent problems which have assumed significance in contemporary society: tribalism, under its modern guise of ethnicity; the position of women in the actual world as distinct from the ideal; and the fragmented lives of political refugees.

The sorry state of contemporary Muslim academic life and the birth pangs of Islamic social sciences are the subjects of chapter 10. The final chapter contains Muslim perceptions of Western – particularly American – society. The concept of individualism in the West is contrasted with Islam's emphasis on the group. The chapter attempts to pull in the arguments suggesting the need to 'connect' between different groups and peoples. The suggestion is rooted in traumatic childhood memories of my family's migration from India to Pakistan in 1947. The *hijra* indicates that the themes of Islamic history repeat themselves.

Viewed together the cases allow us to make sense of Muslim society in the context of its history. They also enable us to see the extent of conjunction between the ideal and the actual in different 'real-life' situations. Sometimes harmony, sometimes contradiction in Muslim societies are perceived through the cases: evidence of a live community living by and up to an ideal. By the end of the book we may not have fully discovered our subject but we will be aware of its diversity, complexity and richness. By juxtaposing Muslim voices, from the earliest days of Islam to the contemporary period, we are allowed to witness the panorama of Muslim history, savour its richness and wonder at the diversity of its society.

The book reflects the times which Muslims live in. The few Islamic voices which speak with learning and courage are isolated. The intellectuals are bankrupt; the saints invisible. We will find answers to the questions posed above only by inquiry and scholarship – and that side of Muslim civilization appears to be dead. The modern Muslim intellectual exists in a state of despair, torn between an ideal world he cannot order and a reality he cannot master.

Revolution, riots and rebellion shake Muslim society. Muslim nations, across the world, confront Muslim neighbours with unease and often hostility negating the concept of Muslim brotherhood. To confuse matters further most of the Muslim nations are ruled by authoritarian figures in or out of uniform often employing an Islamic idiom to support their rule. Ethnicity and nationalism create divisions in the community, destroying the notion of Muslim brotherhood. A chilling sense of Islamic dissolution is setting in. There is thus an urgency in our task of discovering Islam.

PART ONE

The Pattern of Islamic History

2

Muslim ideal: holy Book and Prophet

There is no better way to discover Islam than to climb Mount Hira, a few miles from Makkah. The ascent provides insights into the nature of Islam and its Prophet. On the bleak top the winds blow with ferocity, creating a sense of elemental power, exactly as it must have been in the seventh century. The place speaks of a man looking for solitude, of a man searching for answers. Here the Prophet suffered the agony of rejecting an old religion, and experienced the ecstasy of discovering a new one. There is nothing man-made on the peak. Abruptly loneliness, then awe, and finally exaltation fill the heart. In the most profound sense one is face to face with oneself.

The cave, the Prophet's refuge, is tiny. It points to Makkah and the *haram sharif*, containing the Kaaba, is faintly visible. The drop from the cave is sheer, about 2,000 feet. The climb itself is steep. I, not much older than the Prophet when he received the call to Islam at 40, was stiff the next day. Praying on the spot, in the cave, where Islam was revealed is highly evocative for a Muslim. Away from the crowds, from the signs of our age, Mount Hira is a unique experience – one of the most exhilarating of my life.

When the Prophet was about 40, in 610, on a retreat on Mount Hira he saw a vision. This was the first call. It came in the form of an angel ordering him to read – *iqra* – (hence Quran, reading). 'Read', commanded the angel. Frightened, the Prophet stammered, 'I do not read'. Twice more the angel ordered him to read and the third time replied: 'Read in the name of your Lord, the Creator, who created man of a clot of blood. Read. Your Lord is most gracious. It is He who taught man by the pen that which he does not know.' The Quran was then revealed to him.

The Prophet was the culmination of a long line of prophets – 124,000 of them – many no more than good, exemplary people. He was the last, the seal, of the prophets, the final messenger of God. The prophets did not claim divinity. They were humans entrusted by God to spread the word. The Prophet of Islam had brought the Quran which was, like him, final and cumulative.

The holy Quran

The holy Quran is a collection of divinely inspired utterances and discourses. It is a book of some 300 pages divided into 114 chapters called Surahs. These are arranged roughly in order of length except for the short and popular prayer which constitutes Surah 1, *Al Fatihah*, the opening; Surah 2, *Al Baqarah*, the cow, has 286 verses; Surah 3, *Al Imran*, the family of Imran, has 200; Surah 4, *An Nisa*, women, has 177, and so on down to the final Surahs which have only 3 – 6 short verses. As the Madinan are generally the longer ones the order is not chronological. The formula '*Bismillah ar-Rahman ar-Rahim*', 'in the name of Allah, the Beneficent, the Merciful', is prefixed to every Surah except one.

For our purposes – to explore an ideal of social behaviour – Surah 17, *Al Isra*, the children of Israel, is important. It reflects those aspects of the Prophet's social behaviour we are emphasizing. Be kind to parents, kin, the poor and the wayfarer, exhorts the Surah. Do not be a spend-thrift, kill, commit adultery or cheat, it warns. Boasting and false pride are condemned and honesty lauded. When humans err, and if they are sincere, 'God forgives those who repent.'

The general tone of the holy Quran is sombre and meditative. It is a dialogue between God and humanity. At the core is a moral earnestness. Because it is not an academic thesis it needs no structure, no order, no introduction and conclusion. It is a vibrant outpouring of divine messages, of powerful bursts reflecting different moods. It warns, advises and exhorts in flashes. The Quranic impulses, arriving like claps of thunder, cover the entire gamut of life. Its language is eloquent, its imagery awesome; its scope is humankind and no less. Man and woman are given the highest possible status, that of vicegerent of God on earth. The Quran repeatedly points them to knowledge: *ilm* is the second most used word in the Quran after the name of God. Human beings are told to use their mind and think in at least 300 places.

Forgiveness and compassion are presupposed in the ninety-nine names of Allah contained in the Quran. If we divided the ninety-nine names into those with positive attributes – truth, justice, mercy and compassion – and those with negative ones – suggesting anger and retribution – we would have only four or five in the second category. When man errs Allah is indeed *Muntaqim* (the Avenger). But along with being the Avenger Allah is also *al-Afu* (the Pardoner) and *at-Tawab* (the Accepter of repentance).

Above all, Allah is *ar-Rahman*, the Beneficent, and *ar-Rahim*, the Merciful. By containing these two attributes the common Muslim recitation, *Bismillah ar-Rahman ar-Rahim*, underlines their significance in understanding Allah. In addition, Allah is *al-Mohaymin*, the Protector, *al-Ghaffar*, the Forgiver, *ar-Razzaq*, the Provider, and *al-Ghafur*, the All-Forgiving. Allah is also the Just, *al-Adl*, representing the Truth, *al-Haq*, the Source of All Goodness, *al-Barr*, and the Light, *an-Noor*.

Allah emerges as generous and compassionate. Humanity has been created by Allah and therefore Allah understands its weaknesses. And because Allah is dealing with human beings who are sometimes fickle and sometimes uncertain Allah is *as-Sabur*, Patient. In Allah humans find the source of peace, *as-Salam*, for Allah is Loving, *al-Wadud*, and Wise, *al-Hakim*.

The five 'pillars' – obligatory duties – of Islam sum up its essence: *tauhid*, faith in one God, unity; *salat*, the daily prayers, a constant reminder of the transitory nature of life and *tauhid*; *sawm*, fasting during the month of Ramadan to develop moral and physical discipline; the annual *zakat* to re-distribute wealth to the poorer sections of society; and *haj*, the pilgrimage, once in a lifetime, to be part of the annual congregation of Muslims in Makkah. Islamic ritual emphasized unity among the Muslim community, the brotherhood, the *ummah;* its philosophy emphasized peace, *salaam* (hence Islam).

Islam's appeal lay – and lies – in its simplicity: one God, one Book, one Prophet. It was a tidy, uncomplicated religion with clearly defined ritual. But the simplicity was deceptive. Layers of profundity covered it. As a boy I thought the five daily prayers were meant to instil discipline – the regular washing and waking at early hours in preparation for prayers and the bowing and bending during them. Later, in manhood, I gradually perceived the deeper significance of the prayers. They were a constant reminder of the transient, passing nature of the world. And, related to this, a constant declaration of the permanence of Allah. Muslim prayers can create sublimity around the believer, peace within.

The Muslim ideal rests on the important Quranic concepts of *al-adl*, equilibrium, and *al-ahsan*, compassion. A life based on these is a balanced one. Islam is a religion of balance, equilibrium, of the middle. The Islamic virtues are courage, generosity, cleanliness and piety; and in his life the Prophet exemplifies them.

The Prophet

With the revelation of the Quran Islam came to the world and Muhammad became the Prophet. The Prophet had initially to convert Makkah. Makkah was a busy and wealthy commercial town almost monopolizing the entrepôt trade between the Indian Ocean and the Mediterranean trading centres. This was mainly due to its location on the international trade route from the south to the north, which included the route from Africa. We know that Muhammad's great-grandfather Hashim, who gave his name to the clan, died in Syria while on a trade expedition.

Makkah, where Muhammad was born in 570, was the proud heart of a fiercely inturned Arab tribal society. Arabs prided themselves on their ancestry, *nasab*. For them the Arab was the noblest of nations (*afkhar al-umam*). Among the Arabs the Quraysh considered themselves the aristocrats. The Quraysh,

Genealogical chart: the Prophet's kin.
(Names of those who played an important role in the Prophet's lifetime or immediately afterwards are underlined.)

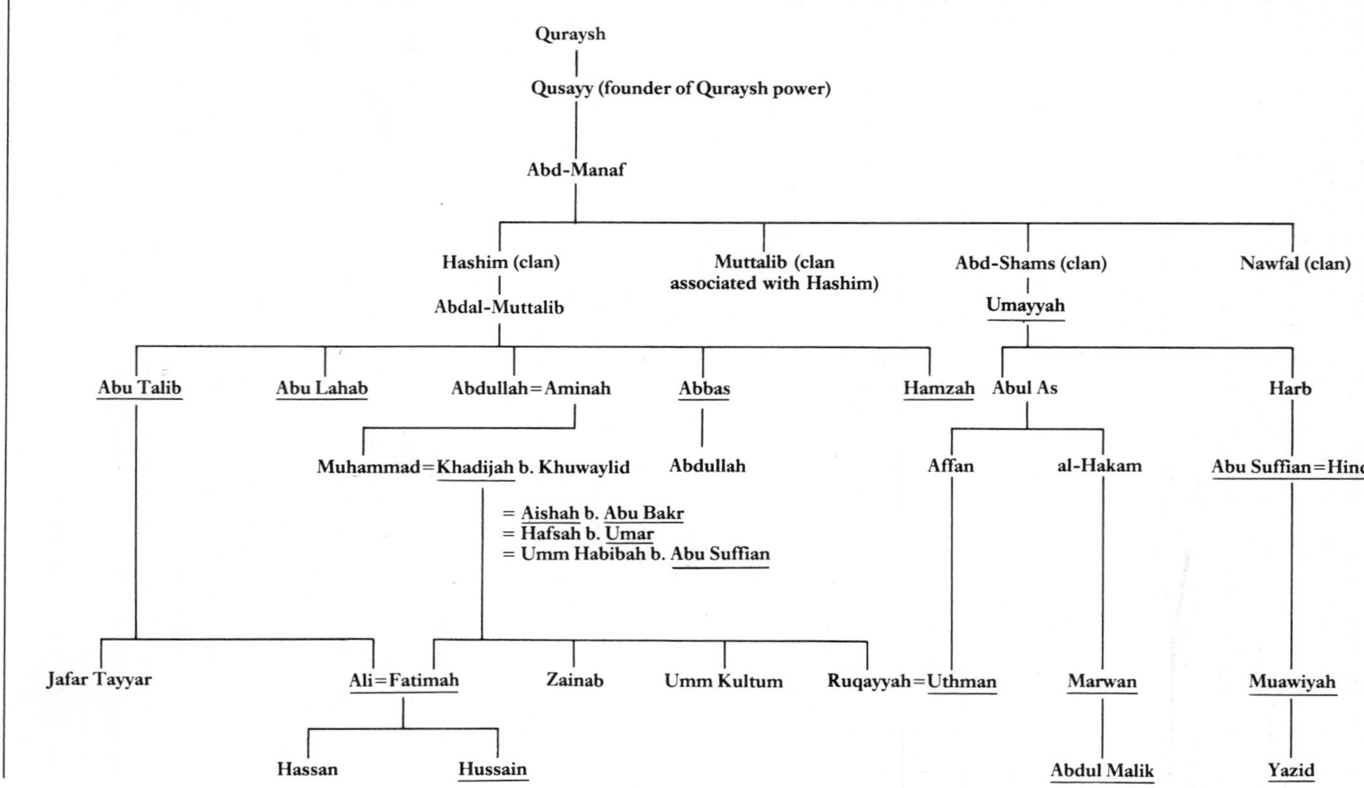

divided into numerous competing clans – our story in chapters 2 and 3 concerns the rivalry between the Hashims and the Umayyads – dominated Makkah. Like recently urbanized groups they held their desert cousins, the Bedouin, in contempt. Exclusive tribal codes, animistic practices, female infanticide, worship of some 360 competing idols, were the characteristics of society. This the Prophet set out to change.

Among the first to accept Islam were Khadijah, the Prophet's wife, allied to the powerful Umayyad clan and his senior in years, Ali, his cousin, then about ten years old, and the venerable Abu Bakr.

After Muhammad announced his mission to the world the Quraysh rulers of Makkah were understandably outraged by his preaching. He was claiming Muslims were equal, 'Like the teeth of a comb.' There were no lineages nor castes in Islam: *la bedawi fil Islam* – 'there is no Bedouinism in Islam'. Muhammad's God demanded 'justice, the doing of the good and liberality to kith and kin.' Worse, his God criticized their wanton ways: 'He forbids all shameful deeds, injustice and rebellion.' Female infanticide, promiscuity and alcohol were all forbidden.

Equality, the status of women, the rights of the less privileged (minorities, poorer working groups) – the shibboleths of our age – were reflected in the Prophet's message. It was a revolution the Prophet wished to bring about, to end what came to be known as the *Jahiliyya*, the dark age. The Quraysh, led by the Umayyads, opposed him resolutely. Hard-headed men, they were also concerned about the effect of his teachings on trade.

The first years after the call were difficult ones for the Prophet. Until recently he had been widely respected as Al Amin, the trustworthy; now he was the object of anger and hate. Abuse and persecution were heaped on him in Makkah by the Quraysh. At one stage the Prophet ordered groups of Muslims to migrate to Abyssinia in order to escape. But there were hopeful signs too. Important conversions took place such as that of Umar ibn al-Khattab in 616. Shortly after this two of the Prophet's most loyal supporters, Abu Talib, his uncle, and Khadijah, his wife, died in 619. Pressure on the Prophet and the small band of Muslims increased. In the forefront of the campaign to discomfit the Prophet was his uncle Abu Jahl. The breaking point had been reached. The Prophet resolved to accept an invitation from the people of Madinah. He was not a complete stranger to the town: his grandmother belonged to the Khazraj, one of its two major Arab tribes.

In the summer of 622 the Prophet left Makkah and arrived in Madinah, a journey that was to change the history of the world. It was called the *hijra*, or migration, and marks the beginning of the Muslim calendar. His party of migrants were called *muhajirs*, refugees, the natives of Madinah *ansars*, helpers. It was an act that has been suggestive to Muslims throughout history, the transition from *dar-al-harb*, the land of war, to *dar-al-Islam*, land of Islam, or peace (see chapter 9, section 3 and chapter 11, section 2).

In Makkah the Prophet had propagated a new message, triumphant over a conversion one moment, concerned over a failure another, always under pressure. In Madinah he arrived as ruler, laying the foundations of a nascent state and religion. He now began to establish his community. One of the first tasks was to provide the charter of Madinah – a sort of Magna Carta – which announced the rights and obligations of all citizens, Jews and Muslims.

A series of important battles followed as the Quraysh attempted to crush the young religion: Badr in 624, Uhud (625), the battle of the Ditches (627), and Khayber (628). Of these perhaps Badr, the first major battle of Islam, is the most critical. Indeed historians rank Badr as one of the most decisive engagements in history. If the Muslims had lost Islam might well have perished. The numbers were small: 313 Muslims against some 900 opponents led by Abu Suffian, the Umayyad. Ali and Hamzah emerged as heroes at Badr. We may obtain an idea of how severely the Quraysh felt their defeat from the fact that Abu Suffian vowed never to wash until he defeated the Prophet. Hind, his wife, forsook fat, perfumes and her husband's bed until that event. Women shaved their hair and whipped themselves into a frenzy declaring a month of mourning in Makkah. But the tide had turned in favour of Islam.

In 630 the Muslims won another victory at Hunayn. In this battle Abu Suffian fought alongside the Muslims, having accepted Islam before the battle. He received the maximum booty, 300 camels, causing comment among older Muslims. Makkah failed to resist the tidal wave of Islam and capitulated. The Prophet finally returned to Makkah in 632. Upon entering he ordered a general amnesty and expressed clemency, but about the idols he was firm. He entered the Kaaba and smashed them, saying, 'truth has come and falsehood vanished'.

We may observe the widening impact of Islam by the increasing numbers involved. At Badr the Prophet fought alongside about 300 men. Less than ten years later, in 632, about 90,000 accompanied him to Makkah. The gathering that received him was about 124,000 in number.

Shortly before his death the Prophet spoke at Arafat at the Hajjatul-Wida, the farewell pilgrimage. In his address he emphasized the unity of humanity – the brotherhood between Arab and non-Arab – and the concept of the *ummah:* 'Allah has made you brethren one to another, so be not divided. An Arab has no preference over a non-Arab, nor a non-Arab over an Arab; nor is a white one to be preferred to a dark one, nor a dark one to a white one.'

The Prophet's words as he lay dying are illustrative of his character. If, he said, he had wronged or insulted or borrowed from anyone, let them come forward to claim their right. One man stepped forward and was given the three dirhams he had lent the Prophet. Martin Lings, the European Muslim scholar, describes the death of the Prophet:

> Many of the older Companions were with the army including 'Umar, and when they were met on their arrival in the city with the news that the death had taken place 'Umar refused to believe it. He had misinterpreted a verse of the Koran which he had thought to mean that the Prophet would outlive them all and other generations to come, and he now stood in the Mosque and addressed the people, assuring them that the Prophet was merely absent in the Spirit and that he would return. While he was speaking thus, Abu Bakr arrived on horseback from Sung, for news had quickly spread over the whole oasis. Without pausing to speak to anyone, he went straight to his daughter's house and drew back from the Prophet's face the cloak with which they had covered him. He gazed at him, and then kissed him. 'Dearer than my father and my mother,' he said, 'thou hast tasted the death which God decreed for thee. No death after that shall ever befall thee.' Reverently he drew the cloak over his face again, and went out to the throng of men whom 'Umar was still addressing. 'Gently, 'Umar!' he said as he approached. 'Hear me speak!' 'Umar paid no attention and persisted, but recognising the voice of Abu Bakr the people left 'Umar and turned to hear what the older man had to tell them. After giving praise to God, he said: 'O people, whoso hath been wont to worship Muhammad – verily Muhammad is dead; and whoso hath been wont to worship God – verily God is Living and dieth not.' Then he recited the following verses which had been revealed after the battle of Uhud: 'Muhammad is but a messenger, and messengers have passed away before him. If he die or be slain, will ye then turn upon your heels? Whoso turneth upon his heels will thereby do no hurt unto God; and God will reward the thankful.'
>
> It was as if the people had not known of the revelation of this verse until Abu Bakr recited it that day. They took it from him, and it was on all their tongues. (*Muhammad*, 1983)

'Tout passe, tout casse, tout lasse' – everything passes, everything perishes, everything palls – must have reflected the feeling of many in the community. Everything except, truly, the name of God.

The Prophet's time on earth had come to an end. In a short span he had played the role of father, husband, chief, warrior, friend and Prophet. His respect for learning, tolerance of others, generosity of spirit, concern for the weak, gentle piety and desire for a better, cleaner, world would constitute the main elements of the Muslim ideal. For Muslims the life of the Prophet is the triumph of hope over despair, light over darkness.

Ideal Muslim behaviour

For the twentieth-century imagination a Biblical prophet is someone from a Cecil B. De Mille film. A towering, fierce figure he is wont to thunder, which he does often and long, about hell and damnation, while his eyes blaze and his wild, flowing, white beard bristles with frenzy. It is wise not to cross him; he can convert a staff into a snake with ease and, when pressed, part the waves in the sea. Our Prophet, then, the last in the line of the Semitic prophets, the seal of all prophets, must be an even more imposing and fearsome figure, it may reasonably be conjectured. Nothing is further from the truth.

Piety, forbearance, courage and judgment – required in some degree by any leader – the Prophet had, and displayed, in abundance. But what is striking about his behaviour and temperament is the most unexpected quality in tribal life, gentleness. It is a quality the critics of Islam overlook and its supporters take for granted; the omission partly explains why images of Islam as a religion of hate and rage flourish.

Whether consoling a child who lost an animal, or not being able to control his tears when breaking bad news to the wife of a friend, or requesting that the bitch which had delivered puppies be kept warm, or telling Aishah 'softly and gently please' when she was rough to an obstinate camel, this aspect of the man emerges. Added to the gentleness was a distinct vein of humour, a capacity to smile at the incongruous and unexpected. Upbraiding Abu Bakr – 'look at this pilgrim' – for being harsh to a camel on a pilgrimage or the lifting of a serious mood with Aishah's suggestion that if she died he would feel no remorse and after the burial immediately take another wife, this trait of the Prophet inspired devotion and love. It would make him, in the words of the Quran, 'a mercy to the worlds'.

The gentle affection for the weak in society – women, children, orphans – may have sprung from the Prophet's own childhood. His father, Abdullah, died before his birth and his mother Aminah, when he was six. His grandfather, in whose charge he was left, died when he was eight. His last public address at Arafat advises Muslims to 'treat your women well and be kind to them'. 'Paradise', he thrice repeated to a questioner who wished to find a short cut to heaven, 'lies under the feet of the mother.' In early Islamic history Khadijah and Aishah, his wives, and Fatimah, his daughter, play important roles.

The Prophet's kindness to women forms the content of many stories. One concerns his wife, Maria, the Christian Coptic slave girl, sent to him by the head of the Coptic church in Cairo. His attentiveness towards her had provoked his other wives into arguments and bad temper. They made life unbearable for him. In protest he withdrew from them for a month, sleeping on the floor of a small, mud store-room and refusing to see anyone. Umar, when he finally succeeded in seeing him, broke into a cry of anguish, threatening to cut off his own daughter's head for having brought the Prophet to this point. But by now the women had learnt a lesson. They promised there would be harmony in the home if he came back. Another man in those times and in that society would have been excused for taking the cane to his wives.

The Prophet's gentleness presupposed a forgiving and tolerant nature. This is confirmed by historical – and momentous – examples. Hind, the implacable foe of Islam as we saw above, in a gesture of hatred and contempt ate the raw liver of Hamzah, a hero of Badr and brother of the Prophet's father (see genealogical chart). It was widely assumed that the Prophet would never forgive her. Hamzah was one of his dearest relatives (and destined to be a favourite Muslim hero in distant parts of the world; for instance, as we see in chapter 6, 'Islam of the periphery', in Indonesia). When Makkah was finally conquered and Hind taken captive the Prophet forgave her. Overwhelmed by his generosity she became a Muslim, declaring he must be a prophet and no ordinary mortal (her progeny would reap the dividends: Muawiyah, her son, founded the Umayyad dynasty as we shall see in the next chapter).

After the conquest of Makkah the Prophet announced a general amnesty. Those who had abused, humiliated and injured him were forgiven, much to the chagrin of those Muslims thirsting for revenge. The conquest of Makkah cost less than 30 lives. The final victory of Islam – comparable in historical significance to the great revolutions, French, Russian and Chinese – is the cheapest in terms of human life.

The charge of those critics who accuse the Prophet of the deaths of a poet who wrote satirical verse and of the Quraiza, a Jewish tribe of Madinah, will not hold. An over-zealous Muslim infuriated by his verses set out to silence the poet in the first case. In the second the arbiter chosen by the Quraiza condemned their fighting men to death – or apostasy – for breaking a treaty in a critical battle which almost destroyed the entire early Muslim community. Harshness and violence were simply not part of the Prophet's nature. Yet on religious matters he was firm and unequivocal, showing no vacillation or doubt.

Along with the virtues of gentleness and tolerance his behaviour exemplified that of humility. Once he was persuading a leading Quraysh aristocrat to become a Muslim when Ibn Umm Makhtum, the blind, asked him to recite the Quran. The blind man's insistence disrupted the conversation. The Prophet, barely concealing his anger, frowned and moved on. Shortly after, a rebuke appeared in a Quranic verse: 'He frowned and turned aside when the blind man approached him.' The verse reprimanded the Prophet for paying attention to the 'disdainfully indifferent' at the cost of one who came in fear and reverence. Muhammad was chastised. A lesser man would have concealed or embroidered the episode to show himself in a better light.

For the first time in Arab society a sense of proportion, of decency, of human kindness, was institutionalized. For instance, regarding war, the Prophet's sayings include: 'Looting is no more lawful than carrion', 'He has forbidden looting and mutilation' and 'He has forbidden the killing of women and children'. To pressure corrupt rulers to change their policies: 'He who commends a Sultan in what God condemns has left the religion of God.' Such sayings would in time provide a charter for action, revolution and constant renewal for Muslims.

In time the Prophet's sayings and actions – *hadith*, traditions – came to be accepted as the truth by Muslims. The problem lay in locating a genuine *hadith*. It is said Imam Hanbal narrated one million. Al Ghazzali earned his title *hujjat al-Islam*, the authority of Islam, by memorizing 300,000. The accepted authority, Imam Bukhari, after a lifetime's work, selected about 7,300 from 600,000 in 97 books. Collecting *hadith* became an Islamic science.

The Prophet's actions and customs are *sunna* (from custom) – hence *ahle-sunna*, Sunni, or followers of the *sunna*. The *sunna* includes a wide range of Muslim responses. Across the world his followers would imitate the Prophet with affection in every kind of activity – abstaining from alcohol and pig's meat, colouring a man's beard with henna, using green for clothes and flags, enjoying honey, talking softly, eating moderately and sleeping little.

The wealth of *hadith* and the minutiae they address raise an important question: do the *hadith* mean that every action of Muslims is predetermined and fixed forever? The answer lies in the discourse between the Prophet and Muadh ibn Jabal, a *qadi*, on his way to al-Yaman as judge.

Prophet: How will you decide a problem?
Muadh: According to the Quran.
Prophet: If it is not in it?
Muadh: According to the *sunna*.
Prophet: If it is not in that either?
Muadh: Then I will use my own reasoning.

The Islamic principles which encourage adaptability and rational choice based on *ijtihad*, independent judgment, *shura*, consultation, and *ijma*, consensus, are reflected in the exchange (also see 'The masters of Islamic law' in the next chapter). Clearly, rationality and man's own judgment play a part in arriving at decisions.

For Sunnis the role of the Prophet, his virtues and his words, is complemented by that of his companions, particularly the first four caliphs – the *Khulafa-e-Rashideen* – the rightly guided caliphs. Their behaviour, along with six other named 'companions', *Sahaba*, was acknowledged by the Prophet as the closest approximation to the ideal Muslim. The ten were promised paradise: 'my companions are even as the stars: whichsoever of them you follow, you shall be rightly guided.' Ali, whose extraordinary qualities shone even in that extraordinary company, was singled out: 'I am the city of knowledge and Ali is its gate.'

The template was provided by the Prophet and his companions, particularly the ten. They provided examples of correct behaviour for every aspect of life. By investing correct behaviour and judgment in the ordinary Muslim, Islam dispenses the need for a priesthood. The Prophet was emphatic – 'there is no monkery in Islam.' In one sense every Muslim is a priest, answerable directly for his actions to God. This was to provide Muslim society with an unending source of vitality and help explain the process of renewing faith through individual action.

The ideal would be recognizable in spite of differences of society, economy, social structure and organization throughout the world, even outside the mainstream and established Muslim heartlands. It would be recognizable in the tropical jungles of Africa, in the steppes of Central Asia and in the humid forests of the Far East. Over 1300 years later it is recognizable in Muslim communities whether in Chicago, London, Cairo or Tokyo.

The life of the Prophet as scholarship

Recognizing the central role of the Prophet, critics of Islam have attacked him and his character. They focus on his numerous marriages and certain incidents in his life, namely the deaths of the vituperative poet and the Jewish group Quraiza (see above). From Voltaire to Gibbon, there is a long list of the writers and scholars of Europe who participated in the attack. In Dante's *Divine Comedy* the Prophet is constantly split in two as eternal punishment for the sin of religious schism. Francis Bacon popularized the apocryphal story which ridicules the Prophet in the saying 'if the hill will not come to Muhammad, Muhammad will go to the hill'. 'Muhammad remained in his moral corruption and debauchery a camel thief, a cardinal who failed to reach the throne of the Papacy and win it for himself,' declared the French *Encyclopédie Larousse.* Pope Innocent III identified him as the Anti-Christ.

The Royal Chaplain and Father Confessor of Spain, Jaime Bleda, writing in the early years of the seventeenth century, triumphant at the final expulsion of the Moors, in what became a standard history, introduces the Prophet as the 'deceiver of the world, false prophet, Satan's messenger, the worst precursor of the Anti-Christ' ('Morisco diaspora: a study of racial and religious intolerance at the time of the expulsion', R. Abdul Wahab Boase, lecture delivered at the Centre for Islamic Studies, Oxford, 1986). Other Spanish authorities were equally zealous in debasing the Prophet. They claimed he was the incestuous adulterous offspring of the Jewess 'Emina' and her brother, Baeyra. Pictured as the Beast of the Apocalypse, he possessed the two horns of a lamb, the voice of a dragon. The ghastly images reveal as much the minds of the priests, locked in medieval prejudice and ignorance, as their hatred against the vanquished Moors.

By diminishing the Prophet, his critics hoped to demolish the foundations of Islam. He was not only the Prophet, the seal of the Prophets, who traced spiritual genealogy to Abraham and Adam, but also the mortal vehicle for the holy Quran.

In an historical perspective we are now better able to understand that the attack on the Prophet was also part of the European intellectual attack on their own churches and priesthood. The intensity of the attacks on the Prophet is partly explained by the need in Europe to check the church.

Orientalists, such as Montgomery Watt, by imputing authorship of the Quran to the Prophet who was unlettered, complained of the lack of logic and method in its arguments. For Carlyle it was 'a wearisome, confused jumble, crude, incondite'. However, for Muslims the power and sublimity of the Quran remains unaffected over the centuries. It is the 'inimitable symphony, the very sound of which moves men to tears and ecstasy' (Marmaduke Pickthall; chapter 8, section 2). Little wonder that when his detractors demanded proof of his divine message in the form of miracles, the Prophet pointed to the holy Quran. Let them, he challenged, produce ten verses like it or accept the Quran as a miracle.

Recently more realistic assessments have been made of the Prophet in the West. A Western study placed him first in '*The 100': A Ranking of the Most Influential Persons in History* (M. Hart, 1978). Indeed the Prophet's name, Muhammad, is probably the most popular in the world. ('Muhammad' – praiseworthy – is derived from the root '*hamd*' which means 'praise'.) There are more Muhammads – or its derivative Ahmed – than any other name. (My father's first name is Muhammad, last name Ahmed.) The name is repeated millions of times daily. It is a central part of the Muslim declaration of faith – 'there is no God but Allah and Muhammad is His Prophet' – repeated during the five daily prayers.

If certain non-Muslims aimed to demolish the Prophet, his ardent followers wrote of him with reverence. The style of Muslim biographers was hyperbolic, the content hagiography. For example, the *Pakistan Times* on 6 December 1984, on the Prophet's birthday, carried two main articles: 'The Perfect Man' – for Muslims he is *insaan-i-kamil* – and 'The Prophet: man or miracle?' *Akhbar-i-Jahan*, a popular Pakistan journal, for the same birth anniversary had articles titled 'The lord of the two worlds: whose mention is the fragrance of roses'. These reflect the high status the Quran gives him 'as a mercy for all creatures'.

Biographical and hagiographical works on the Prophet continue to flow from the pens of Muslims. A Professor in Multan recently compiled a list of 2,713 biographical books and pamphlets in Pakistani languages under the title 'Voice of Truth'.

Muslim writers still fall into the trap of first condemning Western sources as biased and then citing them whenever favourable. Perhaps this is a lingering sense of inferiority from the colonial days. Sarwar's *Muhammad the Holy Prophet*, published in Lahore, begins with the impassioned plea that the West has always misunderstood the Prophet. Yet his book concludes with an entire chapter, 'excerpts from European writers on Muhammed and Islam', which has a heading 'Muhammed was sincere and not an impostor'. *Gulha-e-aquidat*, published in Lahore, is a similar collection of testimonials by non-Muslims. These testimonials are demeaning; they were once carried during the colonial period by cooks and gardeners seeking employment. The Prophet deserves to be treated with dignity; he does not need such citations and testimonials.

Both positions, the one depicting the Prophet as a devil, the other as an angel, are unfair to him. Perhaps fairer are those more realistic studies like M. H. Haykal's *The Life of Muhammad*, translated from the Arabic by Ismail al-Faruqi (1976). These treat him as a mortal, exposed to the range of human experience and feeling pain, uncertainty, joy, anger; and through his behaviour and struggle succeeding with his mission.

Analysis of the Prophet's life

Numerous points emerge from the life of the Prophet which were to have consequences both for the ideal of Islam and subsequent history. One of the main contributions of Islam was the concept of universalistic humanity transcending tribe and clan. There is no doubt that the tribe provided security to its members and a kind of stability to society. But its jealous exclusiveness based on *nasab*, ancestry, created and perpetuated divisions among people. These divisions assumed mythical proportions. Many acts of the Prophet support the claim that Islam was supreme to the tribe: his marriages outside the clan, his preference of Bilal, a black slave, as the first *muezzin* of Islam, and explicitly, for history to hear, his words at Arafat decrying race and caste divisions.

Caste, class or race would never be barriers to attaining the Muslim ideal or the highest status in Islam. A person was judged by his behaviour not his lineage – 'nurture' not 'nature'. Apart from Bilal, who is something of a cult figure in Africa, many of the Muslim rulers in the Arab, Indian and Ottoman dynasties were sons of slaves. The station of 'God's viceroys on earth', the Quran's description of good human beings, is reached after *jihad*, striving and not through caste or lineage.

The Prophet was acutely aware of tribalism as it permeated his life. His support came from either his immediate kin – father's brothers, Abu Talib and Hamzah or cousins like Ali, son of Abu Talib – or his in-laws, Abu Bakr, Umar and Uthman related by marriage. His main enemies, too, were close kin (see genealogical chart). Abu Lahab was his father's brother and Abu Suffian a relative. Within a few years of the Prophet's death, the once dominant Umayyads, who had been overshadowed by their Hashim cousins because of

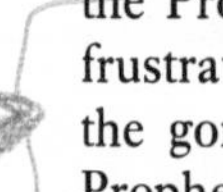

the Prophet, re-emerged. Muawiyah, the son of Abu Suffian, succeeded and frustrated Ali, the fourth ideal caliph. Muawiyah's dissolute son Yazid provided the gory climax to the tribal rivalry by killing Hussain, the grandson of the Prophet, just fifty years after the Prophet's death.

The importance of marriages in forming political alliances is illustrated in the Prophet's life. In particular, the Prophet's own marriages – once a central source of controversy for critics of Islam who wished to portray him as a debauch – are a good example of this. The importance of these marriages may be gauged from the fact that the Prophet was father-in-law to two and son-in-law to two of the four ideal caliphs. The Prophet's marriage to the daughter of Abu Suffian, one of the leading enemies of the early Muslims, helped to win him over to the cause of Islam. The Prophet's marriages also illustrate the possibility of alliances above tribalism. Some of his wives were neither kin nor of his social group. Maria the slave girl is an example. She gave birth to Ibrahim, the only male child who survived into infancy and whose death caused him unending sorrow.

An entire range of universal issues, indicating the balance between sets of opposites that maintain organized life, emerge from the Prophet's life: the struggle between the needs of *din* (religion) and *dunya* (world), between *al-akhira* (the judgment day) and *dunya*, between *dar-al-harb* and *dar-al-Islam*. These issues form the theme of Muslim history from the very beginning. The life of the Prophet balances neatly – and he constantly warned his followers on this score – *din*, religion, with *dunya*, the world. The Muslim lives in the latter by the principles of the former. He does not abandon the one for the other. He is neither blinded by the world nor rejects it to become a hermit or ascetic. Islam, the holy Quran tells us, is the middle path. It talks of the good life for human beings. In Islam the Hindu or Buddhist renunciation of the world, *dunya*, is not encouraged.

Finally, the ideal – with its emphasis on universal values – encouraged the building of bridges connecting groups and peoples. In trouble the Prophet had sent Muslim groups to seek the protection of the Negus of Abyssinia. In the Kaaba when the idols were swept aside certain sources aver that he protected an icon of the virgin and child. His courtesy when receiving the Abyssinians was noted by his contemporaries. His relations with the Coptic Archbishop of Egypt were cordial (the latter sent him the white mule Duldul and Maria the slave girl). The Prophet was building bridges for Islam. His example would be followed by Muslims, culminating in the practice of the Sufi saints whose motto was *sulh-i-kul* or peace with all, and who would attract followers from all walks of life and religions.

For the Prophet the years of tribulation were brief; success followed in abundance. Within his lifetime he had established a religion and a state. Within decades of his death the banners of Islam flew on the Atlantic coast at one end of Africa, and on the banks of the river Indus in South Asia. One hundred years after his death the Islamic empire was greater than Rome at its zenith. That year it was stopped at Poitiers by Charles Martel; otherwise Europe might well have been included. Still, it stretched from the Bay of Biscay to the Indus river, from the Aral sea to the lower cataracts of the Nile. The ancient and glittering city of Damascus was the heart and capital of the empire. The world would not forgive Islam its rapid success; Muslims could not forget the memory of their early triumphs.

3

A theory of Islamic history

There are two traditional methods of interpreting Muslim history. In the first Ibn Khaldun proposes a cyclical theory. It is an attractive idea because it is so simple: hardy tribesmen, fresh from the hills, invaded towns in the plains and, over time, succumbed to city ways and lost their tribal cohesion. Becoming effete they were vulnerable to a fresher wave from the hills. The cycle repeated itself every three or four generations.

In the second interpretation, Islamic history is depicted as a rapid, dramatic, rise in seventh-century Arabia and a tortuous – inevitable – decline. Conservative Muslim scholars date the downfall from the time of Ali's assassination in 660, after the period of the four ideal caliphs. The more orthodox scholars of this school go back earlier. Shah Waliullah, for instance, places the downfall after the reign of the first two caliphs calling it *Khalifat-e-Khass*, or the special caliphate. The decline continued to the middle of the thirteenth century in the Middle East. The Mongols in 1258 captured and sacked Baghdad. That year is seen as the cut-off point, the end, of Islamic history. The rest is despair and decline. From then on, it is argued, Muslims faced a steady decline making European colonization almost inevitable. This is not only a Eurocentric view of history – Spengler, Toynbee and Bernard Lewis subscribe to it – but also an Arabcentric one.

The decline and fall theory has a wide following. Among its protagonists are unlikely companions, such as Bernard Lewis and Imam Khomeini. The Imam explains:

> Unfortunately, true Islam lasted for only a brief period after its inception. First the Umayyads and then the Abbasids inflicted all kinds of damage on Islam. Later the monarchs ruling Iran continued on the same path; they completely distorted Islam and established something quite different in its place. The process was begun by the Umayyads, who changed the nature of government from divine and spiritual to worldly. Their rule

> was based on Arabism, the principle of promoting the Arabs over all other peoples, which was an aim fundamentally opposed to Islam and its desire to abolish nationality and unite all mankind in a single community, under the aegis of a state indifferent to the matter of race and colour. It was the aim of the Umayyads to distort Islam completely by reviving the Arabism of the pre-Islamic age of ignorance, and the same aim is still pursued by the leaders of certain Arab countries, who declare openly their desire to revive the Arabism of the Umayyads, which is nothing but the Arabism of the *Jahiliyya*. (*Islam and Revolution*, 1981)

In an important sense the traditional view was correct. The Prophet and the cluster of his companions provided the highest and best form of Muslim behaviour. After them a decline was inevitable. The Prophet himself said: 'The best of my people are my generation; then they that come after them, then they that come after them.'

Both schools have one main strand in common. They believe in the theory of the rapid rise and equally rapid downfall of Islam. They take the easy way out, blaming 'outside' forces, Mongols or Europeans. It is tempting to view history in this light. For an Arab 1258 truly marks the end of world domination. For Europeans it establishes the arguments for a disintegrating, decadent, corrupt Muslim Orient waiting for reform and a superior, Western, civilization. This is an incorrect reading of Muslim history. These theories are part of established wisdom; they are also a substitute for thought and inquiry.

We view Islamic history, it is suggested, not as the rise and fall of the Arab dynasties. Instead we discover a rhythm, a flux and reflux, a rise and fall, peaks and troughs, in Muslim society attempting to live by the Islamic ideal. Islamic history may be interpreted as an attempt to live up to and by the seventh-century Muslim ideal. So, whereas Muslim dynasties or empires rise and fall, never to emerge again, the ideal is constantly renewed by groups and individuals in different places and in different times. The farther from the ideal, the greater the tension in society. Muslims would interpret success in worldly endeavours as a sign of divine approval.

God does not play dice with the universe, Einstein had said; nor, we may add, with human history. There appears to be a rhythm in history and in the evolution of society which is as symmetrical and balanced as the universe Einstein contemplated. Once we have comprehended the key to our universe we are able to understand its structure and organization. Birth, rise and decline then become comprehensible. There is science and meaning beneath apparently random patterns of history and society: Islam disintegrating in one place, reviving in another, fading here, growing there; but Islam always a factor, a force providing the dynamics to society. As well known, random examples, Delhi was taken for the first time by Muslims in 1192, after Muhammad Ghori defeated Prithvi Raj at the battle of Thanesar; Baghdad was lost to the Mongols shortly afterwards. In another century, Islam, driven out of the Iberian peninsula in Europe, was, across two continents, establishing itself successfully in the Deccan in south India, after finally vanquishing the powerful Hindu kingdom of Vijayanagar on the fields of Talikota. Muslims finally took Constantinople in 1453 and re-named it 'Istanbul' – the city of Islam – and finally, in 1492, lost Granada, which became a Christian city. That year Christopher Columbus, with a subsidy from Queen Isabella, sailed across the Atlantic to discover America and claimed it as the new world for the Christians; a few years later Babar crossed into India to establish the Mughal dynasty which attracted Muslims from all over the Muslim world. Or consider the bleak nineteenth century when the Muslim empires disintegrated, and the Islamic capitals of Delhi, Kabul and Cairo were occupied by Europeans. During this period Usman Dan Fodio, Ummar Tal Al Haji and Muhammad Ahmad, the Mahdi, organized Islamic states in different parts of Africa; Imam Shamyl did likewise in the Caucasus and Sayyed Ahmad in Peshawar; and the Akhund laid the foundations for one in Swat.

More recently, in the last decades, certain revolutionary movements shook the established order across the Muslim world. The flashpoints were at Kano, Cairo, Makkah and Wana, involving major Muslim nations, Nigeria, Egypt, Saudi Arabia and Pakistan respectively (see also 'Mahdism and millenarian movements,' later in the chapter). Imam Khomeini's dramatic success has overshadowed many of these and pushed them into obscurity. Islam in Iran finally had its 'modern' revolution, that, for the world, was the wonder; it had joined the ranks of France, Russia and China.

The leaders of these movements led desperate, unsuccessful, bloody revolts against the established order. They were neither Mahdis, as some of their followers proclaimed them, nor did they represent a new trend in Islam. Rather, they were Muslims motivated by the Islamic vision and burning with a desire to correct the social order and move towards the ideal. 'I killed the pharaoh,' said al-Islambuli in jail, unrepentant after assassinating Anwar Sadat. They echoed Usman Dan Fodio: 'Islam has been flagrantly abused by corrupt rulers. We must return to the Golden Age.'

With the rapid expansion of Islam the quality of Muslim behaviour would be uneven. At such times the gap between the ideal and the actual would be wide. It was the law of diminishing returns: the greater the number of units, the less satisfactory the results.

To place our theory of Islamic history in context and to identify the main developments, we will create six socio-historical categories. These broad categories, overlapping and borrowing from each other, also identify distinct social characteristics correlating the time and place within which Muslims lived. It is a frame to help us view Muslim history and society simply, an otherwise formidably complex task. Although a clear common theme, the move towards the ideal runs through them, the categories are culturally and socially distinct from one another. Each possesses a characteristic way of looking at the world. The six categories are:

1 The time of the Prophet and the ideal caliphs.
2 The Arab dynasties.
3 The three Muslim empires.
4 Islam of the periphery.
5 Islam under European rule.
6 Contemporary Islam.

Viewed as a whole the categories suggest the range of Muslim history and help to explain the complexity of Muslim society.

1 IDEAL CALIPHS

We have already seen the time of the Prophet. Let us now turn to that of the four ideal caliphs. Immediately after the Prophet's death the critical issue of succession arose. A council, board – *al-Shura* (consultation of elders and companions) – selected the caliph. Succession was thus not hereditary. Abu Bakr was elected and the title *Khalifat Rasul Allah* – the successor of the messenger of Allah – was applied to him. This title was shortened to Khalifa – caliph – a title which designated the rightful ruler of Islam. The institution in time would become central to Islamic politics and religious doctrine. With his simple and absolute faith in the new religion Abu Bakr won the title *al-Siddiq*, the believer; Siddiqis claim descent from him.

Abu Bakr lived by the highest Muslim standards of behaviour. This is reflected in his accession speech as recorded by Ibn Hisham in his *Sira:*

> Then Abu Bakr spoke, and praised the lauded God as is fitting, and then he said: O people, I have been appointed to rule over you, though I am not the best among you. If I do well, help me, and if I do ill, correct me. Truth is loyalty and falsehood is treachery; the weak among you is strong in my eyes until I get justice for him, please God, and the strong among you is weak in my eyes until I exact justice from him, please God. If any people hold back from fighting the holy war for God, God strikes them with degradation. If weakness spreads among a people, God brings disaster upon all of them. Obey me as long as I obey God and His Prophet. And if I disobey God and His Prophet, you do not owe me obedience. Come to prayer, and may God have mercy on you.

Abu Bakr, also in the same year, laid down the rules of war reflecting the principles of the Prophet:

> O people! I charge you with these rules; learn them well! Do not betray, or misappropriate any part of the booty; do not practise treachery or mutilation. Do not kill a young child, an old man, or a woman. Do not uproot or burn palms or cut down fruitful trees. Do not slaughter a sheep or a cow or a camel, except for food. You will meet people who have set themselves apart in hermitages; leave them to accomplish the purpose for which they have done this. You will come upon people who will bring you dishes with various kinds of foods. If you partake of them pronounce God's name over what you eat. Go, in God's name, and may God protect you from sword and pestilence. (Al Tabari, *History of the World*)

The forces that were unleashed by Islam now pushed out irresistibly from the Arabian peninsula. Within two years of the Prophet's death Islam fought the Christian Byzantine army at the battle of Ajnadayn and moved on to Damascus. Abu Bakr, already an old man at his accession, died and was replaced by Umar. In Umar's time Iraq, Persia and Egypt were added to the Muslim domain. The battle of Qadsya, fought in 635 against the Persians, was one of the most critical battles in history because it would reverberate up to the present. In the same year the Muslims decisively beat the Christians at Yarmuk.

The confidence and panache of the early Muslims were unbounded, full of the freshness of the desert air. They were bringing a message of salvation to the world – moving in the path of Allah, *fi sabil Allah*. Khalid wrote to the chiefs of Persia:

> In the name of God, the Merciful and the Compassionate. From Khalid ibn al-Walid to the border-chiefs (*marzuban*) of Persia.
>
> Become Muslim and be saved. If not, accept protection from us and pay the *jizya*. If not, I shall come against you with men who love death as you love to drink wine. (*Ibid.*)

Uqbah ibn Nafi, sweeping victoriously westwards along the north African coast – the area Arabs would call the Maghreb, the west – stopped where the land ended. Galloping into the Atlantic he brandished his sword. 'If there were more worlds left to conquer I would do so in the name of Allah,' he cried to the heavens.

But the Islamic world was changing rapidly. Wealth and numbers that were difficult to conceive in the early days now multiplied to boggle the imagination. At Ajnadayn Muslims faced an enemy of 100,000 and at Qadsya 120,000. At Yarmuk the enemy dead alone numbered 140,000. With conquest came vast booty. At Qadsya, the Persian capital, the total booty was estimated at 9 billion dinars. Each soldier received 12,000 dinars. Soon even privates owned one to ten servants each. After Qadsya, within three years of the Prophet's death, the problems and scope of Islam had changed.

As long as he lived Umar's moral authority was undisputed. Al Tabari records:

> 'Umar said to Salman: 'Am I a king or a Caliph?' and Salman answered: 'If you have levied from the lands of the Muslims one dirham, or more, or less, and applied it unlawfully, you are a king, not a Caliph.' And 'Umar wept.

Umar owned one shirt and one mantle, both noted for the patchwork on them. The glory of Islam was his only concern. Many anecdotes are related to illustrate his commitment. Perhaps his order to scourge his son to death for immorality best illustrates Umar's character. In one story he reduced Islam's victorious general, Khalid ibn Walid, to a soldier, in another he ordered Saad, the victorious governor of the eastern provinces to pull down a gate outside his residence which looked ostentatious. At the height of his faculties, in 644, a Christian Persian slave assassinated him in the mosque.

Islam's rapid success carried within it the seeds of crisis. Uthman, who succeeded Umar, was in a sense a victim of these. He was finding it difficult to cope with the changing world and its scale. In the summer of 656 he was killed by rebels from the garrison town of Fustat in Egypt and Kufa in Iraq. His body lay unburied for three days as the assassins plundered the treasury. The Islamic revolution was turning sour:

> Abul-Tufayl Amir ibn Wathila called on Muawiyah [then Governor of Syria] who said to him, 'O Abul-Tufayl, you are one of those who killed Uthman.' 'No,' he replied, 'but I am one of those who was present and did not help him.'
>
> 'And what prevented you from helping him?' asked Muawiyah.
>
> 'What prevented me', he replied, 'was that the Emigrants [*muhajirs*] and the Helpers [*ansars*] did not help him, and I did not see anyone who did help him.' (Al Baladhuri, *Ansab al-ashraf*)

Ali, who succeeded Uthman, faced the full brunt of the crisis of changing times. The moral authority of Ali, as the rightful caliph, challenged and confronted the material power and wealth of his rival Muawiyah, the governor of Syria. Ali's governor was turned back by Muawiyah, at the borders of Syria and battle declared. At the battle of the Camel for the first time Muslims fought Muslims. When it was over 10,000 Muslims lay dead on the battlefield. Within a generation of the Prophet's death Muslims had begun to slaughter Muslims. A year later, in 657, Ali's army of 70,000 faced Muawiyah's of 90,000. The numbers were swollen by non-combatants.

Those who remembered the times of the Prophet were horrified. New wealth, new sects and old tribal rivalries were tearing society apart. Abdullah bin Sabah had declared that Ali was God, much to Ali's embarrassment, while he himself was the Prophet. A group calling themselves the Kharijis decided to wipe the slate clean and make a fresh start. Not for the first time in Islamic history would an attempt be made to revive the time of the Prophet, already seen as the Golden Age.

The Kharijis planned to kill simultaneously the three most important men in Islam, Ali in Kufa, Muawiyah in Jerusalem and Amar in Fustat. Of these only Ali was killed, while praying in the mosque. Muawiyah, now adopting the precaution of living in heavily guarded enclosures, became the caliph of Islam and first ruler of the Umayyad dynasty.

Islamic politics had collapsed. Three of the four righteous caliphs were assassinated while performing prayers. For the caliph public prayer had become a hazard. Not the *al-Shura* but the assassin's blade decided succession. The impact of these events on Muslim history became enormous making itself felt up to our times. Henceforth, whatever achievements might be made in art, literature and architecture, Muslim politics would display signs of instability. However, the lessons were seen not only in the politics but in the values, morality and behaviour of the early caliphs.

The behaviour of the four caliphs approximated to the original ideal: Abu Bakr, wise and pious, Umar courageous and just, Uthman gentle and religious, Ali brave and scholarly. Muslim scholars label each caliph thus: in piety, Abu Bakr, who wore a single garment pinned together and was known as the 'man of the two pins'; in power, Umar, who lived on bread and olive-oil, his clothes patched in a dozen places (some of the patches were of leather), arriving in Jerusalem as conqueror on foot with his servant astride the camel, or lashing his son to death for a crime; in simplicity, Uthman, who was like one of his slaves in dress and appearance, who when questioned upon being seen coming out of one of his gardens with a faggot of firewood on his shoulders said 'I wanted to see whether my soul would refuse; on the battle field and in death Ali, forgiving his assassin as he lay dying of a poisoned blade. When Ali succeeded, he bought a waistband for four dirhams and a shirt for five dirhams; finding the sleeve of the garment somewhat long, he went to a cobbler and, taking his knife, cut off the sleeve level with the tips of his fingers. The four attempted, and largely succeeded, in living up to the ideal of Islam. They inspired others to do so too. When al-Zubair died, he left behind him debts amounting to more than 200,000 dinars, all contracted through liberality and extravagant generosity. Talha ibn Ubaid Allah gave away all his possessions, even his family jewels, to beggars.

Makkah and Madinah

With the ideal caliphs the political importance of Makkah and Madinah came to an end. For over a thousand years – until the emergence of Saudi Arabia in the middle of this century (chapter 8) – these towns would lie in what became the Muslim backwaters. Their history, however, would be chequered. Muslim invaders would commit sacrilege, burning, pillaging and killing here. Natural calamities like earthquakes and fire would destroy them. The Carmathians, Shias from Bahrain, just three centuries after the Prophet's death, in a drunken frenzy killed some 2,000 male pilgrims, enslaved their families and took away the Black Stone from the Kaaba. They kept it for 22 years and returned it in a damaged condition only after their leader had contracted leprosy.

Over a century later, in 1162, Nur al-din Zangi, a Turkish prince, heard the Prophet in a vision calling to him for help. Without delay he rode to Madinah in time to foil a Crusader's plot to desecrate the tomb of the Prophet. Since then the tomb has been sealed with ebony and lead. A century later, in 1256, a fearful earthquake caused a fire in Madinah which burnt every item from the time of the Prophet including his bench. People predicted the end of the world. Two years later the Mongols took Baghdad, the capital of the Arab world, and threatened Makkah and Madinah. The predicted end of the world seemed imminent. Then, miraculously, the Mamluks turned the tide in favour of Islam. Where Christian Crusaders and animistic Mongols failed, Muslim followers of Sheikh Wahab almost succeeded (chapter 8). Fiercely iconoclastic, they threatened to destroy the holy sites in the towns as they distracted from the worship of the one God. In particular their focus was the tomb of the Prophet which, for thousands of illiterate pilgrims, possesses an almost mythical, magical quality.

While on the one hand man and nature conspired to destroy the towns there were, on the other hand, always from the beginning those who dedicated their lives to them. The saintly Abdullah, named by the Prophet himself, and the grandson of the Caliph Abu Bakr, was one of the earliest builders of the Kaaba. The Umayyads rebuilt it in gold. The Caliph Al Walid, son of Abdul Malik, sent Byzantine architects who built with opulence, tearing down the old. Later, Roman and Persian influences can be detected as distant caliphs sent their finest architects. The last and most important influence, still clearly visible, was that of the Ottomans. Sulayman the Magnificent sent the most renowned Muslim architect of the age, Sinan.

But throughout the vicissitudes and calamities, the two towns provided a model of piety, a place of retreat for the faithful. Scholars, saints and pilgrims came for inspiration and renewal. The saint Sheikh Abdul Gilani lived here (so bad were the floods that year that he had to swim round the Kaaba). So did the scholars Malik ibn Anas, Arabi, Rumi and Al Ghazzali (a vision of the Prophet here inspired Al Ghazzali's greatest work, the *Ihya* – see the next section). The men of the sword came to be inspired before (Sayyed Ahmad Barelvi) or after (Imam Shamyl) their holy wars against the enemies of Islam.

For them, as for the ordinary pilgrim, Makkah and Madinah provided direct, living, meaningful reference points to the Muslim ideal.

2 ARAB DYNASTIES: UMAYYADS AND ABBASIDS

The Arabs before Islam constituted a traditional, tribal community led by respected patriarchs and elders. People knew each other, their parentage and their social ways – it was what is called a face-to-face society. Both in Makkah and in the deserts beyond, customs were tribal. Like tribal societies elsewhere they were a frank, warm, earthy people. They had a sense of humour, the hallmark of confidence whether in an individual or in a society. It was a society with a defined social – and on the peninsula, geographical – arena. Islam's success and emergence from the peninsula changed all that.

Arab society now slipped into the established imperial patterns of the defeated Byzantines and Sasanids. These two empires, the most powerful of the age, were characterized by an arrogant bureaucracy, powerful armies and the total power of the rulers. Within a century Arab rule would be identified by these very characteristics (providing Karl Wittfogel material for *Oriental Despotism*, 1981). The Islamic ideal and the actual position of the Muslims, inheritors of these complex systems, now fluctuated. Henceforth each generation would need to redefine itself anew in relation to the ideal.

Umayyads

We saw that in 660 three key assassinations were planned in the three key garrison towns of Kufa, Jerusalem and Fustat which would change the course of Islamic history and shift its location outside the Arabian peninsula. As a result Muawiyah became caliph with his power base outside the Arabian peninsula. The Arabs on the peninsula were about to fall into a deep sleep from which they were to awake only in the late twentieth century.

The rule of the Umayyads, the first of the two Arab dynasties, was not long, lasting until 750. Fourteen Umayyads ruled during this period. The Umayyads followed the practices of those they had succeeded, Persians and Romans. Dynastic succession, a centralized and all-powerful caliph, complex revenue systems and administrative policies reflected how far Islam had moved from the place of its birth. In particular the pre-Islamic tribalism of the Umayyads surfaced, which we will discuss below and on the subject of which we have already heard Imam Khomeini.

Among the notable caliphs of the dynasty were Muawiyah, the founder, Abdul Malik (685–705), Umar II (717–720), Hisham (724–743), and Yazid III who, unlike Yazid I and II, was pious and ruled in 744 just before the Abbasids took power. In particular Umar II, like his ancestor and namesake Umar, the second caliph of Islam, approximated to our ideal. He placated the

Shias, stopping the condemnation of Ali which Muawiyah had instituted in the pulpits, and treated all Muslims, whether Arab or not, alike.

The rule of Yazid, son of Muawiyah, a short three years, is memorable for the massacre at Karbala (which is discussed in section 5), the plundering of Makkah and Madinah, and the introduction of the principle of hereditary rule. Sulayman (715–717) was a debauch. His cruelty established methods that would be imitated later, particularly the hacking of captives with dull swords. It was in his reign that Musa, Tariq and Muhammad bin Qasim, successful commanders and heroes of Islam, were publicly dishonoured.

Yazid II, who ruled briefly, spent his time in song and dance. By the time of Yazid III the Umayyad's sphere of influence had shrunk to Damascus. Rebellion and disorder had eroded the authority of the caliph. The structure was to collapse like a house of cards before the onslaught of the Abbasids.

Already with the first Umayyad, the disintegrating influence of tribalism – or nepotism in politics – is established. Ibn Khaldun, never at a loss for a sociological theory, presents an explanation:

> After Muawiyah, caliphs who were used to choosing the truth and to acting in accordance with it, acted similarly. Such caliphs included the Umayyads Abdul Malik and Sulayman and the Abbasids as-Saffah, Al-Mansur, Al-Mahdi, and Ar-Rashid, and others like them whose probity, and whose care and concern for the Muslims are well known. They cannot be blamed because they gave preference to their own sons and brothers, in that respect departing from the *sunna* of the first four caliphs. Their situation was different from that of the (four) caliphs who lived in a time when royal authority as such did not yet exist, and the restraining influence was religious. Thus, everybody had his restraining influence in himself. Consequently, they appointed the person who was acceptable to Islam, and preferred him over all others. They trusted every aspirant to have his own restraining influence.
>
> After them, from Muawiyah on, the group feeling [of the Arabs] approached its final goal, royal authority. The restraining influence of religion had weakened. The restraining influence of government and group was needed. If, under those circumstances, someone not acceptable to the group had been appointed as successor, such an appointment would have been rejected by it. The [chances of the appointee] would have been quickly demolished, and the community would have been split and torn by dissension. (The *Muqaddimah*, translated Franz Rosenthal, 1967)

Nepotism also meant arbitrary and capricious punishments. Tariq, who destroyed the Christian force in Spain, thus laying the foundation of conquest on the Iberian peninsula, was whipped and disgraced by his commander, Musa, when he arrived in Spain in 712. In turn the caliph disciplined Musa by ordering him to stand in the sun until exhausted, confiscating his property and stripping him of rank. Musa and Tariq were seen as beggars in the capital. The same Musa once owned untold wealth; he had captured 300,000 captives from Ifriqiyah – Africa – and from the Spanish Gothic nobility 30,000 virgins. At the other end of the Muslim world similar arbitrary punishments were meted out. The young conqueror of Sind, Muhammad bin Qasim, a relative of the powerful governor Hajjaj, was sewn in a sack of hide on a false charge and brought home to his death when his patron fell from power.

The acquisition of vast properties and sums of money helped the growth of a new class – the *mawali* (singular *mawla*). A *mawla* was a Muslim who was not a member of an Arab tribe by descent, a Persian or an Egyptian, for example. The term did not include non-Muslims, *dhimmis*. Indeed Christian Arabs were preferred to Muslim non-Arabs. The greatest poet in the capital, Damascus, was Al Akhtal (640–710), the Christian panegyrist of the Caliph Abdul Malik. The *mawali* settled around the Arab Amsar, the early garrison towns, and provided services as artisans and merchants. They soon outnumbered the Arab conquerors. As Muslims the *mawali* were theoretically equal to the Arabs. However, during the Umayyad period this equality was not fully conceded. The tension between Arab and *mawali* found a natural expression in the Shia movement of the Abbasids which was to terminate Umayyad rule.

Abbasids

The Abbasids rode a wave of popular sympathy against the Umayyads. They declared themselves an Islamic kingdom as distinct from the Arab dynasty of the Umayyads. They saw themselves as Imams, the holy inheritors of the Islamic tradition, burning with the desire to avenge Ali and his descendants. Black – the colour of death and mourning, for Ali and his family – became associated with the Abbasids and they were called, as far away as in China, 'the black-robed ones'. The first caliph referred to himself as as-Saffah, the bloodshedder, which became his sobriquet.

The temper of the new dynasty is illustrated by the dinner they organized for their Umayyad rivals. The Abbasid general Abdullah invited eighty leading Umayyads to dinner on a hot night in June 750, at his home near Jaffa. When the guests sat down to eat they were set upon by soldiers. After the slaughter of the Umayyads retainers spread carpets on their squirming, dying bodies and the guests continued to eat and make merry.

Even the dead and buried were not spared. Tombs of Umayyad caliphs were ransacked, only that of the pious Umar II being spared. The youthful Abdur Rahman, a grandson of Hisham, the tenth Umayyad caliph, escaped to Spain to establish a glorious dynasty there.

The Abbasids are the longest-lived Arab dynasty, their rule stretching over five centuries. But this is deceptive. Within the first hundred years the zenith had been reached, symbolized by the reign of the renowned Haroon-ur-Rashid. Then the slow, fitful decline began, a winding, complex, process of palace coups, provinces breaking away, and rebellious dynasties emerging. Towards the end the caliph's authority would be restricted to Baghdad. Around the year 1000 the Abbasid areas were already ruled by the Fatimids (in Egypt, Palestine and south Syria), Hamdanids (north Syria, parts of Iraq), Buwayhids (Iraq and Iran), Samanids (eastern Iran and western Afghanistan), and Ghaznavids (Afghanistan). The Fatimids in Egypt and the branch of the Umayyads who survived the Abbasid onslaught in Spain are the most notable of the dynasties whose rule coincided with the Abbasids.

Of abiding interest for Muslims is the rule of the Umayyads in Andalusia, Spain, started by the young Abdur Rahman. It reached its glory in the poetry, literature and learning of Cordova and Granada. The colleges in Andalusia were to provide a model for those at Oxford and Cambridge.

With its baths and libraries, poetry and chivalry, Andalusia was the symbol of high Muslim civilization. Nothing better symbolizes Andalusia than the town, now a ruin outside Cordova, built by Abdur Rahman III for his favourite Zahra, and called after her, Madinah-at-Zahra.

The end for the Muslims on the Iberian peninsula was abrupt. They were given a clear choice: conversion to Christianity or migration. Many of the migrants to the Maghreb in North Africa, such as those who founded Salé in Morocco, still keep the keys of their houses in Spain, a symbolic gesture of their expulsion. The Inquisition in Spain ensured the extinction of Muslim civilization even in its most superficial aspects. Its collapse was as poignant as its zenith was glorious, and created in Muslims an Andalus syndrome which still haunts them (chapter 8).

Notable shifts took place in society and culture early in the Abbasid period. Arab supremacy faded and first Persians and then Turks were in the ascendant. Arabic died out as a court language, a process begun from the time of Al Walid (705–715), who could not speak it. A new capital, Baghdad, was started by Al Mansur in 762. It cost about 5 million dirhams, took four years to build and involved 100,000 architects, craftsmen and labourers. The caliph became a mystical, semi-divine figure shrouded in court etiquette and lost in bureaucratic procedure.

The rule of Haroon-ur-Rashid (786–809), caliph of the thousand and one nights, is famous for its wealth and colour:

A goodly place, a goodly time.
For it was in the golden prime
Of good Haroun Alraschid

sang Tennyson in the *Recollections of the Arabian Nights*. (It is Haroon's rule which provides material to Karl Wittfogel.)

As Turks, Arabs and Persians jostled for influence and the *ulema* led restless citizens pressing for Islamic reform, the rulers wishing to escape these wearisome pressures, shifted their capital to Samarra. Samarra about 60 miles north of Baghdad, was occupied for less than sixty years in the ninth century. The ruins stretching for twenty miles along the Tigris river bear testimony to the wealth, energy – and extravagance – of the Abbasids.

The purity of Arab blood – the celebrated Arab *nasab* – was destroyed forever by these rulers. Among the Umayyads only Yazid III's mother was a non-Arab, a Persian princess; Abbasid preference for concubines and harems destroyed the principle of racial purity. Of the long Abbasid line only three caliphs were sons of free mothers. The rest were descended from Greek, Persian and Berber slaves (like Haroon-ur-Rashid, the son of Al Khayzuran).

Arabization is the true wonder of the early part of the Arab dynasties. By the eleventh century Arabic – although dead at court – had become the main language from Persia to the Pyrenees, superseding older languages like Coptic, Aramaic, Persian, Greek and Latin. As the language spread the distinctions between Arab conqueror and non-Arab faded.

The establishment of the Abbasid empire with its thriving capital, Baghdad, and its provincial cities, from Qairawan to Bukhara (for the farthest west, the Maghreb and Andalusia, disowned the claim of the Abbasid to rule all Islam), created a situation of relative stability and ushered in the birth of an affluent society. Byzantium was contained and would eventually be mastered, although under very different conditions, Europe was still in the Dark Ages, India no menace, and the east, from where the Mongols would come, asleep.

During the Umayyad and early Abbasid period women remained in the forefront of public life. Arab maidens as stateswomen, as commanders of troops, as poets and as musicians were prominent. Of these Al Khayzuran, Al Mahdi's wife and Haroon's mother, Zubaydah, Al Amin's mother, and Buran, Al Mamun's wife, were examples. Women sank to the low level depicted in *The Arabian Nights* due to the extensive concubinage, laxity and luxury of the later Abbasids.

The Arab empires continued to increase in wealth, as trade went farther and farther afield; the wealth was concentrated in the hands of the grasping few, who relished an affluence which would have amazed their Bedouin ancestors. Marvellous palaces and lavishly-appointed mansions adorned the capital, Baghdad, and the provincial centres of Bukhara, Samarkand, Balkh, Shiraz, Damascus, Aleppo, Jerusalem, Cairo, Tripoli, Tunis, Fez, Palermo and Cordova. Slave boys and singing girls, amenities rare in tribal Arabia, provided Muslim gentlemen with novel pleasures and the poets with a new vocabulary. Wine was forbidden by unambiguous prohibition but the wealthy indulged to the full, and their minstrels vied with one another to sing its praises.

For all the manifest corruption, for all the scandal of flaunted riches and abused power (see 'Decline and Fall', below), the Islamic search for the divine way, the truth, was maintained. From the life of the Prophet, another way to the truth had been shown, the path of direct experience of the Divine. This was the way of the Sufis and it attracted simpler people. Ascetic beginnings and ecstatic climaxes led to theosophical speculation, as the Sufis came under the all-pervading influence of neo-Platonic thought. Abu Yazid of Bistam, a Persian, claimed to have met and conversed with God, indeed to have been absorbed into God. Al Junaid of Baghdad, an Arab, worked out with Quranic texts and dicta of the Prophet a doctrine of spiritual union. His disciple Al Hallaj would declare '*ana-al-Haq*', 'I am God' (as we will see in chapter 5).

In the midst of royal opulence and corruption there were examples of ideal behaviour: Caliph Al Kamil publicly acknowledged the Sufi poet Al Farid although the latter snubbed him by refusing the caliph an audience; Al Kamil also patronized the Coptic church visited by Saint Francis of Assisi; Saladin – whom we meet below – left behind after his death 47 dirhams and a gold piece; Caliph Abu Jaffer was summoned to a court on the complaint of camel-owners and paid the penalty ordered by the judge. For these, as for the countless humbler Muslims, the ideal inspired and attracted.

The distinctive characteristic features of this period included the assimilative power of Arab culture, wrongly misrepresented as imitative. For the first time in history vast territories, from the borders of China to those of France, were united. A new kind of society had emerged. Drawing from existing, older, sources it none the less bore the characteristic imprint of Islam. The *beau idéal* of the Arab gentleman reflected clearly the Islamic ideal. In behaviour, proper (*adab*), in virtue manly (*muruah*), and in manner elegant (*zarf*), he made no cheap jokes and he was clean in appearance.

The diversity of Muslim society underlined the Islamic feature of tolerance. Apart from certain minor social marks of distinction in token of Islamic primacy, non-Muslims, *dhimmis*, were left to themselves. Non-Muslims enjoyed religious, economic and intellectual freedom and the opportunity to make a contribution to the larger civilization. 'Unlike his Western contemporaries, the mediaeval Muslim rarely felt the need to impose his faith by force on all who were subject to his rule,' acknowledged Bernard Lewis, an Orientalist not known for his love of Arabs, in *The Arabs in History* (1967).

Muslim society also reflected another Islamic feature, the importance of knowledge which was prized: a caliph's minister refused an attractive post in Persia because he would need 400 camels to carry his books. In 891 there were a hundred bookshops in Baghdad.

The industry of the Muslim scholars astonishes us even in our period of electric typewriters, dictaphones and personal computers: the historian Al Tabari wrote forty sheets daily for forty years. One of his major works is the 30-volume *Tafsir* – commentary – on the Quran. Western Orientalists plan to edit his *History of the World* into 38 volumes. Al Masudi after a lifetime of scholarship spent the last ten years compiling his 30-volume history, *The Meadows of Gold*. As we saw in the last chapter, Imam Hanbal narrated a million traditions, *hadith*, while Al Ghazzali memorized 300,000.

In spite of bad-tempered kings and invasions by hordes with no respect for learning the scholars seem to have lived long lives. Al Farabi, Malik ibn Anas, Imam Hanbal, Al Beruni, Firdausi and Ibn Khaldun – to name some who appear in the text – lived to about 80 years. We know of at least one section of society whose longevity contrasts with the 50–odd years Muslims are expected to live in our times. Following the Islamic ideal men of learning pursued knowledge with passion. Rulers acknowledged them and ordinary people revered them. These features help explain the extraordinary cultural and intellectual richness of the Arab dynasties.

3 THE FLOWERING OF ISLAMIC CIVILIZATION

Three ancient streams fed the Islamic river of learning and knowledge. These were Hellenic, Persian and Indian. Hellenism meant mainly Greek philosophy (the Arabic word *falsafa* derives from the Greek) – Plato, Aristotle, Euclid and neo-Platonic commentaries, and medical treatises such as those of Hippocrates and Galen. Within a hundred years the Greeks had been translated into Arabic. Then, via Spain and Sicily, the Arab world returned the gift of Greek learning to Europe augmented by their own considerable achievements, which helped to trigger the European renaissance. The Persian influence was restricted to art and belles lettres suffused with mysticism. Astronomy, mathematics and later the decimal system were inspired by India. Al Mansur ordered Muhammad ibn Ibrahim Al Fazari to translate *Siddhanta* (Arabic *Sindhind*) about 800 and Al Fazari thus became the first astronomer in Islam. His contemporary Al Khwarizmi, the first great mathematician of Islam, spread the use of the Hindu numeral system (called in Arabic *Hindi*) through tables. The oldest text on algebra, in which over eight hundred examples are presented, is Al Khwarizmi's chief work.

It was the time of Muslim genius. Four scholars would be outstanding in any company (Al Beruni – with Ibn Khaldun who belongs to a later period – will be discussed in chapter 5). The first, Abu Bakr Al Razi, the Rhazes of medieval writers, was born at Raiy near Tehran in 864 and died there in 925. He devoted himself in particular to the study and practice of medicine, which he pursued mainly in Baghdad. His work is distinguished by meticulous research – 176 contraceptive and abortifacient methods, including coitus interruptus, for which he located numerous *hadith*, were listed. Razi's major work, the encyclopedia of medicine called in Arabic *al-Hawi*, the *Comparative Book*, and translated into Latin by Farragut under the title *Continens*, was published five times between 1488 and 1542, but the original text had to wait until the 1960s to be printed for the first time. In it Al Razi cites Greek, Indian, Persian and Arab opinion on diseases before presenting his own ideas. Fifty of his works are extant. His adventures into philosophy earned him the wrath of orthodox theologians. In his later years, threatened by blindness and disabled by partial paralysis, he defended his reputation against his critics.

Abu Nasr Al Farabi, the ascetic, was born of Turkish stock in Transoxiana and died in Damascus at nearly eighty years of age in 950. A pupil in Baghdad of Christian scholars who had themselves played a prominent part in the first renaissance of Greek learning, he directed his interest to logic and politics as parts of philosophy. His most famous and influential book is the *Ideal State*, in which he attempts to Islamize Plato's *Republic* and *Laws*.

Abu Ali ibn Sina, Avicenna (980–1037), a giant among men of science and learning, came from Bukhara. Like other Muslims of his age he was a many-sided genius. His exhaustive *Canon of Medicine* was translated into Latin and used more than Galen and Hippocrates until the end of the sixteenth century. At one stage he was imprisoned by the Buwayhids. It was said there was no philosopher in the eastern Muslim world after Avicenna (Ibn Rushd, Averroes, who made a greater mark on Christian Europe than the Islamic world, belonging to the western part).

The work of Abu Hamid Al Ghazzali (1058–1111) represents the zenith of Arab intellectual thought. The intellectual crisis for Muslim Arabs between orthodox and Sufi forms of Islam, complicated by Hellenistic intellectual and other ideological influences, was resolved by Al Ghazzali after intense soul-searching which left him in despair. Intellectualism had failed him and in desperation he turned to Sufism. After twelve years of retirement he returned to teach in Baghdad. There he wrote his major work, *Ihya-ulum al-din*. The book was inspired by a vision of the Prophet seen in Makkah. It is said of this book that 'if all the books of Islam were destroyed it would be but a slight loss if only the *Ihya* of Ghazzali were preserved.' Al Ghazzali has been called by scholars of Islam like Professor Anne Marie Schimmel 'the greatest Muslim after the Prophet Muhammad'.

With Al Ghazzali the three currents – theological, philosophical and mystical – made confluence to attempt an all-embracing harmony, an end to dispute. Orthodox Islam, though suspicious of the mystics, and prepared even to execute the extremists, finally accepted the Sufis as allies against the far more dangerous enemies, the freethinking philosophers. Al Ghazzali, eminent jurist, theologian and practising mystic, routed from the field the followers of Razi and Avicenna.

Muslim literature

Islamic intellectual activity was not all dry religious philosophy and staid medical treatise. A new literature which combined instruction and entertainment evolved. It saw the world through brilliantly twinkling human eyes and was widely referred to as *adab*, meaning 'manners', 'proper behaviour'. Al Jahiz (780–869) compiled *The Book of Animals*. It was not a treatise on zoology but a collection of stories, anecdotes and folklore from Greek, Persian, Arabic and Indian sources. The *dolce vita* of the gilded aristocracy is sparklingly portrayed, as it was lived in Andalusia on the eve of the Norman conquest of England, in *The Ring of the Dove*, a highly sophisticated manual of courtly love composed by an eminent theologian, Ibn Hazm. Ibn Qutayba, a serious, orthodox *qadi* influenced by Imam Hanbal, wrote *The Fountains of Story;* Ibn Rabbihi, *The Unique Necklace.*

Adab was amply illustrated in Arab historians, for instance in the *History* of Al Yaqubi (d. 897), the *History of the World* of Al Tabari (d.923) and *The Meadows of Gold and Mines of Gems* of Al Masudi (d. 956), which Ibn Khaldun would use as a base for his own work (chapter 5). Muslim historians used a wide canvas but provided fascinating details of everyday life. Not only Islamic but pre-Islamic Arabic, Persian and Biblical sources, along with folk stories and anecdotes, are cited.

Among the followers of Razi and Avicenna was Umar Khayyam, famous in the West through Edward Fitzgerald's sometimes arbitrary but delightful translation of his quatrains. Hedonism, pantheism, mysticism and Sufi philosophy mix freely in the verses:

Come, fill the Cup, and in the Fire of Spring
The Winter Garment of Repentance fling:
The Bird of Time has but a little way
To fly – and lo! the Bird is on the Wing.

The verses make for a continuously and widely popular Western perception of Persian Sufi poetry. Generations of schoolboys, experiencing the first flush of adolescence, have memorized and quoted Umar Khayyam. But in wanting 'A flask of Wine, a Book of Verse – and Thou' the translator, snuggled 'beneath the Bough', betrays Victorian romanticism. Fitzgerald's poet is a parody. Sufism, as we will see in chapter 5, is intrinsically austere and intensely devotional. Umar composed his shafts of wit and shapes of beauty in his native Persian, which by the tenth century had recovered from the stunning blow dealt it by Arabic. Generations of thinkers, scholars and poets of Persia had been constrained to express themselves – and they did so supremely well – in Arabic, seen as the language of the victor. Then provincial autonomy, symptomatic of the break-up of central government, encouraged a new growth of native literature. The mystics made a large contribution to Persian poetry and prose. Persian prosody followed closely the patterns invented by the Arabs; the poetic forms of ode and lyric were eagerly adopted, with their full complement of rhetorical embellishments. Additionally, the Persians developed a genre which the Arabs had known but scorned to encourage, the rhyming couplet, so that the epic and the idyll enjoyed unrestrained popularity. The couplet suited admirably the requirement of didactive and narrative, both necessary to mystical instruction. The lyrical poems of Hafiz, the greatest of Persia's poets, do not become fully comprehensible until it is realized that the references are as much to the preceptor in his circle of mystical disciples as to the prince and his courtiers. Thus it came about that whereas in Arabic literature only one truly great mystical poet, Ibn Al Farid, emerged, Persian produced a constant succession – Sanai, Attar, Jami – and perhaps the most famous – Rumi (whom we will meet in chapter 5, 'Sufis, saints and mystics').

There was also the development in Persian literature of a distinct 'nationalist' position and a Persian *adab*. It found its most popular expression in the work of Abul Qasim Mansur or Firdausi.

Firdausi (935–1020) is considered the greatest poet in the Persian language and his *Shah Nama, Book of Kings*, the most enduring form of the national epic. The *Book* begins with mythical times and covers the period up to the reign of Khosrau II (590–628) and the overthrow of the Sasanids by the Arabs in the middle of the seventh century. It includes the rise of Zoroastrianism and its prophet, after whom the religion is named. The *Book*'s 60,000 verses took 35 years to complete and it draws heavily on pre-Islamic sources, employing the minimum of Arabic words. Firdausi completed the epic in 1010, when he was 75 years old, and presented it to Mahmud of Ghazni who then ruled Khurasan, Firdausi's home province, expecting a handsome reward. Mahmud's response was tardy. It is suggested that the response was coloured by his Sunni and the poet's Shia belief. This may be so, but Mahmud's relations with Al Beruni were equally prickly (chapter 5). In any case Firdausi, in a gesture of contempt, distributed the reward between two attendants, one at a bath-house, the other at a wine-cellar. He then went into hiding, writing pungent satirical verses about Mahmud. Years later Mahmud, while returning from one of his numerous campaigns in India, was reminded of his poor treatment of the poet. Repenting, Mahmud sent 60,000 dinars worth of indigo – one for each verse – on royal camels to the poet's town, Tus. As the camels entered from one gate the bier with the poet's body left from another. A preacher had inflamed passions against the poet, disallowing his burial inside the town. The poet's daughter proudly refused the king's offering. The sad nature of Firdausi's death would be overshadowed by the influence of his work. The *Shah Nama* would become an inexhaustible source for future Persian nationalism (chapter 4).

Firdausi's life makes a poetic story, especially the ending. It also illustrates the uneasy historical relationship between rulers and men of letters in Muslim society.

However, it was in jurisprudence – not philosophy or *adab* – in which the most impressive achievements were made during the early Abbasid period, and which would have far-reaching consequences. The four main schools of Islamic jurisprudence were established by four scholars widely revered as Imams.

The masters of Islamic law

Abu Hanifa (chronologically the first, 700–767), Malik ibn Anas (710–795), Muhammad ash-Shafi (767–820) and Ahmed ibn Hanbal (780–855) are the four Imams on whose work rests the foundations of Islamic jurisprudence and law. Although Hanifa's is the earliest, most tolerant and largest school – almost half of the Sunnis are influenced by it – Shafi created the discipline of *usul al-fiqh*, principles of jurisprudence, which laid the foundations for the first 'school', influencing the others. The principles rest on the Quran, *sunna*, *ijma*, consensus, and *qiyas*, analogical reasoning. (See also the conversation between the Prophet and Muadh ibn Jabal in the last chapter.)

In Arabic each school was called a *madhhab*, and had slightly differing views, for example on inheritance, private prayers and public worship. All four were, none the less, acceptable to Sunnis (see section 5 of this chapter for a discussion on Shias). A school tends to dominate an area: Hanifi in what would be the Ottoman and Mughal Empires, Maliki in North Africa, Shafi in lower Egypt, east Africa, southern Arabia and South East Asia, Hanbalis in Saudi Arabia (where the Wahabis of Najd followed the principles of Ibn Taymiyah, 1263–1328, a follower of Hanbal; see chapter 8). But two or more schools co-exist in the large cities like Cairo.

Although the active part of the lives of the Imams spans a short century, their work, along with the corpus of traditions, *hadith*, to a large extent moulded Islamic civilization and dominated its intellectual activity. Indeed their vast erudition and penetrating perception so awed their followers that they elevated the Imams to the status of saints and declared 'the gates of *ijtihad*, independent judgement, henceforth closed.' Muslim intellectual activity would thus be discouraged and pushed towards the direction of stagnation.

The lives of the four Imams make several points for us. First there is the quality of Muslim scholarship. In spite of prison, floggings, frequent changes of residence and sometimes material poverty the standards of scholarship would be of the highest. These scholars were not living in ivory towers. Their problems were to discover the principles for organized life, to apply Islamic law to real-life situations. A solid base for future scholarship was thus laid.

Second is the endurance of the human spirit in the face of brute state force. Hanifa died in prison, Malik was stripped and flogged, Shafi, appearing before

Haroon-ur-Rashid, narrowly escaped a death sentence but not prison, Hanbal was beaten and imprisoned. But none of them relented. In their lifetime the Imams were revered as saints and evoked wide affection – for example, almost a million men and women attended Hanbal's funeral in Baghdad. Today their ideas dominate ritual and intellectual thinking among millions of people while their tormentors are forgotten figures in history books.

Finally we must note their struggle to achieve the Islamic ideal, which would provide lessons for future scholars. Stay away from the men of wealth and power, the Prophet had warned. Each Imam would be in grave trouble with the ruler of the day for refusing to subordinate Islamic principles to temporal authority. Hanifa refused to serve as a *qadi*, judge, Malik and Shafi opposed the Abbasids. Hanbal refused to co-operate with Al Mutasim and Al Mutawakkil. In the end he was allowed to leave Samarra, old, sick and tired, to die in Baghdad. Like the captains of Islam in the preceding century the Imams were struggling 'in the path of Allah'.

Muslim rulers

For the privileged few, the aristocrats of birth, wealth or wit, Muslim society offered a way of life different indeed from our austere Islamic ideal. However, power and luxury were enjoyed under the constant threat of disaster. Conspiracy ending in assassination for the caliph, and intrigue followed by disgrace and often enough by execution for his intimates, was always a possibility. The razor's-edge uncertainty perhaps stimulated the desire for sensual pleasures.

In their high, inaccessible palaces the royalty seemed cold and aloof; perhaps they had no hearts underneath the glittering gold and silk they wore. But they felt jealousy, melancholy and love like ordinary mortals, as the following story told by a courtier of the Caliph Al Wathiq illustrates.

The caliph loved Faridah, a concubine, to distraction. He had similar sets of clothes made for both of them. One summer evening, when the courtier was present, the caliph appeared lost in thought. Faridah played a musical instrument which failed to dispel his gloom. Without warning he struck her with force across the chest. She ran out of the chamber, crying. Later he called her and with tender words presented her with a rare pendant. The courtier, intrigued, kept his silence. The caliph then explained his unhappiness: 'One day I will not be here. And I cannot bear to think of Faridah sitting in the same place, on a similar evening, playing to another man.' The caliph was murdered shortly afterwards at the age of thirty-three and succeeded by his brother, Al Mutawakkil (the same who tortured Imam Hanbal), and the prediction of Al Wathiq came true. It was a similar evening and Faridah was present with her instruments before the caliph. The courtier watched with interest. But Faridah refused to play. The caliph's anger was becoming uncontrollable when she broke the instruments and fled. The caliph was amazed and asked the courtier what this meant. 'I know not, my lord, ' replied our discreet courtier.

To ordinary folk the power of the caliph appeared supreme. In fact much of the caliph's authority was illusory. The confessions of a tenth-century caliph in Al Suli's *Akhbar* are revealing:

> Al Radi said to us one day, 'By God, I suppose people ask, Is this caliph content (*radi*) that a Turkish slave should run his affairs and even control finance and exercise sole power? They do not know that this authority (of the caliphate) was already ruined before my time and that certain people put me in it without my desiring it. I was handed over to the life guards and palace guards, who acted insolently toward me, demanded audiences several times a day, and even came to seek me during the night. Every one of them wanted me to favour him above his fellows and to have his own treasury. To save my life I played no tricks on them, until at last God rid me of them. Then Ibn Raiq seized power and acted even more insolently than they in the treasury. He had no peer in drinking and pleasure. If he or his predecessors were told that one parasang away there were horsemen looting property and killing people and if they were told to travel one parasang to fight against them, they would first ask for money and demand arrears of pay – and even so, they might well have taken the money and then not moved. Any one among them or among their companions might commit an offence against my subjects or even my intimates, and if I ordered action against him, my order was not obeyed or carried out or put into effect.'

This honest if self-pitying caliph is one kind of ruler, another was Saladin. Although not an Abbasid he also represents that age. Moreover, he represents the Muslim ideal.

Saladin, ideal Muslim ruler

Saladin (1138–93) – a European corruption of Salah-al-din, rectitude of the faith – perhaps more than any figure in Muslim history has captured the Western imagination, featuring in popular novels (notably those of Walter Scott and Rider Haggard) and films (Rex Harrison's Saladin, performed with all the gusto of a star of the Black and White Minstrel Show, is not easily forgotten). Among Muslims, too, he remains a favourite (my father's middle name, which I inherited, is Salah-al-din).

Saladin's encounters with Richard Coeur de Lion – battling against him one day and exchanging gifts the next – added to the lustre of his name. To the European he came to symbolize ideal, romantic Muslim chivalry. It is no wonder that the French General in 1920, representing a victorious Europe partitioning the Arab lands, knocked on his tomb in Damascus saying, 'Awake Saladin, we have returned.' The continuity of the Crusades in one form was explicit in the General's statement.

Saladin, a Sunni from a somewhat obscure Kurdish background, made his way to the key post of Vizier in Shiite Egypt, eventually becoming its ruler. He patronized scholars, built dykes, dug canals and founded schools and mosques. Among his surviving architectural monuments is the Citadel of Cairo. Soon after becoming ruler he emerged as the champion of Islam, uniting Egypt and Syria against the European Crusaders. The high point of his career was the re-taking of Jerusalem in 1187, well covered by historians and novelists. His legendary generosity was displayed when he allowed the Christian priests to stay on and keep their churches – this in spite of the fact that some had encouraged Crusaders to acts of barbarity like eating Muslim corpses.

In spite of his worldly success he remained a simple man, preferring the company of holy and learned men. He possessed the heroic Islamic virtues of courage, generosity and piety. He appeared to inspire affection among his followers. Not many rulers in history at their death could move their friends to say: 'For I know that had our sacrifice been accepted, I and others would have given our lives for him.'

As these lines are written Arabs are under a state of military siege in Lebanon. Once again we are reminded that towns and cities are but pawns on the Middle East chess board. Jerusalem has been but recently lost by the Muslims. The description of Saladin vowing in illness to recapture Jerusalem, whatever the cost in men and money, thus gains added poignancy for Muslims.

4 DECLINE AND FALL

The nearer a man is to government, the further he is from God; the more followers he has, the more devils; the greater his wealth, the more exacting his reckoning, said the Prophet. But in the palaces and harems of the rulers few were heeding him.

The splendours and sensual gratifications in the seraglios and pavilions are familiar to all who have read the stories of *The Arabian Nights*. But fact was stranger than fiction. Al Mutawakkil (who has already appeared in the text) had 4,000 concubines all of whom shared his bed. *Ghilman*, male slaves including eunuchs, following Persian precedent, became a social institution. They wore rich uniforms and beautified and perfumed their bodies in effeminate fashion. The Caliph Al Amin established their use for homosexual purposes. A judge under Al Mamun used 400 *ghilman*. Poets like Abu Nuwas wrote verses in their praise. Al Mustain's mother ordered a rug which cost 130 million dirhams. It had figures of birds in gold with eyes of rubies and diamonds. According to Al Masudi, Caliph Al Mutazz, the thirteenth Abbasid caliph, was the first to appear on a golden saddle in golden armour. Haroon-ur-Rashid inscribed his name on the most famous ruby in the Arab world, the counterpart of the *Koh-i-noor* in India, after acquiring it for 40,000 dinars.

Here is Ibn Khaldun on Arab weddings, his sociological composure undisturbed by the extravagance:

> Looking at the reports of Al Masudi, Al Tabari, and other (historians) concerning the wedding of Al Mamun to Buran, daughter of Al Hasan b. Sahl, one will be amazed. They tell about the gifts Buran's father made to the retinue of Al Mamun when the caliph came by boat to (Al Hasan's) house in Fumm as-silh to ask for Buran's hand. They tell about the expenditure for the wedding and the gifts Al Mamun gave her. On the wedding day, Al Hasan b. Sahl gave a lavish banquet that was attended by Al Mamun's retinue. To members of the first class, Al Hasan distributed lumps of musk wrapped in papers granting farms and estates to the holders. Each obtained what chance and luck gave him. To the second class, he distributed bags each of which held 10,000 dinars. To the third class he distributed bags with the same amount in dirhams. In addition to all this, he had already spent many times as much when Al Mamun had stayed in his house. Also, Al Mamun gave Buran a thousand hyacinths (rubies) as her wedding gift on the wedding night. He burned candles of amber each of which weighed one hundred *mann* – a *mann* being one and two-thirds pounds. He had laid down for her carpets woven with threads of gold and adorned with pearls and hyacinths. One hundred and forty mule-loads of wood had been brought three times a day for a whole year to the kitchen in readiness for the wedding night. All that wood was consumed that very night. Palm twigs were set alight by pouring oil on them. Boatmen were ordered to bring boats to transport the distinguished guests on the Tigris. The boats prepared for that purpose numbered 30,000, and they carried people back and forth all day long. There were many other such things.

A historian, speaking of the Wazirs, remarks:

> They were cruel rascals, inventors of a thousand injustices, arrogant and presumptuous. They were famous neither for their knowledge nor for their religious spirit. They were the scourges of their age, always with a causeless insult ready in their mouths. Their existence, passed exclusively in oppressing the people of their time, was a disgrace to humanity. When Sultan Barsbay convened the four chief Qadis of Cairo and asked them to authorise new taxes over and above those laid down by the Holy Law, one of them was reputed to have replied: 'How can we authorise the taking of money from the Muslims when a wife of the Sultan wore on the

> day of her son's circumcision a dress worth 30,000 dinars; and that is only one dress and only one wife.'

Harems, debauchery, gold and rubies – we are a long way from the ideal. Power was corrupting and the absolute power of the caliphs corrupted absolutely. Ordinary Muslims in the eighth century were disgusted with what they saw and heard. Their murmurings were to lead to an unending series of revolts and rebellions. Ibn Qutayba records:

> Sudayf, a *mawla* of the Banu Hashim, said, 'By God, our booty, which was shared, has become a perquisite of the rich; our leadership, which was consultative, has become arbitrary; our succession, which was by the choice of the community, is now by inheritance. Pleasures and musical instruments are bought with the portion of the orphan and the widow. The *dhimmis* lord it over the persons of the Muslims, and evildoers everywhere govern their affairs. O God, the seed of falsehood is ripe; it has reached its limit. O God, open the hand of the Reaper of the Right to split falsehood asunder and destroy its being, so that right may appear in the fairest form and most perfect light.' (*Uyun al akhbar*)

The decadence would fuel the fire for Islamic revolt. Ibn Al Athir's *Kamil* contains the following account of Islamic orthodox revivalism in the tenth century. It could be a description of contemporary Iran or Saudi Arabia (see chapter 8):

> In the year 323 (AD 935) the Hanbalis became active and their power became great. They began to raid the houses of the commanders and of the common people, and if they found wine, they poured it away, and if they found a singing girl, they beat her and broke her instruments. They interfered in buying and selling and with men going with women and boys. When they saw this, they asked the man who his companion was, and if he failed to satisfy them, they beat him and carried him to the chief of police and swore a charge of immorality against him. They raised tumult in Baghdad.

Orthodox action created a popular reaction among people. They had had enough of orthodoxy, as Al Athir notes:

> A rescript of the Caliph Al Radi was issued against the Hanbalis, denouncing their actions and accusing them of believing in anthropomorphism and other doctrines, in which it was said: 'You claim that your ugly and disgusting faces are in the image of the Lord of the World and that your vile appearance is in the image of His; you talk of His feet and fingers and legs and gilded shoes and curly hair and going up to heaven and coming down to the world – may God be raised far above

> what wrongdoers and unbelievers say about Him. Then you revile the best of the Imams and ascribe unbelief and error to the party of the family of Muhammad, may God bless and save him. Then you summon the Muslims to religion with manifest innovations and erroneous doctrines, not attested by the Quran; and you reject visits to the tombs of the Imams and abuse those who visit them, accusing them of innovation, but at the same time you yourselves assemble to visit the tomb of a man of the common people, without honour or descent or reason in the Prophet of God, may God bless and save him, and you order people to visit his tomb and you claim for him the miracles of the prophets and the favoured of God. May God curse the devil who enticed you with these abominations and that which led him astray. Now the Commander of the Faithful swears by God a mighty oath which must be fulfilled, that if you do not turn away from that which is pernicious in your doctrines and crooked ways, he will surely punish you with beating, exile, death, and dispersal and use the sword against your necks and fire against your dwellings.'

Helpless or powerful, pious or debauched, the ruler of Islam represented a disintegrating society. The enemies of Islam clearly saw the corruption in Muslim society. The envoys of the Mongol Halagu Khan used Muslim arguments, supported by references from the holy Quran, to justify their actions. Halagu wrote in a letter: 'Prayers against us will not be heard, for you have eaten forbidden things and your speech is foul, you betray oaths and promises, and disobedience and fractiousness prevail among you. Be informed that your lot will be shame and humiliation. "Today you are recompensed with the punishment of humiliation, because you were so proud on earth without right and for your wrongdoing" (Surah 46, *Al Ahqaf*, the wind-curved sandhills). "Those who have done wrong will know to what a (great) reverse they will be overturned" (Surah 26, *Ash Shuara*, the poets).' Halagu predicted with accuracy: 'You will suffer at our hands the most fearful calamity, and your land will be empty of you.'

For Muslims Halagu was the manifestation of the Mongol eruption from Mongolia. Their great leader Chenghiz Khan in the early years of the thirteenth century established himself as one of the most successful military commanders in history. Massacring entire populations – their pyramids of skulls appeared to symbolize their philosophy – destroying established empires, levelling ancient cities within weeks, the Mongols moved inexorably to the heart of the Muslim world.

It is significant that many of the established contemporary scholars of Islam opposed the rulers of Baghdad, even joining the Mongol advance. Khawaja Nasir al Din Tusi, one of the most renowned of all Shia scholars (1201–74) and admired by Imam Khomeini, also joined the entourage of the Mongol conqueror Halagu when he was passing through Iran on his way to Baghdad. This led to accusations of complicity in the conquest.

When the Mongols captured and sacked Baghdad, the capital of the Abbasids, they destroyed not Islam, but a corrupt and decadent society. That event in 1258 terminated the Arab dynasties. The Arabs were destroyed by tribesmen who, as they once did, rode out of isolated deserts to destroy more established systems. But there was one fundamental difference in the two situations: the Mongols brought with them no universal ideology beyond tribalism. They would, therefore, soon succumb to Islam and emerge as its champions.

The Mongols were finally repulsed at Ain Jalut in Syria by the Mamluks in 1260. The Mongol tide was stemmed after this event. Within decades their empires would shrink, their force be spent. 'Few Europeans realized the fate from which their Islamic rivals had saved them,' notes the *Readers Digest Library of Modern Knowledge* (vol. 2, 1981).

It is widely accepted that the vogue of mysticism which Sufism fosters enabled Islam to survive the catastrophe of the Mongol invasions. The practice of fortitude and contemplation, and the hope and realization of experiencing the love of God, sustained men's hearts and souls through the terrible thirteenth century. By then the Baghdad caliphate had vanished in the holocaust. But in the end the bonds of the Sufi orders were more enduring. When Persia finally emerged as a strong and independent kingdom the founders of the Saffavid dynasty took pride in their Sufi origin, as we will see in the next chapter.

In a sense the Abbasids were destroyed by similar factors which would weaken the great Muslim empires in our next socio-historical category. They ran the state as a family affair; the *Shariah* was not applied to them; they had poor communications to cover vast territories; their financial management was disastrous; and they were energetically opposed from abroad, in the case of the Abbasids from the west, indirectly, by the Crusaders and from the east, directly, by the Mongols. It would be another two to three centuries before Muslim destiny would again take firm shape in the form of the three great empires. But that would be another time, the action would take place in other arenas and the world of the Arab dynasties would have been long dead and buried.

5 SHIAS: REVOLUTION IN THE REVOLUTION

Islam carries within it the seeds of renewal and revolution and Shiaism, in particular, may be seen as a revolution within a revolution. Particularism, esotericism, idealism and iconoclasm characterize Shiaism, and Shias make up about 10 per cent of the Muslim total. Their main concentration is in Persia

– now Iran – and South Asia (discussed in the next chapter and chapter 8 respectively). A sense of exclusiveness identifies the Shia: 'The Shi'i saw themselves as an "elect" (*al-khassa*) living among the generality (*al-'amma*) of the Muslims', notes M. Momen (*An Introduction to Shi'i Islam*, 1985).

Shia belief revolves round the figure of Ali, also widely revered by Sunnis (see next section, 'Mahdism and millenarian movements'). Ali's charisma, comprised of personal chivalry and charm, is undisputed. As the Prophet said, 'I am the city of knowledge and Ali is its gate.' Indeed the word Shia means 'one who loves and follows Ali and his descendants', explains a leading Shia Sheikh (Sheikh M. Husayn Al Kashiful-Ghita, *History and Principles of Shiism*, 1985.) Loyalty to the *ahl al bayt* – the house of the Prophet, or Ali and his descendants – is at the core of the sect. The notion of the hidden Imam, descendant of Ali, merely reinforces the loyalty. Shiaism's focus on the tragedies of early Islam, the points of departure from Sunni Islam – Ali's assassination, the deaths of Hussain and his family – gives it passion and creates commitment among its followers. The Shia heartlands would remain in the region where the deaths of Ali and Hussain took place – present Iraq and Iran.

The Prophet, Fatimah, Ali, Hassan and Hussain are the five key figures in Shia theology and history. These are the 'the pure five' of the Shias, *panj tan pak* in South Asia. The five are symbolically represented by a hand-print in most parts of the Shia world. For purposes of our argument in this section it is important to note that three of the five figures were martyred in the cause of Islam. Death, martyrdom, tears and sacrifice therefore form the central part of Shia mythology. Followers are thus expected to respond with fervour to a call for sacrifice. A sense of sectarian uniqueness, of group loyalty, faith in the leadership, readiness for sacrifice, devout ecstasy, divine ritual, marks the community. The ecstasy and passion create 'the Karbala paradigm' (Michael Fischer, *Iran: From Religious Dispute to Revolution*, 1980).

The position of the five figures, *panj tan pak*, in the Shia ideological universe is so enlarged as to eclipse the other actors in the early drama of Islam. Abu Bakr, Umar and Uthman, the first three caliphs of Islam, and Ali's predecessors, are therefore seen as usurpers by Shias. In particular Umar, revered widely by Sunnis, is cast as a villian. Extremists among the Shia magnify the role of Ali sometimes larger than that of the Prophet. One small group even elevate him to the level of Allah. For them the Shia *kalima*, the central Muslim declaration of faith, includes the words 'Hazrat Ali is the friend of Allah'. A further example illustrates the nuances of schism in Islam. One of Allah's ninety-nine names is *al-Ali* or Most High. 'Ya-Ali' is an invocation to Allah for assistance. The cry 'Ya-Ali' for Shias thus becomes a political statement suggesting a subtle play on the name.

Shia history

For Shias, history went awry at the source; a sense of injustice is thus rooted in the way the community perceives the world. There is no substantial difference between the core theological beliefs of Shia and Sunni. Both believe in the central and omnipotent position of Allah; both accept the supremacy of the holy Prophet as the messenger of Allah. The holy Quran is revered by both as the divine message of Allah. The Sunni ideal also holds for the Shia.

The problems are rooted in the history not theology of Islam. Islamic history, Shias maintain, began to go wrong when Ali, married to Fatimah, daughter of the Prophet, was not made the first caliph after the death of his father-in-law. To make matters worse Ali was assassinated. Ali's two sons, Hassan and Hussain, following in their father's footsteps, opposed tyranny and upheld the puritan principles of Islam. Both were also martyred. Hussain was killed, facing impossible odds on a battlefield with his family and followers, at Karbala.

Hussain's challenge of Yazid and his death at Karbala are among the more significant events in Muslim history. 'The greatest cause of the advancement of Shiaism, however, was that bloody event which revolutioned the Islamic world,' observes Sheikh Ghita (1985). About 70 men, including Hussain's infant son, Asghar, were slaughtered by an army of thousands. The only male member to survive was Zain-ul-Abedin, Hussain's son, who was ill at the time, and from whom come the Sayyed, the descendants of the Prophet. After the battle was over Hussain's head was cut from his body and brought to Yazid's governor. The governor, playing about with it, provoked a reprimand from an old Muslim: 'I have seen this very face being kissed by the Prophet.'

Hussain's action established anew the principle of challenging at all costs any authority deviating from the Islamic ideal. The struggle between Hussain and Yazid is the classic confrontation between good and evil. Hussain represented the virtues found in the ideal of Islam. Yazid symbolized despotism, dynasty and temporal power. Although the incident provides Shias, the main Muslim sect after Sunnis, with their exclusiveness, Sunnis, too, mourn for Hussain and are chastised by the manner of his death.

The deaths laid the foundations for Shia mythology: Hussain's *alam*, flag, horse and *tazya*, representation of his shrine at Karbala, are universal symbols of mourning. The very names of Hussain's family would become common in Muslim, particularly Shia, households: Fatimah and Zainab, his mother and sister, and Abbas, Zain-ul-Abedin and Asghar, his brother and sons. The immense sacrifice ensured the perpetuation of the myth of Karbala; its political content has made it a powerful and emotional rallying point against tyranny and oppression. An Urdu poet summed it up in verse: '*Islam zinda hota hay har Karbala key bad*', 'Islam is reborn after every Karbala.'

When Islam was brought to Iran by conquering Arabs at about the time of Karbala, Persian separateness asserted itself by supporting the Shia sect. The current Iran-Iraq war – one of the longest in our times – thus has deep historical roots explaining the animosity it generates between the antagonists (major Iranian offensives are called Karbala and sequentially numbered 1,2,3). In time an entire set of differentiated customs, rituals and even forms of prayer evolved. Most of these are only marginally different to Sunni practice. For example, opening and closing of the fast during Ramadan at slightly different times or washing the feet first rather than at the end of the daily prayers. However, they act as social diacritica to widen the gap between Shia and Sunni.

A characteristically Shia institution which marks it from Sunni Islam is the *muta*, temporary marriage. 'Marriage for a fixed term and usually for a predetermined financial arrangement is considered allowable by Shi'is. The marriage may be for any length of time, even for a matter of hours' (Women, *op. cit.*). Sheikh Ghita explains the logic behind *muta* by raising a question: 'How should the traveller behave especially when he happens to be young and subject to strong sexual urges?' The Sheikh considers 'only two alternatives possible': 'he should either control his passion or must indulge in unlawful relationships'. But 'It should be stated that excessive control and suppressing of sexual desires sometimes causes serious physical and mental illness', he warns. By practising *muta* 'the honour of man and woman would be saved, the Muslim community would grow in number, the world would be rid of illegitimate children and moral values would be strengthened.' Sunnis scoff at the *muta* deriding it as a lustful act concealed under a religious cover. The historical differences between Shia and Sunni even affect the *muta*. Ali, Shias aver, supported, Umar opposed it: 'It was Hadrat Umar who prohibited *muta* during his rule', notes the Sheikh with disapproval.

In countries where both Shia and Sunni live, conflict between them is endemic. In Pakistan, where about 20 per cent of the population of about 100 million are Shias, these differences can degenerate into armed clashes. This is especially so during the month of Muharram, and in the ten days of Shia mourning for the events of Karbala. During this period Shias mourn, flagellate themselves, bring out processions symbolic of Karbala, and recite moving poems of the tragedy at Karbala which reduce those present to tears and quivering rapture. Conflict with Sunnis is often sparked as a result of overzealous Shias abusing figures respected by Sunnis such as Umar and by Sunnis denigrating the *tazya* and other symbols of the Karbala martyrs.

Women in Shiaism

An appreciation of the five central figures for the Shias will help us in understanding the role of women in that community (also see chapter 9 section 2, 'Muslim Women'). Among the five the role of Fatimah is central. 'The more accommodating attitude to women expressed in Shi'i law over divorce and inheritance is attributed to the important position held by Fatimah among

Shi'is' (Momen, *An Introduction to Shi'i Islam*, 1985). Always a great favourite of her father Fatimah provides the link between her father and husband and between her sons and their grandfather. The Sayyeds, those claiming descent from the Prophet, do so through Fatimah. So do the twelve Imams, revered by the Shia. In addition, Fatimah's mother and the Prophet's first wife, Khadijah, is also an object of reverence.

Two other women feature in Shia mythology. Neither of them is popular. They are Aishah and Hafsah, both wives of the Prophet. The reason for their unpopularity is linked to the question of Ali's succession. Aishah was the daughter of Abu Bakr and Hafsah of Umar, the two who preceded Ali as caliph. Aishah is singled out because she opposed Ali actively after the death of the Prophet.

As we note, one of the five revered figures, *panj tan pak*, for the Shia is a woman. Among the Sunnis a similar listing, of the Prophet and the first four caliphs, consists entirely of males. In other matters, too, Shia women are better off than Sunnis. Shia women often inherit shares equal to that inherited by male kin from their parents. Among the educated Sunni, women receive, at best, one-half of what a male inherits; in the rural areas they seldom inherit. In Shia ritual women play a leading role. Shia women are more active than their Sunni sisters in other religious functions too: 'the *sufra* (literally tablecloth) . . . consists of an invitation by the hostess to a number of other women to join her for a meal which is usually preceded or followed by a discourse by a *mulla* (often female) on a religious theme' (Momen, *op. cit.*). The organization and the enactment of the death dramas of Karbala involve the active participation of women. Shia women are thus in the forefront of religious practice and belief.

The Shia search for the ideal

The saints and scholars of Shiaism are revolutionaries, exhorting, pointing towards the ideal. They either live in or are inspired by Iran. Learning is prized. A hierarchy ranking on the basis of reputation and scholastic attainment is recognized: *mullah, mujtahid, Ayatullah*, sign of God, and *Ayatullah al-Uzma*, the supreme Ayatullah of the age.

One of these, the Ayatullah al-Uzma, Imam Khomeini, states the case for Shiaism:

> The Shi'i school of thought, which is the prevalent one in Iran, has had certain distinguishing characteristics from the very beginning. While other schools have preached submission to rulers even if they are corrupt and oppressive, Shi'ism has preached resistance against them and denounced them as illegitimate. From the outset, Shi'is have opposed oppressive governments. (*Islam and Revolution*, 1981)

The Imam compares Shia belief and practice with that of Sunnis, throwing light on recent events in Iran:

> In countries other than Iran, where either there are no Shi'is or the Shi'is are in the minority, the earlier traditions of submission to the rulers have prevailed. The rulers are obeyed as the legitimate holders of authority (*ulu'l-amr*).
>
> Many Sunnis, however, may regard this rebellion against oppressive government as incompatible with Islam; for example, we find the Azhar opposing us and condemning the Iranian people. That is because of the belief that even an oppressive ruler must be obeyed, a belief that is based upon an incorrect interpretation of the Qur'anic verse concerning obedience.
>
> In contrast, we Shi'is, who base our understanding of Islam on what we have received from Ali (upon whom be peace) and his descendants, consider only the Imams and those whom they appointed to be legitimate holders of authority. This view conforms to the interpretation of the Qur'anic verse on authority made by the Prophet himself.
>
> This is the root of the matter: Sunni-populated countries believe in obeying their rulers, whereas the Shi'is have always believed in rebellion – sometimes they were able to rebel, and at other times they were compelled to keep silent. (*ibid.*)

The Shia striving for the ideal is reflected in a central feature of the Islamic constitution in present day Iran. The *Vilayat-e-fiqih*, supreme over government, a post held by Imam Khomeini, need not be from Iran as long as he is a good Muslim. The Islamic principle is superior to the national one. This is a unique provision; not even the most advanced Western democracy could match its spirit.

In the West contemporary Shiaism is known widely for terrorism and anarchy because of the politics of Iran and Lebanon. This is an incorrect reflection of Shiaism. I will cite experts from America to support my contentions, because that country is usually the target.

American experts make three important points, which are contrary to the stereotype, in their recent book on Shia Islam (Cole and Keddie, *Shi'ism and Social Protest*, 1986): first, 'Shi'ism is not now and never has been a monolithic movement, nor have either the *ulama* (religious scholars) or the followers of this branch of Islam always been activists or united in their views'; second, 'Indeed, one of the conclusions indicated by several contributors . . . is that nationalism has often proven stronger than obvious religious or sectarian allegiances, even in states with weak national identities.' The content of Imam Khomeini's foreign policy – *nah sharq nah gharb*, neither East nor West – is as much a nationalist reflex as an Islamic one. Third – acting as a corrective to the Fischer 'Karbala paradigm' thesis – 'In the past several years the word Shi'i has often, especially in the United States, taken on the connotation of "fanatic" or "terrorist", and we are often told that Shi'is have a "martyr complex" that makes them welcome death in pursuit of their cause. In fact, the majority of the world's assassins in the past century have been Europeans of Christian background, and with the exception of the medieval "Assassin" sect, which belonged to a different line than today's politicized Shi'is, Shi'is were not known until very recently for either terrorism or special devotion to offensive holy wars (which most Twelver *ulama* have held were forbidden during the occultation).'

Consideration of the next phase of Islamic history includes the Saffavids, the Shia dynasty par excellence. The Saffavids would constantly be at war with their Sunni neighbours, the Ottomans in the west and the Mughals in the east (chapter 4).

6 MAHDISM AND MILLENARIAN MOVEMENTS

Islam is a *jihad* – struggle, fight – to improve the world, to bring it into accord with the ideal. The Prophet had promised there would be reformers to renew and revive faith: 'God will send to this community, at the head of every hundred years, one who will renew for it its religion.'

As chapter 1 indicated throughout Islamic history and wherever Muslims lived Muslim leaders would preach a move to the ideal. Calling themselves – or more correctly called by their followers – Mahdis, they gave expression to often vague ethnic, social or political movements. Many of these movements were motivated by an ill-defined but firm conviction that in the near future society would blossom into the ideal based on justice, equality and truth. In common belief a cycle – a hundred years or a thousand years, hence millenarian, was most popular – would bring change and relief for the majority. Chiliastic, eschatological and populist arguments found their way in these beliefs. The Islamic concept of *jihad* thus easily translates into Mahdist and millenarian movements.

From the assassination of Ali the idea of the Hidden, Infallible or Rightful Mahdi (or Imam) took root. This person divinely appointed, would avenge wrong, correct injustice and restore the Islamic ideal. The obscurity of his origins and vagueness surrounding him enhanced his mystique. It ensured the success of the idea, for any person, however lowly, could appropriate the role if the circumstances were right. In its romantic simplicity the idea provides vast scope for Mahdist and millenarian activity. The basis was laid for the entire schismatic gamut in Islamic thought from the Shia, with offshoots like the Ismailis, to more temporary movements.

Muslim history is replete with Mahdis leading revolts against established authority and often dying for their efforts. Mahdis appear early in history. A rising in Syria in 752 declared the coming of the Mahdi. A decade later Muhammad claiming descent from Ali declared himself the Mahdi and was eventually defeated and killed in Madinah.

Although religious in form and idiom, Muslim movements in history have been motivated by ethnic, political and economic factors, sometimes a combination of these. The rebellion led by Sonpadh in 755 combined millenarian ideology and ethnic resentment. His followers, Muslim peasants of west Persia and Zoroastrians, numbered about 100,000. Sonpadh invoked the memory of Abu Muslim who had preached the coming of a just Islamic order. He was seen as having been betrayed by the Abbasid caliphs he had assisted in obtaining power. Persian hostility to Arabs played a major part. Although the Caliph Mansur's army defeated Sonpadh, the movement simmered on in Khurasan.

More dangerous for the Abbasids was the movement of Muqanna, the Veiled One, who forms the subject of an episode in Moore's *Lalla Rookh*. Muqanna was so called because he concealed his face, to hide its radiance according to his followers, to hide its deformity according to critics. A Persian peasant, his following spread throughout Central Asia and Khurasan between 776 to 789. The orthodox accused him of practising and preaching communism of property and women.

The rebellion of Babak (816–837), which also created problems for the Abbasids, was an economic one. Babak's followers were poor villagers. His sect, the Khurramiya, had orders 'to attack the landowners and plunder their possessions'. Four of the generals of the Caliph Mamun were defeated.

Even more serious was the rebellion between 869 and 883 of the Zanjis, the black slaves. East of Basra on the salt marshes worked gangs of slaves to drain land for agriculture and extract salt. These gangs, between 500 to 5,000 strong, were mostly Africans and worked in appalling conditions. Not far from the marshes were the wealth, glitter and corruption of urban Arab life (see section 4 above). Owner and slave were both Muslim. Resentment in the latter was high and only a spark was needed to light the fuse. It was provided by Ali ibn Muhammad who claimed to be descended from Ali. Al Tabari, the Arab historian, describes the Zanji movement and its leader. One imperial army after another was defeated by them. Basra was sacked in 871 and in the next few years the Zanjis were raiding the outskirts of Baghdad.

The Zanjis built their own capital, calling it the Chosen, Al Mukhtara. Their territory covered south Iraq and they expanded into south-west Persia. They believed their Islam to be nearest to the ideal. The best Muslim – even an Abyssinian slave – had the right to be caliph. Other Muslims were seen as infidels. Black troops sent to quell them changed sides and supported their cause. The Abbasids finally succeeded in assaulting and capturing Al Mukhtara in 883. Ali's head was brought on a pole to Baghdad.

Most of the movements were marked by an ephemeral nature. But one that would flourish was led by Ismail and therefore called Ismaili. Claiming descent from Ali, Ismail and his son Muhammad organized their devoted followers into a well-knit group. Their doctrines, many of which were kept secret, included neo-Platonic and Indian ideas. Their head was an infallible, religious Imam. The sect has endured to the present day, and now, because of the attitudes of their forward-looking Imam, Prince Karim, they command wide respect and influence.

'I am not the Mahdi', declared Dan Fodio after his successful *jihad* and defeat of the Hausas, and just before his retirement after disillusionment to a life of contemplation. 'But', he added, 'I am clothed in his robe. Every era has a Mahdi. Like the wind heralding rain, I stand in relation to him.' And indeed Muslims would rise in every era to face the challenge.

The last century has witnessed a profusion in Mahdis. Across the Muslim world – from Sudan to Somalia to Swat to Indonesia – they have challenged authority, a stimulus being provided by European colonization. General Gordon's opposition to the Sudanese Mahdi, Muhammad Ahmad, and his dramatic death in Khartoum are the subject of film and novel. The Mahdi to many in the West is only Muhammad Ahmad of Sudan. This, as we see, is not so.

The fervour of the Mahdis invited an easy label from their critics: the mad mullah. Thus Europeans came to know – and dismiss contemptuously – the Mad Mullah of Somalia, of Swat, and of other Muslim areas of rebellion (see chapter 7). Although the Mahdi's role overlaps at an early stage that of the mullah it is incorrect to view him, a man burning with a vision to change society and prepared to challenge authority, as a mullah. The mullah is a religious functionary, supervising the village mosque and rarely rising above village politics, far removed from millenarian thought.

Contemporary Muslim society, too, is riven by Mahdi-like figures: Muhammad Marwa in Kano, Nigeria, Khalid al-Islambuli in Cairo, Juhaiman Ibn Saif Al Utaiba in Makkah (chapter 8, section 1) and Noor Muhammad in Wana, Pakistan. In the last decade they have led bloody revolts against central authority. For their followers they had the qualities of the Mahdi. Non-Muslim – particularly Western – values stimulate and provoke Mahdism, providing the preconditions for the emergence of Mahdis.

The significance of Mahdism and the movements lies in their Islamic form and content as interpreted by the leader and his followers. Although we clearly see underlying economic, political or ethnic factors for revolt, it is important that their expression is Islamic. Nowhere is Islam rejected. The movements wish to impose an ideal Islam on society. Indeed, so marked is the attempt to legitimize the movement in an Islamic framework that most of the leaders claim descent from Ali. Another significant point is the ethnic and social background of the leader. Leaders have often been poor peasants and from deprived ethnic groups. Using Islamic idiom has reinforced their sense of deprivation and consolidated the movement.

The official scribe or historian, paid by the royal treasury, condemned the rebellious Mahdi and movement. Using the Islamic argument he dismissed them as unorthodox, deviant or anti-Islamic. They thus have a bad press in history. But the movements often reflect genuine discontent in society and their expression acts as a safety valve. The very vagueness and simplicity of the notions of Mahdism ensure that millenarian and populist movements will mark Muslim society. Until the ideal is achieved the *jihad* will agitate Muslim society, disturbing the sleep of arrogant and corrupt rulers.

4

The great Muslim empires: Ottomans, Saffavids and Mughals

We will look in this chapter for those features in three Muslim societies, in different parts of the world, which are explained by their regional culture and history. The three societies, which were contemporaneous, represent the three great Muslim empires, Ottoman, Saffavid and Mughal. The first section draws brief, impressionistic pen pictures of the empires, highlighting major events and drawing attention to their characteristic features. The second points to certain similarities between them and the central obsession in each of these societies created by the confrontation with a major alien ideology which already existed. Christianity for the Ottomans, Sunni Islam for the Saffavids and Hinduism for the Mughals were to provide the obsession, the main theme and the neurosis. In some cases there was synthesis, in others stimulation, but the obsession could not be dismissed. In an important sense the three empires were supplanting these older, established systems which they confronted. They were thus usurpers, but successful usurpers.

1 OTTOMANS: FACING EUROPE

The Ottoman – from their ancestor Uthman (a namesake of the third ideal caliph), thus Osmanli and eventually Ottoman – was one of the largest and longest-lived dynasties the world has seen. Starting with Uthman, in the direct male line, 36 sultans ruled from 1300 to 1922. The empire probably reached its zenith with Sulayman, the Magnificent, in the sixteenth century. This was the greatest time of expansion. The North African conquests date from this period – all of North Africa, save Morocco, formed part of the empire. It stretched from Budapest to Yemen, from Baghdad to Algeria. In 1529 Sulayman came close to taking Vienna.

In poetry, art and architecture, a peak was also reached. Yet the obsession with Christianity was never far from the surface. When Constantinople – named after Constantine the Roman Emperor, who shifted his capital here from Rome – was taken in 1453 it was renamed 'Istanbul', the 'city of Islam'. In these exchanges church was converted to mosque and mosque to church as fortunes changed. The most famous example of conversion being that of Santa Sophia, one of the best known churches in Christendom (when its builder, Justinian, saw it on completion he thought of the Temple of Jerusalem and exclaimed, 'Ho, Solomon I have surpassed thee'). Sinan, the most celebrated architect of the empire, built the Sulamanyih mosque, deliberately to exceed Santa Sophia by 16 feet (80 of Sinan's buildings are extant).

The Ottoman empire was eclectic. Persian notions of absolute monarchy, the tradition of constant warring from Central Asia, Byzantine ideas of government and, above all, the Arabic script, sciences and religion formed its character. Perhaps the most pervasive influence came from the last source. The Arabs were to the Ottomans what the Greeks were to the Romans.

The association of Islam and the Ottomans is perhaps not fully appreciated today. The Ottoman flag was a crescent and star, adopted since by many Muslim nations. The proudest possessions of the Topkapi Palace are the mantle and staff of the Prophet brought by Sultan Salim from Cairo in 1517. And in the heart of the harem, in the main bedchamber of the sultan, Quranic verses in exquisite tiles exhorted women to be God-fearing and virtuous.

The eclectic nature of the empire allowed, indeed demanded, promotion and status to be rewarded on merit, irrespective of caste or class. Turk or Arab, Slav or Armenian, once they became Muslim were eligible to the highest posts in the land – save that of the sultan, the only position determined by birth. Thus birth and genealogy, old families, or landed aristocracy became irrelevant.

The Janissaries – Yeni Ceri, new soldiers – who played such a key role in Ottoman history were almost entirely born Christian but raised as Muslim soldiers. They knew only discipline and their loyalty to the sultan and Islam was legendary. Some of the most famous historical figures were not Muslim by birth. For example, Sinan, and Barbarossa, the victorious admiral, were born Christian. Ali Bey who became Sultan of Egypt and Syria in the late eighteenth century was the son of a Caucasian Christian priest. The Ottoman administrative system was the first to be based entirely on merit.

The heart of the Ottoman empire was the Topkapi Palace in Istanbul. The Topkapi was for 400 years the seat of Ottoman power and is now advertised as 'the largest and richest Museum in the world'. The palace itself is spread over 30 acres and overlooks three seas.

Eating like a canker in the heart was the harem. The harem was designed for one man, the sultan. He lived, played, and died here. He also ruled from here. Protocol around him was rigid, inherited from the Byzantine emperors.

His silk robes were worn once only to be discarded, he shifted his chambers nightly for fear of assassination.

Here demented sultans, captive concubines and scheming eunuchs lived in the 350 warren-like rooms. The harem is advertised today as 'the most secret and inaccessible palace on earth'. It is the most fascinating part of the Topkapi for visitors. I also found it one of the most depressing.

Women of all colours and castes were brought, bought or kidnapped to the harem ensuring that the sultans had very little Turkish blood in their veins. Once they entered the harem there was no escape for the women. Their fate was sealed. Their lives, waiting for the sultan's notice, were empty. The jealousy, intrigue, and squabbles were, like the rooms, claustrophobic. Women jockeyed for favour. Favourite sons were suddenly elevated to rule vast territories, out-of-grace sons were locked away in cage-like rooms in the harem to go mad slowly in isolation. Over 1,200 concubines were kept in the seventeenth century. In the same century Sultan Ibrahim, mad with drugs or rage, ordered 280 of his women to be sewn in weighted sacks and thrown into the Bosphorus. The Turks have a saying, 'a fish begins to rot at the head'.

In 1683, a second attempt was made to capture Vienna. It also failed. Now the long, slow, tortuous process of decline began. Turkey became 'the sick man' of Europe. Expanding and vigorous European powers made attempts to devour what they could of the Ottoman empire. Slowly bits and pieces began to fall off; nationalism claimed some, European colonial avarice took others. It is little wonder that the first thing Ataturk did was to abolish the Ottoman caliphate and move the capital from Istanbul to Ankara. He was consciously rejecting the past.

It was during the sick phase of the empire's history that the Ottomans inspired the popular caricature of the Oriental in the minds of Europeans. Orientals were seen as debauched, lazy and ignorant. Their foods were said to induce debauchery (Ottoman names of sweets which survive are suggestive: 'lady's navel' – *hanim gobegi* – 'lips of a beauty' – *dilber dudagi*), their lives prodigality (harems and seraglios). Modern tourist guides, hoping to capitalize on these images and unaware of the academic controversy raging around the images of Orientalism, advertise night life in Istanbul as 'sequins shimmer with the twinkle of tiny cymbals as Oriental dancers express the age-old seduction of the East'.

Writers confirmed the images of the Oriental, poets sang of them. In particular, the attempts of the Greeks to break away from Istanbul evoked strong emotional support in Europe. Greece was, after all, the cradle of Western civilization. Shelley and Byron sang of Greek valour and denounced Turkish atrocities. 'And musing there an hour alone, I dream'd that Greece might still be free', pondered Byron. Statesmen condemned the Turks: '[The

Turks] one and all, bag and baggage, shall, I hope, clear out from the province they have desolated and profaned' (Gladstone in the House of Commons).

The very word Turk became synonymous with treachery and cruelty. It was a land where people bore – and still bear – the name Attila with pride. 'A malignant and turban'd Turk' (Shakespeare), 'the unspeakable Turk' (Carlyle), became a prototype in Europe (in the mid-1960s, centuries after Shakespeare, I recall a popular restaurant in Cambridge called 'The Turk's Head').

For Europe, the Turkish bath, Turkish coffee and Turkish kebab were among the few positive images of the land. It was the harem and the seraglio, where pale-skinned, over-fed women reposed on divans, which were fixed in European minds through images of Orientalist literature and art.

Although to the Europeans the Sunni façade of the Ottoman empire appeared monolithic it contained interesting unorthodox Muslim sects. The Alevi are an example. Nur Yalman, a Turkish anthropologist at Harvard University, has studied the Alevi who historically live in eastern Turkey bordering Iraq and speak Turkish and Kurdish ('Islamic reform and the mystic tradition in Eastern Turkey' in *European Journal of Sociology*, 1969). Alevis emphasize the role of Ali – hence Alevids – in addition to the oneness of Allah and prophethood of Muhammad. They fast for only twelve days of the year in memory of the twelve Imams, rejecting the month of Ramadan; they dismiss daily prayers, bowing only twice annually; and they see no need of the pilgrimage to Makkah, considering the real pilgrimage internal and in one's heart. The ritual for Eed, the Muslim celebration, the Feast of Abraham, is known as *mum sondu*, 'candle blown out', a term 'associated with the myth of communal sexual intercourse and incest'. A key element of the ritual involves members approaching the Dede or spiritual leader on all fours, like lambs, to kiss the hem of his coat. Twisting the five features of Islam beyond recognition Alevis were condemned by Sunnis as non-Muslims.

As a consequence of the Turkish decline curiosity about and respect for the West were genuine. From the eighteenth century onwards attempts to imitate Western institutions were made. A school of military engineering with a French director was started. Other training institutes, particularly for the army and navy, were run by European, mainly French, instructors. French and Italian were studied. European literature was widely translated into Turkish under government patronage. The fascination for European ways was thus deep, laying the foundations for the obsession with Christian Europe.

The Turks were not the first to challenge Europe. The Moors, crossing from Gibraltar, had ruled Spain for centuries. Sicily, too, was ruled by Arabs. So were large parts of Russia. But over the centuries their dynasties weakened, their will exhausted, these Muslims had been expelled from Europe. Only the Turks remained. For the Europeans they were the hammer of Islam.

Once ruling vast parts of eastern Europe, even knocking on the gates of

Vienna, the Turks had been driven out relentlessly from their European territories. But they clung on to Istanbul and its hinterland, and by so doing they remained in Europe. This achievement was due almost entirely to the military genius of one man, Kamal Ataturk, the father of the Turks and of modern Turkey.

Repelling invading armies, selecting a new capital, forming constitutions and governments, Ataturk burnt himself out prematurely and died when he was only fifty-five. In his brief lifespan he had created a modern nation but in doing so he had to sever the Ottoman connection.

Ataturk, consciously, furiously, rejecting the past, succumbed to the European obsession. From the profound to the trivial he Europeanized Turkey's cultural, social and religious life: the Santa Sophia mosque was converted to a museum, the fez was banned and replaced by European hats, Sufi and dervish orders were suppressed, Islamic law superseded by European legal codes and Latin not Arabic letters were used for the Turkish script. In order to communicate his message, emphatic – sometimes crude – symbolism was used. A new Turkey, Europeanized, purged of its past, was to be born. Affiliation with the past almost became a crime. Even today a woman covering her head or a man cultivating a beard, both suggesting Islam, risk termination in government service.

Ataturk's picture is everywhere, in houses, cafes and government offices. On the anniversary of his death, 10 November, at five minutes past nine in the morning, the exact moment of his passing, the whole nation stands still. He is officially called the Eternal Leader. As if to guard his revolution, Ataturk stares in statues and busts, in European dress usually wearing a bow-tie, in public places. In Ataturk's Turkey the obsession with Europe found its fullest expression and through Ataturk's deeds was sublimated.

2 SAFFAVIDS: SHIA STATE

The Saffavid dynasty originated in the Sufi order founded by Safi-al-din (1252–1334). During the fifteenth century the order converted to a revolutionary movement. Shiaism was its faith and charter. The Turks, with the Uzbegs on the eastern front, would be the constant enemies of the Saffavid soldiers, the Qizilbash or red-heads. The Saffavids wore red turbans with twelve folds commemorating the twelve Shiite Imams.

In 1501 Shah Ismail I, only fourteen years old, was proclaimed ruler after defeating a Turkish army. The most important decision of the Shah was to declare that the official religion of the state would be Twelver – *ithna ashari* – Shiaism. The Saffavid state was to be a theocracy, Shah Ismail personified the twelfth Imam in the flesh. Shah Ismail conducted a vigorous campaign to convert the predominantly Sunni population to Shiaism. The Sunni *ulema* either fled or were killed. Shah Ismail thus became the Sufi master and the Qizilbash, the main officials, his disciples. The state thus reflected the Sufi order from which it derived its origin.

Shah Ismail's son, Shah Tahmasp, was an ascetic. None the less, he was enough of a military strategist to resist five Uzbeg invasions of Khurasan and four Ottoman invasions of Azarbaijan. Tahmasp's grandson, Shah Abbas the great (1588–1629), coming to the throne when he was seventeen, brought Saffavid fortunes to their peak. By 1606, he had decisively defeated the Uzbegs and the Ottomans.

Shah Abbas's achievements are not limited to the political and military fields. Peace was brought to the countryside, art and industry – especially the manufacture of carpets and silks – flourished. Ambassadors and traders thronged to the court of Shah Abbas. He patronized one of the finest flowerings of the Persian artistic genius and compares well with his contemporaries, Akbar of India and Elizabeth of England.

Like Akbar in India, who created a new capital at Fatehpur Sikri, Shah Abbas ordered his capital at Isfahan. It symbolized the wealth and artistic achievements of the Saffavids. Assisting him was Sheikh Baha al-din Muhammad Amali, theologian, philosopher, astronomer, poet and engineer. Isfahan became one of the world's beautiful cities and, for its time, one of the largest with about one million people. It boasted 162 mosques, 48 madrasas, 1,801 caravanserais and 273 public baths. Water, trees and parks delighted the eye. 'From whatever direction one looks at the city it looks like a wood,' marvelled a French visitor.

In an age of Islamic renaissance, the Saffavid princes were themselves poets and artists. Shah Ismail was a poet and Shah Tahmasp a painter. Most important, they patronized the arts. Shah Abbas would hold the candle while his favourite calligrapher, Ali Riza, was at work. To encourage the arts, artists were induced by attractive offers or coerced to join the court from distant provinces. Brilliant miniature paintings reached new heights of excellence with the illustration of classics such as Firdausi's *Shah Nama* and Jami's *Haft Awrang*. Perhaps the high point was the series of 250 miniatures which illustrated the *Shah Nama* commissioned by Shah Ismail for his son Tahmasp.

Tahmasp spent his early years in Herat, studying how to paint. Painters were among his closest companions, although this did not prevent him from cutting off the nose of one painter who ran off with his favourite page boy. Sensuality became increasingly prominent in the later Saffavid paintings and eroticism blatant. A more realistic style, dealing with everyday themes, was evolving.

By the eighteenth century the Shia *ulema* were beginning to challenge the theory of the divine right of kings, the concept that the shah was the Imam incarnate, the shadow of God, *zilallah*, on earth. Mullah Ahmad Ardabili confronted Shah Abbas with the thesis that he did not rule by divine right but as a trust on behalf of the Imam. The *ulema*, he warned, would decide whether that trust was being honoured or not. Soon the *ulema* were vigorously arguing that the Imam must be a genuine *mujtahid*, a man of learning and impeccable character. The *ulema* were bidding to take control of the Shia state which the Saffavids had created.

Henceforth, politics would oscillate between two points, secular rulers jealously guarding their authority while discovering their roots in imperial pre-Islamic Persian history, and aggressive religious scholars claiming a share of it. Where the rulers emphasized Persian language and custom especially drawing on the Pahlavis – Firdausi's *Shah Nama* was a rich source – the *ulema* spoke of a universal Islam. In an important sense the base for contemporary politics in Iran was being laid.

Most of the seventeenth and eighteenth centuries were taken up by the rule of four drunken shahs claiming to be the shadow of God on earth. Late in the seventeenth century Muhammad Majlisi, a precursor of Imam Khomeini in the twentieth century, challenged the Shah successfully and imposed Shiaism on the court. Hundreds of thousands of wine jars in the royal cellars were smashed. Under Majlisi the power of the *ulema* would be at its height.

Majlisi became Sheikh al-Islam of Isfahan in 1687 and Mullabashi – Head Mullah – in 1694, the same year that Shah Sultan-Husayn started his reign. Although he would end his days as a drunken debauch Sultan-Husayn was initially pious, holding the Sheikh in great respect. Majlisi was acknowledged as the foremost Shia scholar of his time. He wrote more than sixty books. He initiated a campaign against Sunnis and Sufis which opened with an effort at their expulsion from Isfahan. Although missing the lessons of tolerance and gentleness, Majlisi's ideal was none the less the Prophet: *Bahar al-Anwar*, accepted as his magnum opus, is an encyclopedic collection of *hadith*. Shia fervour brought to and maintained at a pitch by the Saffavids left little room for compromise or compassion; by the end its intensity had drained away the vitality of the state.

When Mahmud of Kandahar attacked Isfahan in 1722 the empire fell like a rotten apple into his hands. Nadir Shah, a Khurasani bandit, grabbed the reins of power in 1736. His short reign is noted for the campaigns against his Sunni neighbours which culminated in the sacking of Delhi.

The Saffavid period marks a turning point in Shia politics and society which would permanently affect the way Shias see themselves and the outside world. For centuries after the initial activity in the early history of Islam Shia politics had remained low-key and localized. The ascendancy of the first Saffavid monarch in 1501 was to change all that.

A major development during the Saffavid reign was the end of the mutual toleration between Sunnis and Shias that existed from the time of the Mongols.

The common form of Saffavid abuse was to curse Abu Bakr and Umar for having 'usurped' Ali's right to be caliph. The hatred served two purposes: it reinforced Shia sectarian identity as it underlined Persian against Arab ethnicity. Another development was the Shia rejection of Sufism and concentration on law and the external observances of religion and ritual. There was also the widening cleavage between the state and the increasingly meddlesome *ulema*. By the time of Shah Abbas I's death in 1629 the myth of a semi-divine monarch or a representative on earth of the Hidden Imam was fading. Certain customs such as prostration before the king remained but these reflected the hollow values of court. The shift begun by Shah Abbas I in Twelver Shiaism from Arab – Najaf and Karbala (present-day Iraq) – to Iranian centres of learning such as Isfahan was completed. Finally came the growth and establishment of a centralized, pyramidal and hierarchical priesthood. The bureaucratic structure included written and *viva voce* examinations to determine promotions. The powerful, rigidly organized nature of the priesthood was far removed from early ideal Islam – recall the Prophet's saying 'there is no monkery in Islam'.

The above developments in Saffavid Persia would reverberate in society and politics up to the present times. Persia – Iran – became the largest, most powerful Shia state in the world, the source and inspiration of Shia dogma, the champion of its destiny. The Saffavid period thus determined, as it accurately reflected, the shape of things to be in what is now Iran.

The contemporary need to redefine and reassert Shiaism, from the point of view of a religious scholar, thus has its sources in history:

> According to Shi'i belief, only the Imams or those who act on their behalf are the legitimate holders of authority; all other governments are illegitimate. The belief has been expressed throughout history in Shi'i uprisings against different governments. Sometimes it was possible to resist; at other times, it was not. If the Iranian people are now rising up against the Shah, they are doing so as an Islamic duty.

The speaker is Imam Khomeini (*Islam and Revolution*, 1981). His opponents, the Pahlavis, consciously employed pre-Islamic symbolism, including the institution of the 'Shah' itself. Khomeini's final victory over the Shah is in an important sense the logical culmination of the movement of the Saffavid *ulema* towards power in Iran.

3 MUGHALS: ENCOUNTER WITH HINDUISM

Islam in India presents seemingly intractable problems. In India alone, Islam met with Hinduism, a polytheistic, ancient and sophisticated religion, and here it assumed its most extravagant forms: Akbar, the Great Mughal, creating a new creed, the Deen-e-ilahi; Ali transformed into an avatar with four arms;

Duldul, the Prophet's mule, equated to Hanuman, the monkey god. Flying holy men, starving saints, divine figures with human attributes – or humans with divine ones – were locked into a coherent if unbounded and malleable philosophy in Hindu India. With the conversion to Islam of South Asian peasantry these notions, altered and adapted in transition, found their way into Muslim society. In India Islam faced its most interesting set of challenges.

The clash between monotheistic Christianity and Islam in Europe and the Middle East resulted in clear-cut social and political boundaries. The irresistible force of Islam met the immovable object that was Christianity in historical encounters that still colour the relationship. In the Buddhist areas of Central Asia Islam's victory was total. However, the clash between Hinduism and Islam in South Asia was never conclusive.

Symbolizing this clash, mosque replaced temple, and temple in turn mosque, often on the same site and using the same building materials. A case in point is the renowned mosque, Quwat-ul-Islam, in Delhi, said to be the earliest in Delhi. It revealed the elephant heads and lotus flowers of a temple when the plaster on the columns peeled off. Historically Hinduism absorbed the shock of Islam and, as best it could, survived. The secret, as Nehru noted, was synthesis.

It is tempting to exaggerate the uniqueness of Indian Islam. But Professor Francis Robinson suggests and I will argue (in chapter 6) that we resist the temptation, as

> all Islamic societies contain a mixture of local pre-Islamic practice and high Islamic culture. In Java Muslims are known to pray to the Goddess of the Southern Ocean as well as to Muslim saints and to God himself (Ricklefs, 1979). In Ottoman Turkey, the Bektashi Sufi order, which was powerful in the Balkans and Anatolia and closely associated with the famed Janissary corps of once Christian slave soldiers, recognised an Islamic Trinity of Allah, Muhammad and Ali, and included a version of the Christian communion service in their rites (Birge 1937: 210–18). Further, in nineteenth century southern Arabia the Swiss Arabist and traveller, Johann Burckhardt, noted that the Bedouin still observed the pre-Islamic practice of sexual hospitality (Burckhardt 1829: 453). ('Islam and Muslim Society in South Asia' in *Contributions to Indian Sociology* N.S.17,2, 1983)

The mutual stimulation and synthesis between Islam and Hinduism were most notable during Mughal rule in India. Inscribed in marble in the Diwan-e-Khaas, the private audience chamber of the Mughals, in the recesses of the Red Fort in Delhi, are the lines 'If there is paradise on earth it is here, it is here, it is here,' and during the Mughal era India was indeed paradise for the Muslims. Their buildings were exquisite, their gardens perfect and their lives appear charmed.

The Mughals were remarkable. Their vitality alone is extraordinary. Princes and princesses, warriors and courtiers, artists and writers, sages and scholars jostled in creativity, and towering above them, inspiring and stimulating them, stood the figure of the emperor. The first six – from Babar, who founded the dynasty in 1526 by gaining Delhi and who claimed the blood of Chenghiz Khan and Taimur flowed in his veins, to Aurangzeb who died in 1707 – were larger than life. After them would come a long line of pale dwarfs. The end would be abrupt and ignominious in the removal of the last emperor, Bahadur Shah Zafar, in 1857 by the British. The emperor was exiled to Rangoon where he died and was buried. Zafar, a poor shadow of his hardy ancestors is none the less a Mughal in his poetic sensibility. His lines sum up the Mughal end and destiny in India:

how unfortunate is Zafar, for his burial
he did not even obtain two yards of earth in his beloved's lane

kitna hai bad naseeb Zafar, dafan key ley
do gaz zamin bhi na milli ko-e-yar mein

At their best the Mughals possessed perceptive minds and brave hearts. Courage, piety, poetry and love were reflected in their lives. Above all they expressed themselves in writing. They were passionate bibliophiles. Their women, never far behind the men, have left behind literature of high quality. Babar is the best introduction to the Mughals. Brimming with curiosity, vitality and charm, he sets the pace for his successors. Among them would be scholars, saints, drunkards and warriors.

To whatever extent the Mughals dabbled in religious adventurism they saw themselves, and were largely seen, at least formally, as champions of Islam. Jahangir's title was *Nur al-din*, light of religion, Shah Jahan's *Shihab al-din*, bright star of religion, and Aurangzeb's *Muhyi al-din*, life-giver of religion. Akbar's friend and publicist, Abul Fazl, went one step further. The Emperor Akbar was the summation of the major spiritual and religious tendencies of the Islamic world. He was Perfect Man. For contemporary historians and scholars the Mughals are ideal Muslim rulers. A blind eye is turned discreetly to imperial excesses.

It was not love at first sight for the early Mughals in India. Babar, who grew to manhood in the bracing climate and open spaces of Farghana, did not like India. He was not impressed by its charms. In his delightfully frank autobiography he complains:

Hindustan has few pleasant things in it. Its people are not handsome or at all friendly; they know nothing of sociable visiting. They have no genius or manners or understanding of mind. In handiwork they have

> neither ingenuity nor sense of planning; in building they have no skill at design. There are no good horses or dogs, no good grapes or melons – or prime fruit of any kind – no iced or cold water, no fine meats or bread in their bazaars. They have no hot baths, colleges, candles or candlesticks. Instead of candles they have a dirty gang they call lampmen, holding a wick in one hand and pouring oil from a gourd in the other. If you call for a light at night, these lamp slaves run in and stand around you.
>
> Except for rivers, they have no water channels, or water in the gardens or houses. These houses have no charm, good air, or fine design.

Indian dress offended him:

> Peasants and other low-class people go around with only a strip of cloth hanging down two spans from their navels. Women tie one cloth around their waists and throw another over their heads.

The attractive points of India were few and listed perfunctorily:

> As for pleasant things – it is a large country and has great quantities of gold and silver. When it rains, the air is fine. Yet the dampness ruins good bows, armour, books, and cloth and even the houses themselves. Another good thing is that Hindustan has numberless workmen of every kind. There is a fixed caste for every sort of work, or anything done – sons doing the work of their fathers.

Even his men disliked the place. His army was homesick and threatened to return home: 'Because of all this most of the *begs* [nobles] and trusted warriors became unwilling to stay in Hindustan, and even set their faces for leaving.'

Not long afterwards India claimed Babar. Gulbadan, his daughter, has left behind a record for us of the circumstances of his death. Traditional prayers had failed to cure his son and heir apparent, Humayun, who was gravely ill. Some courtiers suggested that the *Koh-i-noor*, the most dazzling of precious stones, freshly won from the Hindus (and now in the crown of Queen Elizabeth in London), be offered as sacrifice. 'I shall not offer a stone to God,' Babar replied. 'On that Tuesday,' Gulbadan records, 'and from that day His Majesty walked around Humayun, in prayer. He lifted his head in intercession to the saintly *Karim illah*. He made his intercession, anxiously and deeply distressed, from Wednesday. The weather was extremely hot, and his heart and liver burned. While going around the couch he prayed, saying something like this: "Oh, God! If a life may be taken for a life – I who am Babar – I give my life and my being for that of my son, Humayun" '.

Others in the room heard Babar exclaim, 'I have taken it away. I have taken it away!' At the end of the day Babar became weak and ill, while, when water was put on Humayun's head, he could rise up. In the torment of the heat and the darkness of the sick chambers the women prayed in silence, not knowing what most to fear after the sacrifice.

Babar's one Indian act cost him his life. Before then he is uncomfortable with India and Indian ways. Always honest, he complains extensively of both. He yearns for his homeland in the north, for the simple and straightforward life. A man accepted life, as he accepted death, with resigned dignity; with no complaints. But faced with the prospect of a dead son and successor, just when he had finally won an empire, he allows local council to prevail. The supreme sacrifice is suggested. Characteristically, he accepts. Walking around the sick bed, chanting a formula, life drains away from him and into his son. Islamic faith or Hindu science, the cure worked: son lived and father died.

Renunciation, migration of souls, death rituals – we are, in the short span of a few years, already far from the Islam of Babar's land in the north. The older, sophisticated and complex civilization of India has made its influence felt. If Babar's life represents untrammelled Islam, his death suggests the encounter with Hinduism. By the time of his grandson, Akbar, Hindu influences – astrology, caste, magic – would be commonplace in daily life. The introduction of the foreign element was the cost Islam paid for the transition, the passage, to India.

And in India the idea of religious synthesis was seductive. Akbar himself had dabbled with the idea of creating his own religion, borrowing from the major world religions, in particular Islam, Hinduism and Christiantiy. Now Akbar's actual name was Jalal, majestic, which is one of the ninety-nine names of Allah. The Muslim orthodox accused Akbar of heresy when his followers at court greeted each other with the words '*Jalla Jalala-hu*', a traditional recitation reflecting the Majesty of Allah. They saw this as Akbar's desire to have himself elevated to the level of a deity by a clever employment of his name.

For all the accusations and innuendoes of apostasy by the orthodox Akbar remained a Muslim. Proof lies in various official acts. In an order – *farman* – his governors were asked to spend their spare time reading Al Ghazzali and Maulana Rumi.

However tarnished their reputation – and many would be drunks and drug addicts – the Mughals had a keen eye for beauty. Here is Jahangir, widely regarded as a drunkard who allowed his wife Noor Jahan to run the empire, describing Kashmir: 'a garden of eternal spring . . . a delightful flowerbed . . . wherever the eye reaches there is verdure and running water. The red rose, the violet and the narcissus grow of themselves.' Like a professional ornithologist he observes birds in detail. Mansur was ordered to paint birds, animals and flowers. 'Such a master in painting that he has the title Nadir al-Asr (Wonder of the Age),' acknowledges the emperor.

Jahangir's glittering empress, Noor Jahan, at the centre of the most glittering period of the Mughals, was all too aware of the passing of power, the fading of glory. The Persian lines she is said to have written for her own desolate mausoleum, outside Lahore, predict its condition:

on the tomb of we, the poor, no candle is lit no flower laid,
neither the moth burns its wings nor the nightingale sings

bar mazar ma ghariban ney chiragey ney guley
ney par parwana sozad ney sadaey bulbuley

Then there is Jahangir's son and successor, Shah Jahan, combining poetry and architecture. Shah Jahan, romantic to the last, immortalized himself and his beloved empress, Mumtaz Mahal, in the Taj Mahal, the monument built for her.

But by the time of Jahangir's grandson, Aurangzeb, it would be clear to a shrewd observer that all was not well with the Muslims. An examination of the late seventeenth century in India would assist us in illuminating some of the relevant questions relating to the Mughal collapse after Aurangzeb and the crisis of leadership in Muslim society at the time. The dilemma facing Aurangzeb, the last great Mughal emperor, in the second half of the seventeenth century was not a new one. All Muslim rulers in the three great empires had to confront it to a degree. Simply put: was Aurangzeb the impartial emperor of a poly-ethnic, multi-religious state or the exclusive Muslim leader of the Muslim community in India, the *ummah*, treating non-Muslims as lowly, conquered subjects? Was Mughal India, for Muslims, the ideal state, *madinat al-tamma*, or the imperfect state, *madinat al-naqisa?* If the latter, was India the *dar-al-harb*, the land of war, as distinct from *dar-al-Islam*, the land of Islam? But unlike his predecessors who could put off the day of reckoning developments in his century forced Aurangzeb to grapple with the issues surrounding the dilemma.

The two types of Mughal leaders

What was happening in the seventeenth century to make it different from the previous centuries? A number of factors combined to create the severe intellectual and socio-political crisis of confidence among the Indian Muslims. It was the beginning of the end of Muslim power in India and corresponded with the emergence of the colonial era of Indian history. The main developments are briefly touched upon below.

Foremost of these was the climax that the political crisis in Mughal India was reaching. The very size of the empire – stretching from Kabul to Chittagong – in those days of poor communications foretold its disintegration. At the height of its greatest physical expanse the empire was at its weakest. Mughal princes, waiting for Aurangzeb's long reign to end, led armies against him and each other, sapping the strength of the empire. But empires have held for centuries, as had the Mughal empire, and we may turn to other factors behind the crisis.

There were important cultural-religious developments which applied internal pressure on the empire. Assertive Hindu revivalist movements were spreading rapidly in India and often assuming an anti-Muslim shape. Tulsi Das writing in Hindi borrowed from the *Ramayana.* The adaptation from Sanskrit provided access to it for the majority. In particular, the *bhakti* movement begun in south India made its impact on northern India. Although the *bhakti* movement had grown with figures like Kabir preaching universal peace, and borrowed certain features of Islam, such as monotheism and egalitarianism, by the late seventeenth century it assumed an anti-Muslim stance.

Perhaps more important, non-Muslim religious movements converted into nationalist-ethnic armed struggle against the Mughals who were identified with Muslim power. The emergence of ethnic identity was a new social-political phenomenon. Whereas previously political conflict was based on dynastic, religious or caste differences now ethnicity was emerging as a major factor. Ethnicity as a political force was destined to grow over the centuries. At the present time it threatens the integrity of the contemporary states in the subcontinent.

Of the ethno-religious movements those of the Marathas and the Sikhs were the most significant in the part they played in debilitating the Mughals. Their leaders, Sivaji and Guru Gobind Singh, after his predecessor was killed by Aurangzeb, were personally committed to fighting the Mughals. Aurangzeb spent the entire second half of his long reign in a seemingly futile attempt to crush the Marathas in the south.

It is no accident that the early eighteenth century produced one of the greatest Muslim scholars and reformers in India, Shah Waliullah, who sounded the orthodox alarm as a result of the social condition of the Muslims. Contemporaneous to the Wahabis in Arabia (see chapter 8, section 1) Shah Waliullah emphasized a reversion to pristine Islam. Rejection of Hindu accretions, such as tomb worship, consulting Brahmans for omens and celebrating Hindu festivals, was advocated by him. Pointedly, he wrote his major contribution to theological dialectics, *Hujjat Allah al-baligha*, in Arabic not Persian. In spite of bitter polemics by the traditional *ulema* he translated the holy Quran into Persian in order that it should reach a wider readership; his sons translated it into Urdu. Shah Waliullah's ideas were to shape the Islamic college at Deoband and influence Muslims of all opinions. Significantly, and logically, one of his heroes was the Mughal Emperor Aurangzeb.

It is believed that Shah Waliullah's urgent letters to Ahmad Shah Abdali may have influenced the Afghan ruler to come to India and challenge the rapidly growing and victorious Maratha confederacy (see chapter 9, section 3). By defeating the Marathas in the third and last battle on the fields of Panipat in 1761 Abdali provided Muslims with breathing space for a while.

The Sikhs, until then a syncretist religion between Hinduism and Islam, thenceforth moved toward the former in their ideological and political position. In the eighteenth and early nineteenth centuries they were to rule with an iron hand large Muslim populations in north India who were constantly in rebellion.

An equally important development, and posing an external challenge, was the appearance of the Europeans in India. Fresh ideas, military techniques and technology from a Europe about to launch into the industrial revolution which would change the map of the globe burst upon the Mughals just when they were at their weakest. Earlier the vigorous Mughals had had nothing to fear from Europe. (The comparative economic position of Mughal India at its height and England is represented by the following figures: the salary of a *mansabdar* of 5,000 – the senior troop commander – was equivalent to £24,000 of English purchasing power when the total revenues of England were less than £1 million.)

By the last decades of the seventeenth century it was clear that the English were winning the colonial race in India against the other Europeans. They had established trading companies, later factories – which soon became organized military forts – in Bombay, Madras and, by 1690, Calcutta. These were to become the future Presidencies, the nucleus of civil and military activity, of the British Indian empire.

The combination of these internal and external developments created a deep sense of crisis among Muslims. Their world was beginning to shrink and crumble. The slow process of decline and political decay would continue for the next few centuries, providing the major themes of lost glory and sense of despair in Muslim literature (see the major poets, Ghalib, Hali and Iqbal).

From the late seventeenth century onwards Muslims faced two choices: they could either firmly re-draw the boundaries of Islam around themselves, shutting out the emerging realities, or allow the boundaries to become elastic and porous thereby effecting synthesis with non-Muslim groups. The two alternatives delineated were clear: legal, orthodox, formality on the one hand and eclectic, syncretic, informality on the other. It is no accident that these two clearly differentiated and mutually opposed choices emerged in the person and character of the sons of the emperor Shah Jahan, Aurangzeb and Dara Shikoh. No such dramatically extreme and opposed positions in the sons of the rulers of Delhi are recorded in earlier Muslim history. One of the two would succeed Shah Jahan to rule India and thereby influence the course of future history, casting shadows on contemporary events in South Asia.

Below are the opposed characteristics of Aurangzeb and Dara Shikoh:

Aurangzeb	**Dara Shikoh**
Orthodox, legalistic, Islam; emphasis on *ummah*, Muslim community; discouraged art (music, dancing, etc.) supports clergy/*ulema*.	Syncretic, eclectic, Islam; universalist humanity; encouraged art; anti-clergy ('Paradise is there, where there is no mullah').
Outward signs of orthodoxy: rejects silk clothes and gold vessels, the Nawroz – the Persian New Year – the solar year, etc.	Constant company of Sufis, Hindu *yogis* and *sanyasis*; his ring bore the legend 'Prabhu', the Sanskrit for god.
Patron of *Fatawa-i-Alamgiri*, most comprehensive digest of Muslim (Hanifi) jurisprudence ever compiled.	Patron/translator of *Upanishads/Bhagavad Gita*, classic Hindu texts, into Persian.
Favourite reading: Quran, Al Ghazzali. Wished Muslim society to revert to orthodox mould, thus drawing boundaries.	Favourite reading: mystics. Wished to expand boundaries of Muslim society into incorporating non-Muslims: equates Michael with Vishnu, Adam with Brahman, etc.

A glance at the characteristics of the two may lead us into the same trap in which many Orientalist scholars have fallen. We may be tempted to reject Dara Shikoh as an apostate. There is no problem with Aurangzeb. For orthodox Muslims he personifies orthodoxy. But how do we deal with Dara Shikoh?

Although the charge sheet drawn up by Aurangzeb on the basis of which Dara Shikoh was executed centres around apostasy, he at no point renounces Islam. His understanding of Islam is wildly extravagant and at times incorrect but in an earlier phase his orthodoxy is irreproachable. For all his syncretism his ideal, like that of Aurangzeb, remained the Prophet of Islam. The dilemma for South Asian Islam becomes acute when both brothers refer to the Prophet. We are thus not talking of two or three types of Islam but of different aspects of Islam.

The adventurism comes later in the life of Dara Shikoh. But even then he wished to extend not reject Islam. Indeed he locates the Hindu holy scriptures – the *Upanishads* and the *Bhagavad Gita* – in the holy Quran. His assertion was based on Islamic tradition. God, as we saw in chapter 2, had sent prophets, messengers, in their thousands, to enlighten and assist people wherever they lived.

The tragedy of Dara Shikoh's life is not the lack of commitment to religious ideals but excess of it. The central obsession, Hinduism, threatened to inundate him.

Aurangzeb, too, is not to be dismissed as a simple fanatic if we are able to read his mind. He reprimanded his religious tutor thus:

> 'Pray what is your pleasure with me, *Mullah-gy* (Mullah-ji) Monsieur the Doctor? – Do you pretend that I ought to exalt you to the first honours of the State? Let us then examine your title to any mark of distinction. I do not deny you would possess such a title if you had filled my young mind with suitable instructions. Show me a well-educated youth, and I will say that it is doubtful who has the stronger claim to his gratitude, his father or his tutor. But what was the knowledge I derived under your tuition? You taught me that the whole of *Franguistan* [Europe] was no more than some inconsiderable island, of which the most powerful Monarch was formerly the King of Portugal, then he of Holland, and afterward the King of England. In regard to the other sovereigns of *Franguistan*, such as the King of France and him of Andalusia, you told me they resembled our petty Rajas, and that the potentates of Hindoustan eclipsed the glory of all other kings; that they alone were Humayuns, Akbars, Jahangirs, or Shah Jahans, the Happy, the Great, the Conquerors of the World, and the Kings of the World.'

In another instance, belying his reputation as a fanatic, he wrote across the petition of a Sunni noble who led the Mughal army against the Marathas and who wished for advancement by abolishing the high post of a Shia, one of the 'accursed misbelievers': 'What connection have worldly affairs with religion? For you is your religion and for me is mine.'

In our quest to make sense of Muslim history we have identified two distinct, opposed Muslim types reflecting two aspects of Muslim society and created as a consequence of socio-political crises in the seventeenth century: orthodox, legalistic, formal, and unorthodox, mystical and informal (a third Muslim type which emerged as a consequence of European colonization and was influenced by British culture is explored in chapter 7). We are drawing firm lines around our example figures for simplification but between them there is overlapping and borrowing.

The sharp differences in behaviour and values between the two – indeed three, as we see below – types in South Asia are explained primarily by the inextinguishable Hindu presence. Hinduism, always an external, ever-present force, stimulated while it provoked, defied as it influenced Muslim society. Remaining insecure, off-balance, the range of responses of Muslims is as wide as it is varied. Our other two empires, the Ottomans and Saffavids, were organized within the context of Muslim societies, although the lines which would form the opposition between Europeanized secular and traditional thinking in Turkey and royal authority and religious scholars in Iran are identifiable. In contemporary South Asia the acrimony and distance between the two example figures are recognizable.

The Mughal connection in Pakistan

Drawing genealogical lines – so to speak – from Aurangzeb and Dara Shikoh to the leaders of Pakistan illuminates the problem further for us. Mr Z.A. Bhutto, the late Prime Minister of Pakistan, in a significant and historical manner – and despite Berkeley and Oxford – reflects the conceptual position of Dara Shikoh. Both were eclectic and syncretist. While Dara Shikoh wished to include Hinduism in Islam, Bhutto attempted a similar exercise with the dominant rival ideology of his time, socialism, evolving the concept of 'Islamic socialism'.

In particular the Sufi elements in the character of the two are worth noting. I do not wish to push the argument portraying Bhutto as a mystic Sufi too far, but his devotion to Sufis, especially to Shah Baz Qalandar, is well known. Bhutto frequently recited the verses of the other Sindhi Sufi, Shah Abdul Latif. His fascination with Shah Baz Qalandar, the 'saint of the beggars' who traced his spiritual lineage to Al Hallaj, converted the devotional hymn – the *dhammal* – about the saint almost into an informal national song. Audiences at public meetings burst into it, accompanied by clapping and often dancing, on seeing Bhutto. The onomatopoeic refrain – *dama dam mast Qalandar* – is known to induce trance-like and ecstatic behaviour. The song's spiritual lineage is blameless as the Qalandar acknowledges the supremacy of Ali – *Ali da pehla number*, Ali is number one.

By his public association with the Sindhi Sufi saints, whose poetry is explicitly populist, Bhutto was making a political point to the dispossessed in society and Sindhis in particular. To the former he appeared as a champion of their rights and to the latter of their ethnicity. Rural Sind, no matter what his politics, would remain loyal to him.

Bhutto's death on the gallows merely confirmed an established Sufi tradition stretching back to the spiritual mentor of Shah Baz Qalandar, Al Hallaj (see 'Sufis, saints and mystics', chapter 5). The Sufi prepares to meet death, and his Maker, as the Persian line on Shah Baz's tomb says, 'dancing on the gallows' (Professor Anne Marie Schimmel, personal communication).

While many saw Bhutto's behaviour as unorthodox, excessive and – at shrines, for instance – ecstatic, others read in it signs of Sufism, no matter that his practical life was not sublimated by mysticism, an observation also made of Dara Shikoh.

Conceptually General Zia is a spiritual descendant of Aurangzeb. He is personally austere, committed to Islam and the *ummah*, and a regular visitor to the orthodox holy places of Islam in Saudi Arabia. The question of adding to Islam 'socialism' – or any 'ism' – does not arise for him as Islam is a perfect and complete system in itself. However, his education at St Stephen's College, Delhi, and career in the elite corps of the army, the Guides, indicate wide networks.

In terms of our arguments above the characteristics of Zia and Bhutto provide an interesting comparison with the previous chart and bring into relief the arguments in this section:

Zia	**Bhutto**
Orthodox formal Islam, prays five times daily, visits holy places in Saudi Arabia regularly.	'Mystical', informal Islam, visits Sufi shrines, dance and ecstatic behaviour.
Personally austere.	Personally extravagant.
Abstains from alcohol.	Drinks alcohol ('I drink alcohol not blood like others').
Ethnicity: culture defined by Islam.	Ethnic culture ('I will not allow Sindhis to become like Red Indians').
Emphasis on Urdu as national language.	Encourages ethnic languages.
Ummah supreme over ethnicity.	Importance of ethnicity.
Dress: formal military or formal national (black coat over white muslin shirt).	Western suits or informal worn by common man (usually with Chinese cap).
State: public meetings formal, protocol (wears military dress).	Informal, mêlée-like (wears informal clothes).
National Assembly called *Majlis-i-Shura* (ideally good Muslims) and nominated.	Elected National Assembly represents all political shades.
Heroes: Prophet and Muslim generals.	Prophet, Napoleon, Mao Tse-tung.

Zia	Bhutto
Wishes to draw boundaries firmly around Islam.	Wishes to expand Islam (to include, for example, socialism).

Critics of both Zia and Bhutto accuse them of exploiting religion to further political ends.

Some anthropologists studying religious behaviour are inclined to be cynical of what they observe. Others are more believing. I am in agreement with the latter position. As social scientists we are interested in basing conclusions on regularly observed – or recorded – social behaviour. So although their critics would accuse Zia and Bhutto of manipulating religion I maintain that Zia's tears when praying in the holy Kaaba in Makkah or Bhutto's as a result of listening to Shah Latif's verses are genuine. In those moments, they are not Presidents and Prime Ministers but worshippers responding genuinely to deeply felt emotion. For purposes of analysis it is interesting to distinguish the different contextual framework of the stimuli that moved them. Both respond to Islam but, significantly, to different aspects of it.

The question that arises is: how accurate are the stereotypes of both, the one a rigid fanatic, the other a syncretic humanist? Are Aurangzeb and Zia the extreme orthodox fanatics portrayed by their critics? Recent historical research indicates that Aurangzeb was not – as popularly supposed – a destroyer of temples. On the contrary, records exist showing numerous grants to Hindu temples. Similarly, although Zia's image in the Western press is that of a harsh Islamic judge ordering criminals to be stoned to death or lashed, and their hands cut off, the facts show a very limited use of these punishments. This type suffers from a bad press.

On the other hand just how far has the other type drifted – consciously or unconsciously – from religion? Here, too, the answer is interesting. This type does not see himself as leaving Islam for non-Islamic ideologies, but rather as bringing the latter into the former. His understanding of Islam may be faulted, not his intentions. With Iqbal, himself a Sufi poet, he believes that 'at critical moments in their history it is Islam that has saved Muslims and not vice-versa' (Presidential address 1930).

It appears that the confrontation between the two types is destined to end by the death of one at the hands of the other. There is no compromise or synthesis between the two. The death warrants signed by Aurangzeb and Zia sealing the fates of Dara Shikoh and Bhutto thus reflect the unresolved dilemmas of South Asian Islam and illustrate the continuity of the tension in historical perspective.

The Muslim malaise in India

Muslims during the Mughal dynasty were on top of the social hierarchy, on top of the *dhimmis*, the non-Muslims, and in a land where status determined the most minor commensal and ritual rules this superior position mattered. But by the end of the Mughal period, in the last century, the Muslims had tumbled down from the top. Their political role was terminated, their language rejected and their very identity threatened. The trauma of this downfall lies at the heart of the Muslim problem in India today (for a fuller discussion see chapter 8, section 2).

To solve the problem of the Muslim malaise is to come to terms with it by confronting it squarely. The Muslim monuments – the Red Fort, the Taj Mahal, at Fatehpur Sikri, and at Sikandra – appear to mock the Indian Muslims. Their present impotence and lowly status are exaggerated by the splendour and scale of the buildings. In spite of unending tourists these monuments appear desolate. The crowds, the beggars, and the pervasive stink of urine underline the changing times, the contemporary demotic reality swamping the imperial settings. This is illustrated nowhere better than at the entrance to the Red Fort.

When I visited the Fort, a cassette of Nazia Hassan played full volume '*Disco Diwana*' (disco mania) '*badan se badan*' (body to body) on the loudspeaker. Garish neons advertised Hindu names and small shops sold plastic Taj Mahals and mildly erotic Rajput paintings. Opposite the Fort the Jamia Masjid, splendid in its perfect symmetry, floats on a sea of shanty shops and huts. In the lanes the foul smells are strong; so is the sense of claustrophobia as the shops strangle the roads to the mosque, swarming up to its very staircase. Amidst the filth and squalor around the mosque is displayed the expensive Saudi chandelier under the main dome, as exquisite as it is irrelevant to the problems of the Muslims.

The Mughals, their passions, their women and the drama of their lives have become part of public property. The guides rattle off anecdotes and thumbnail sketches: 'Aurangzeb' when describing his Moti Masjid (and opinions on him are always divided along religious lines), 'told the mourning procession of musicians to bury music deep so she will not arise again. He was a fanatic. And so the Mughal empire came to a downfall.' At the Panch Mahal of Fatehpur Sikri: 'Akbar had hundreds of wives but his favourite was the Rajput princess. He was the most successful ruler.' The guide's emphasis on liberalism and secularism reflects the official philosophy of modern India.

The guide, worn out by poverty and the heat, vicariously takes pleasure in the sensual images of imperial harems and seraglios. At the Taj Mahal – 'Mumtaz Mahal had fourteen children and died. Shah Jahan was broken-hearted. He built the Taj for her. He wished to build a black one for himself but his son Aurangzeb jailed him and he died'. History is reduced to one-dimensional characters, to bazaar stereotypes. Here the borders between fantasy and reality are blurred.

The history of the Muslims in India is illustrated through ruin lying atop ruin, crumbling capital on crumbling capital, disused mosques and neglected graveyards. The environment does not encourage confidence; it is estimated that 2,000 mosques have been captured by militant Hindu groups or resumed by the authorities. Muslim history is never more poignant than in Delhi, once the heart of Muslim India. Nursing the sense of injury, Muslims are sensitive to suggestions that reflect imagined or real cultural grievances. Sheikh Ibrahim Zauq, one of the best known Urdu poets and teacher of Bahadur Shah Zafar, the last Mughal emperor, lies buried under a public latrine in spite of official protests by Dr Anjum, President of the Zauq Research Institute. Goats deposited their faeces on the grave of Mirza Ghalib, possibly the greatest Urdu poet, in my presence. Such facts generate in the Muslim a feeling of being deliberately neglected if not deliberately injured.

Devoid of contemporary power and still in search of his destiny, the Muslim tends to live in the past. He clings to the fantasy provided by it. But he is also crushed by the burden of this past; and it creates in him emotional anorexia.

4 OBSESSION AND SYNTHESIS

Although located in different parts of the world, the Ottomans partly in and facing Europe and the Mughals in and facing South Asia, the Saffavids touching both, there are interesting points of comparison between the three empires. The most important is a central obsession that would during the time of the empire provide the dynamics in society and, today, help us explain the tension in its successor society. We have seen that for the Ottomans, Europe and Christian civilization and for the Mughals Hindu civilization were these obsessions. Placed between the two, Saffavid Persia was now attacked by Sunni Ottomans, now by Sunni Mughals. The pressures from its neighbours reinforced its own obsession with Shiaism. In these societies the tension between the desire to reach for the Islamic ideal on the one hand and to come to terms with the obsession on the other would remain unresolved. As a result the ideal would be distorted, perverted and in some cases changed beyond recognition.

In Turkey the obsession would pull in the direction of Western liberalism (European education, secularism, rationalism) and technology (artillery, railways, ships), while in India in an opposite direction, towards magic, mysticism and ritual (see chapter 5, section 1). In Turkey if the leaders of society debated the merits of French as against Arabic education, of the replacement of the fez by the bowler, the scimitar by the rapier, baggy pyjamas by pants, then in Indian society holy men fought for ascendancy through extravagant demonstrations of spiritual powers. For the benefit of their disciples they defied gravitation and hunger. The stereotype of the Hindu *yogi* and Muslim *faqir* bore a suspicious resemblance to each other. The more established the saint the more fluid the barriers separating his followers: Hindus and Muslims visited them with equal fervour to request miracles and favours. The saints in India, at Ajmer and Delhi, and Pakistan, at Sehwan, Pakpattan and Lahore are well known examples. While Aurangzeb and Zia reflect the obsession with Islam in its South Asian environment, Dara Shikoh and Bhutto represent its synthesis with that environment, it was pointed out above. Leadership and thought in Muslim society would oscillate between the obsession on the one hand and synthesis on the other. The tension between the two remains the common strand in the history of the Muslims of South Asia.

In Iran the situation is less complex if more intense. The intensity of devotion to Shiaism decided the standing of the citizen in the eyes of the *ulema*. Islam in Iran was locked in an attempt to renew and redefine Shiaism from which it has still to free itself. Here it struggled with itself and was always fiercely cannibalistic.

We may argue that an important source of the stimulation in artistic and intellectual development is to be found in this obsession. Sinan built his mosques, as he admitted, to over-shadow the Christian church, Santa Sophia. Temple on mosque and mosque on temple is the history of India according to one view. The Taj Mahal reflects the Hindu impact on Muslim architecture. Modern Indian historians go one step further, claiming that in fact it is a Hindu monument. The most brilliantly decorated mosque in Iran is at Mashad, built in honour of Imam Raza, descendant of Ali and one of the twelve Imams of the Shias.

Consider the peaks of these societies when a glorious synthesis stimulated by the central obsession produced exquisite art, architecture and poetry. During this time women, especially in the élite, participated in these developments. New capitals were created – Agra, Fatehpur Sikri and Isfahan – or declared – Istanbul, the city of Islam. At the peak their extraordinary vitality and exuberance presupposes a generally contented peasantry and impartial administration. Their very size in area and span in time suggests stability and contentment in the population.

Consider, too, their scale. The three empires covered vast areas encompassing different faiths and peoples, and an extraordinarily long span of time, from the sixteenth to, effectively, the eighteenth century – although the Mughals lasted until the middle of the nineteenth and the Ottomans, probably the longest ruling dynasty in history, from the fourteenth to the twentieth century.

The empires were often Muslim in name only. They were as much at war with Muslims as with non-Muslims. The Mughals conquered and colonized the southern Muslim states of Bijapur and Golkonda while the Ottomans did the same to the Arab lands of Syria, Iraq and most of North Africa. The Saffavids actively persecuted their Arab and Baluch Sunni populations.

The early years of the sixteenth century saw the establishment or origin of these three empires. The Ottomans expanded rapidly during this period, reaching their peak under Sulayman, when the Turks reached Vienna in 1529. The Mughal dynasty was established by Babar's victory at the first battle of Panipat in 1526. Shah Ismail established a Shia state in 1501.

The Saffavids, looking at their Sunni neighbours through Shia eyes, perceived them as threatening and remained in a constant state of nervous vigilance. Border towns and provinces would exchange masters, reflecting the fortunes of the state and abilities of its rulers – the Saffavids now losing a city to the Sunni Ottomans to their west (Baghdad in 1638), now a province to the Sunni Mughals to their east (Kandahar also in the same year) under the drunken Shah Safi; now regaining a loss (Kandahar in 1648) under a vigorous ruler, Safi's son Abbas II.

The empires were firmly established when the world was moving towards modern, European, times and they thus act as a link for us to the past. Consider their downfall. The eighteenth century saw the simultaneous decline of these three empires and the active interference of European powers in their territories.

The Mughal empire was in turmoil. Emperors were murdered and blinded and Delhi sacked more than once in the eighteenth century. Only Oudh and Hyderabad remained as Muslim states and they, too, acknowledged British suzerainty. Never before had so much been surrendered by a ruling group to their subjects in history. When General Lake took Delhi at the turn of that century Shah Abdul Aziz, son of Shah Waliullah, declared that India was no longer *dar-al-Islam* but *dar-al-harb*.

In Iran religious scholars and secular shahs battled for authority. When Nadir Shah grabbed power the empire was at its weakest. Seeking to divert it and enrich himself in the process, Nadir crossed into India to plunder and sack Delhi in 1739; 20,000 people were killed. Less than a generation later Delhi was to be sacked again, in 1761, by Ahmad Shah Abdali, the first king of what we know as Afghanistan (see chapter 9, section 3). Whenever the opportunity arose the Muslim empires aided the process of disintegration by attacking each other.

The final phase of the three empires also reflects their respective obsessions. The Ottomans opted for a Western-style secular government even before Ataturk's abolition of the caliphate in 1924 and his Westernization campaign. In India the All-India Muslim League was formed in 1906 as a response to the Hindu-dominated Congress. The demand for Pakistan and separation from Hindu India was a logical playing-out of the obsession. In Iran the oscillation between royalist-dynastic and orthodox-Shia forms of politics created severe stress. Under the last Shah of Iran and his father society swung to the one extreme; under Imam Khomeini the pendulum swung back to the other.

Of the three great empires two had captured and ruled from capitals with ancient pre-Islamic associations. Constantinople had been Christian for centuries before Islam and Delhi was once the capital of Hindu kingdoms. Today even the name and identity of the three empires has vanished. Delhi is no longer a Muslim city.

Through the rise and fall of dynasties, the uncertainties of expanding empires, there were saints and scholars, princes and paupers – some of whom we meet in these pages – who lived according to the ideal. And in the midst of imperial developments which were a deviation from the Islamic ideal – dynastic principle, the opulence of the court – their example was a reminder to the rulers and an inspiration for the population. Sometimes persecuted – Sheikh Sirhindi jailed by one Mughal emperor, Sarmad decapitated on the orders of another – sometimes honoured – Salim Chishti by yet another – they demonstrated the possibility of living by the ideal.

What we have called obsessions in this chapter have left scars in society, creating cultural mutants but also in part cultural synthesis with non-Islamic systems. In Istanbul the young men and women in jeans and open shirts would look askance – a trifle embarrassed – at a Muslim woman from India wearing a *saree* and a *bindi*, the Hindu circle on her forehead, if she were to say, 'I, too, am a Muslim.' For the Indian woman the young Turks would not only look more European than Muslim but appear to be so in their behaviour. In Tehran today the Shia obsession is particularly intense. As a symbol of orthodoxy the *chaddar*, veil-sheet, must be worn by women. They risk public disgrace, even danger – throwing of acid, for example – without it. These examples reflect perplexity in society and a continuing legacy of the obsessions that once engaged its forebears. The necessity to clarify issues, to make sense of the past, is therefore urgent.

Certain developments during this period were to have consequences for Muslims later for which they would have to pay heavily. Muslim naval armaments and navigational skills were never to be as good as those of the Europeans, for example. Spain and Portugal were thus able to establish their empires based on sea routes at the expense of the Muslims. Most important, the supremacy at sea allowed Europe to colonize what would become the richest and most powerful land mass in the twentieth century, the Americas. Had the descendants of the Muslim soldier who galloped into the Atlantic thinking the world ended here crossed the ocean, the early American explorers might have had names such as Abdullah and Abdur Rahman rather than Cortez and Columbus. The world today would have been a different place.

5

Sufis and scholars

In the stereotype image medieval warriors from Central Asia – hard men with sullen temperaments, sword in one hand and the holy Quran in the other – were the main cause of the conversion to Islam in India. This was not the whole picture. Separately, sometimes alone, sometimes with a few disciples, came Sufi scholars and saints. Their modes of attack were contrary: uncompromising rigorism for the soldier and adaptive, absorbent and pragmatic for the Sufi. With the former Islam secured followers in spite of insisting on purity, with the latter by compromising it.

Whereas the memory of the warriors faintly lingers on in deserted palaces and ruins, the memory of the Sufi saints is kept alive at their shrines. A neat contrast is provided in Delhi at the burial places of the Tughlak king and the saint he opposed, Nizam al Din. The king's tomb is neglected, the saint's shrine bustles with activity and visitors.

The Sufis, saints and scholars are the 'opposition' party, as it were, of Islam. The line between Sufis, saints and scholars is usually a thin one. Identifying with and living by the ideal, this group often finds itself in opposition to the rich and powerful. They have acted as a strong, if indirect, pressure on the excesses of the rulers. Many a well-known clash is recorded between the master of the age and a recalcitrant Islamic scholar. They include those between the four Imams and the Abbasids (chapter 3); Mahmud of Ghazni and Al Beruni and Firdausi; Muhammad V of Granada and Ibn Khaldun (we meet Al Beruni and Ibn Khaldun below); Jahangir, the Mughal emperor, and Ahmad Sirhindi, *Mujaddid-i-alf-Sani*, 'renovator of the second thousand years of Islam'; Aurangzeb, himself revered by many Muslims as a saint, and the mystic Sarmad who was killed on his orders. On the other hand, many rulers felt it wiser to leave these people alone or acknowledge their superiority in religious matters. We thus have examples of the Abbasid caliph attempting to pay homage to the Sufi Farid, and Akbar the Mughal walking barefoot to Sheikh Salim and to the shrine of Muin al Din Chisti.

1 SUFIS, SAINTS AND MYSTICS

Sufism is universalist and humanist Islam striving for spiritual purity. Its foundations are love and peace, *sulh-i-kul*, peace with all. The Prophet's life provides inspiration to the Sufis – his clothes of wool, *suf*, give them their name. The gentleness, contemplative solitude, and universal tolerance of the Prophet are reflected in Sufi behaviour. Ali, too, is a source of Sufi inspiration. The Sufic spiritual genealogy is thus impeccable. Sufism is the endearing – and enduring – side of Islam.

The Sufi, through the key concept of *fana* – negation of self, annihilation – devoted himself to Islam. This the Sufi did sometimes literally. In death the Sufi found life. In the rejection of the world the Sufi was gaining it; the Prophet had said, 'What have I to do with this world?' Poverty was made respectable; austerity desirable. The poor and the dispossessed could thus identify with Sufi values.

The Sufi therefore became, willy-nilly, a rebel figure making the establishment nervous and uneasy. Salvation lay in rejection; success in the extent of rejecting the world. A paradox thus emerged. The greater the rejection of the world the greater the success of the Sufi in the eyes of society. The idea was old. 'Having the fewest wants, I am nearest to the gods,' Socrates had said.

The tripartite way to God is explained by a tradition attributed to the Prophet: 'The *Shariah* are my words (*aqwali*), the *tariqa* are my actions (*amali*), and the *haqiqa* is my interior states (*ahwali*). *Shariah, tariqa* and *haqiqa* are mutually interdependent.' 'Mystics in every religious tradition have tended to describe the different steps on the way that leads toward God by the image of the Path. The Christian tripartite division of the *via purgativa*, the *via contemplativa* and the *via illuminativa* is, to some extent, the same as the Islamic definition of *Shariah, tariqa* and *haqiqa*,' explains Professor Anne Marie Schimmel (*Mystical Dimensions of Islam*, 1981).

The *tariqa*, the 'path' on which the mystics walk, has been defined as 'the path which comes out of the *Shariah*, for the main road is called *shar*, the path, *tariq*.' No mystical experience can be realized if the binding injunctions of the *Shariah* are not followed faithfully first. The path, *tariqa*, however, is narrower and more difficult to walk. It leads the adept, called *salik*, 'wayfarer', in his *suluk*, 'wandering', through different stations (*maqam*) until he reaches his goal, the perfect *tauhid*, the existential confession that God is One.

In order to achieve this exalted position the *salik* faced a series of severe tests including humiliation, hardship and discouragement. Perseverance, the burning desire to move toward perfect unity, *tauhid*, was the key. The methods of humiliating future Sufis were numerous. If they were ordered to beg so that they would be rebuked by the people, the intent was not the material profit derived from begging, but the discipline. Shibli, once a high government official, eventually reached the point of saying, 'I deem myself the meanest of God's creatures,' and only then was he accepted by his Sufi master. A story that illustrates this attitude is told about Majduddin Baghdadi in the twelfth century:

> When he entered the service of a Sheikh, he was made to serve at the place of ablution, i.e. to clean the latrines. His mother, a well-to-do lady physician, asked the master to exempt the tender boy from this work, and sent him twelve Turkish slaves to do the cleaning. But he replied: 'You are a physician – if your son had an inflammation of the gall bladder, should I give the medicine to a Turkish slave instead of giving it to him?'

The disciple would probably not have undergone these trials had he not had absolute trust in his master. It was, and still is, a rule that an affinity, almost atavistic, has to exist between master and disciple. Many Sufis wandered for years throughout the Islamic world in search of a master to whom they could surrender completely.

Before Al Ghazzali reconciled Sufism with orthodoxy one of the most controversial Sufis, Hussain ibn Mansur Al Hallaj, shook the establishment. He has become something of a cult, even populist, figure, symbolizing rejection of the material and the false.

Al Hallaj, born in the province of Fars in 858, grew up in Wasit and Tustar, where cotton was cultivated and where cotton carders (the meaning of *hallaj*) like his father could pursue their occupation. The young man attached himself to Sahl at Tustar and accompanied him to Basra. Later he became a disciple of Al Junaid.

Al Hallaj's father-in-law began to regard him as a 'cunning sorcerer and miserable infidel'. In connection with his first pilgrimage, Al Hallaj stayed in Makkah for a year, undergoing terrible hardships in asceticism. After his return to Baghdad, Junaid foretold, according to legend, an evil end for his former disciple. At this point the tradition relates the following anecdote: 'When he knocked at Junaid's door, the master asked: "Who is there?" and he answered: "*ana-al-Haq*, I am the Absolute [or Creative] Truth [or the True Reality]." ' This sentence, rendered as 'I am God', has become the most famous of all Sufi claims, inspiring Sufis throughout the ages. Al Hallaj was tried by the orthodox and sentenced to the gallows. He went to his death singing: he would be meeting the object of his love.

In *fana*, annihilation, Al Hallaj found *tauhid*, unity; in death immortality. Famed Sufi poets and scholars have honoured Al Hallaj both in the major Islamic languages like Persian, from Faridudin Attar to Jalaludin Rumi, and in regional languages, like Sindhi, from Shah Abdul Latif to Sachal Sarmast. Dara Shikoh, who would lose the Mughal throne and his life to his orthodox brother Aurangzeb, admired and quoted Al Hallaj extensively. Sarmad was executed by Aurangzeb for repeating Al Hallaj's line, *ana-al-Haq*. Louis Massignon devoted almost his entire life studying Al Hallaj and writing about him. So intense was the fascination with his subject that when Massignon died he recited the same Quranic Surah which Al Hallaj recited before his execution.

Al Hallaj became a symbol in the Mevlevi Sufi order, the 'whirling dervishes', whose patron saint was Rumi. One of the flutes used in the ritual dance is called *Mansur ney*. On various occasions in his celebrated *Mathnawi*, Rumi makes use of Al Hallaj's lines: '*uqtuluni ya thiqati inna fi qatli hayati*':

Kill me oh my trustworthy friends,
for in my being killed is my very life.

Although condemned by the orthodox Al Hallaj's dramatic pronouncement of *fana* and merging with the beloved have provided a base for subsequent Sufi mystical development. Rumi describes the same experience in a passage from the *Mathnawi:*

A certain man knocked at his friend's door: his friend asked: 'Who is there?'

He answered, 'I.' 'Begone,' said his friend, ''tis too soon at my table there is no place for the raw.'

'How shall the raw be cooked but in the fire of absence? What else will deliver him from hypocrisy?'

He turned sadly away, and for a whole year the flames of separation consumed him.

Then he came back and again paced to and fro beside the house of his friend.

He knocked at the door with a hundred fears and reverence lest any disrespectful word might escape from his lips.

'Who is there?' cried the friend.

He answered: 'Thou, O charmer of all hearts.'

'Now,' said the friend, 'since thou art I, come in, there is no room for two I's in this house.'

The fusion with God, the blasphemous ambition of Al Hallaj, has been reflected in subtle Sufi poetry down the ages:

I have separated my heart from this world,
My heart and Thou are not separate.
And when slumber closes my eyes,
I find Thee between the eye and the lid.

The Sufis practised the motto *sulh-i-kul*, peace with all. Their intense selfless devotion to God, their rejection of the world, and their love for humanity made them universally attractive figures. Rich and poor, Muslim and non-Muslim, flocked to them.

Sufis in South Asia

V.S. Naipaul felt the rage, and saw hate and anger in Muslim society (*Among the Believers: An Islamic Journey*, 1981). Had he visited Sufis or their shrines he would have witnessed calm, peace and love; perhaps even a touch of magic, the live practice of *sulh-i-kul* demonstrated. The shrine of Muin al Din Chisti in Ajmer, India, is an example.

The shrine and cult of Khwaja Muin al Din – preserver of religion – Chisti, Gharib Nawaz, blesser of the poor, are central to Sufism in India. In them are displayed the characteristic elements of Indian Sufism: mystical, magical, poetic and tolerant expression of faith.

Muin al Din is believed to safeguard the welfare of Muslims in South Asia. For Muslims he is 'The Deputy of the Prophet in India' (Amir Khwurd, *Siyar al-auliya*, reprinted 1885). The fullest exposition of Muin al Din's legend is contained in the seventeenth-century *Siyar al-aqtab* of Ilahdiya Chisti, reprinted in 1889. It is a colourful narrative of how Muin al Din vanquished local opponents by his magical powers, and as a result gained possession of the sacred site at Ajmer. It also describes in the same style the selection of Muin al Din and of the site of Ajmer:

> It is related that the Shaikh was 52 years old when he received the gifts (*tabarrukat*) of his *Pir* (and set out on his own mission). Everywhere he went he customarily lived in cemeteries, and wherever his reputation spread he tarried no longer, but secretly departed from there. After some days he came to the House of the Ka'ba and stayed there for some days. Then he went to Madina the Illuminated, and performed the pilgrimage to the Holy Tomb of the Lord of the World (the Prophet Muhammad). He stayed there for a while, until one day from inside the pure and blessed Tomb a cry came: 'Send for Mu'in al-Din'. The servitor of the Tomb called out the name, and from several places heard the reply:
>
> 'I am here for Thee!'
>
> The servitor went back and stood before the door of the radiant and holy Tomb, and again the cry came forth:
>
> 'Send for Mu'in al-Din Chisti!'
>
> The servitor came forward and told what he had been ordered, and at that moment a strange ecstasy, such as cannot be described, came over the *Khwaja* (Mu'in al-Din). Weeping and crying and invoking blessings, he came to the door of the Tomb and stood there.
>
> The voice cried:
>
> 'Enter, O Polestar (*Qutb*) of Shaikhs!'

> Lost to self and intoxicated, the *Khwaja* went in and was exalted by the sight of the world-adorning beauty of the Presence; and he beheld that Presence speak to him:
>
> 'Mu'in al-Din, you are the essence of my faith, yet you must go to Hindostan. There is a place called Ajmer, to which one of my sons (descendants) went for a holy war. Now he has become a martyr and the place has passed again into the hands of the infidels. By the grace of your footsteps Islam shall once more be manifest there, and the infidels punished by God's wrath.'
>
> Then the Prophet – on whom be Blessings and Peace – gave a pomegranate into the hands of the *Khwaja* and said:
>
> 'Look into this, so that you may see and know where you have to go.' At his command the *Khwaja* looked into the pomegranate, and he saw all that exists between the east and the west; and he looked well at Ajmer and its hills. He humbly offered prayers and sought help from the *Dargah* ('Court') which is the envy of the heavens. Then he set out for Hindostan. (*Siyar al-aqtab*)

The story is part of the legend of Ajmer. It underlines the central place of Muin al Din in Indian Islam, his support by the spiritual authority of the Prophet and the almost supernatural powers that he embodies.

The Muslim presence in India itself is listed as a *karamat* (miracle, grace) of Muin al Din:

> By the arrival of the blessed footsteps of 'that Sun of the People of Belief' . . . the darkness of this land was illuminated by Islam . . . Whoever will become a Musalman in this land, enduring to the Day of Resurrection, as well as their offspring as they are engendered who will be Musalmans; and those who will be brought from infidel territory (*dar-al-harb*) to the land of Islam (i.e. slaves taken from unconverted Hindu territories and converted) – until the day of Resurrection the recompenses of these are added to the lofty court (*bargah*) . . . (of Mu'in al-Din) . . . in obedience to him. (Amir Khwurd, *Siyar al-auliya*)

To visit Ajmer is to obtain benediction. 'The pure earth of the grave of this saint is medicine for the hearts of those in pain. May (they) obtain the good fortune of pilgrimage (*ziyarat*)!'

Ajmer, in the heart of Rajputana, land of drought, famine and proud people, lives in communal harmony in an India torn by ethnic and religious hate. The continuity of Muslim history in India for the last 800 years, when Gharib Nawaz arrived, is reflected here. Gifts by emperors and queens are on display and anecdotes about them abound. One of the early Muslim conquerors, Ghori, after defeating Prithvi Raj in 1192, in one of the most decisive battles of north India, sent envoys to pay homage to the saint. Akbar made several pilgrimages on foot to Ajmer between 1562 and 1579. He donated a cauldron to cook 120 maunds of rice at a time for 5,000 people. His son, Jahangir, presented one which cooks for exactly half the number. Both are in use (on the right and left sides respectively, as you enter). Jahangir's son, Shah Jahan, constructed a mosque, as did his son Aurangzeb. The homage paid by the rich and powerful is recorded. Presidents and their families, of Bangla Desh and Pakistan respectively, visited the shrine in 1983, the same year that I went.

The *urs* or festival of the anniversary of the death of Muin al Din is today the most important pilgrimage festival of South Asian Muslims with the annual number reaching 300,000 (P.M. Currie, *The Shrine and Cult of Muin al-Din*, 1978). The majority of the devotees at the Ajmer shrine are Hindus, I was told by the Sayyeds who tend the shrine, some 3,000–4,000 of the 4,000–5,000 who come daily. Hindu *qawals* – singers – like Shankar-Shambhu move congregations to tears. I heard miraculous stories of Gharib Nawaz's powers from Muslims and Hindus of various social backgrounds. A senior Hindu civil servant recounted, fighting back tears, a personal miracle at Ajmer after being disappointed by doctors and failing to evoke a response from other shrines in India. There is an air of wonder and make-believe in Ajmer.

Some of the miracles are self-induced by the devotees. My companion – a gentle, devout Muslim – recollected a memory from his previous trip to Ajmer as a child with his father before the creation of Pakistan. A man had climbed to the top of a tree in the courtyard and was crying loudly. He demanded from Gharib Nawaz 5,000 rupees, a great deal of money then. From the crowd stepped a Hindu Raja, requested the man to climb down and paid him the sum on the spot. The miracle remained fresh in my friend's mind after forty years.

Invitations to Ajmer and permission to leave it are given with the blessings of the saint, it is believed. After completing our visit we left for the railway station. Berths had been booked days in advance and the tickets were with us. Before the arrival of the train the porters – Hindus, we learned later – enquired, 'Have you asked Gharib Nawaz that you may leave?' We smiled tolerantly. When the train arrived there was no booking for us and in spite of spirited arguments we could not board it. The porters stood around with a quiet air of triumph. Chastened, we returned to the shrine to obtain 'permission'. We left the next day. Bureaucratic inefficiency or magic? – in Ajmer it was difficult to tell.

Magic has always been part of Sufism in India. Sufi masters used magic to combat the forces of evil and darkness. The basis for the existence and use of supernatural powers is explained by Ali Hujwiri, the most venerated saint in Pakistan, the Datta Sahib of Lahore. The Datta is one of the earliest Sufis to have come to India, even before Muin al Din to whom only he is second in the Sufi hierarchy of South Asia:

> God has saints (*auliya*, plural of *wali*) whom he has especially distinguished by His friendship and whom He has chosen to be the governors of His kingdom. . . . He has made the saints the governors of the universe . . . Through the blessing of their advent the rains fall from heaven and through the purity of their lives the plants spring up from the earth and through their spiritual influence Muslims gain victories over unbelievers. (*Kashf al-Mahjub*, translated R.A. Nicholson, 1911)

A strong, almost blind, belief in the miraculous permeated society. The learned and the powerful were not immune. *Karamat* (grace, miracle) was proof that the Sufi sheikh had attained the status attributed to him. The sheikh's interventions in the ordinary course of nature extended from trifling affairs of individuals, to whom they supplied amulets, to an influence over major political events. In the opinion of their followers they held powers for the making and unmaking of kings and kingdoms (Amir Hasan, *Fawaid al-fuad*, reprinted 1966). In a dated and unquestionably authentic narrative of the individual conversations of Nizam al Din of Delhi, close behind Muin al Din and Ali Hujwiri in the Sufi hierarchy, we find a succession of anecdotes illustrating the use of magic: of a preacher in a mosque who was so transported by his own eloquence that he flew away from the pulpit (*mimbar*) to a neighbouring wall; of meetings in deserted places with Khwaja Khidr who has everlasting life; of various 'fairy people' like the *abdals* who physically fly above the territories which they protect from harm; of a holy man circling around the vault of the chief mosque at Delhi through the night till the dawn, and of the *mardan-i-ghaib*, 'men of the unseen', who appear and disappear, and sometimes call away a mortal to join them (*Fawaid al-fuad*). Nizam al Din and his successor at Delhi Sheikh Nasir al Din Mahmud shared these folk-beliefs with their followers.

The question as to why Nizam al Din did not perform the *haj* intrigued scholars. The answer lies in the magical powers Sufi masters possess. Nizam al Din had access to a means of transport not available to the ordinary person. A camel arrived at his *khangah*, lodge, on Friday evening to transport him through the air to Makkah, where he was observed at prayer by a witness (*Siyar al-auliya*).

Along with magic the other characteristic of Indian Sufism is its devotion to poetry and singing. The tradition derives from Persia. In the Persian-speaking world the connections between poetic sensibility and Sufism are almost inseparable. The verses of the greatest of Persian poets, Rumi, Sadi and Hafiz, as well as those of many of their predecessors, contemporaries and successors, would often have been unintelligible without some knowledge of

Sufi concepts and practice. Even when the poet himself had worldly connections and employment, and did not live the life of a Sufi sheikh, he had claims to their company. This was the case of Amir Khusraw (1253–1325), one of the most notable of the Indo-Persian Sufi poets, an intimate companion of Nizam al Din, and of his rival Amir Hasan, author of *Fawaid al-fuad*, the record of Nizam al Din's conversations.

The appeal of poetic sensibility spread in spite of the discouragement and deprecations of the orthodox. The sensibility was shared by all the Chisti sheikhs. So charged are the emotions, so intense the ecstasy, aroused at a *sama* or Sufi gathering, that death is known to occur. The second sheikh of the Chisti *silsila* – genealogy, chain – Qutb al-din Bakhtyar Kaki, is alleged to have expired after four days of violent ecstasy at the recital of a Persian *bait* (couplet):

For those slain by the dagger of belief
Every time from the Unseen there is new life. (*Fawaid al-fuad*)

kushtagan-i khanjar-i taslim-ra
har zaman az ghaib jan-i digar ast

The event is said to have occurred in 1235. Down to the twentieth century there have been attested examples of death through ecstasy at *sama*.

Magic, tolerance and devotional poetry lay at the heart of Sufi practice in India. This explains the appeal of Sufism to the majority Hindu population which was already predisposed to them. The poor, the dispossessed, those in need, regardless of caste and religion, came to the Sufi or his shrine to find solace. Sufi Islam conquered hearts through love. At this level Islam in India is serene, untroubled and secure. It is a tribute to the saints of Islam and a testimony to *sulh-i-kul* and the universality of mystic love.

2 TWO SCHOLARS OF ISLAM: AL BERUNI AND IBN KHALDUN

Scholars, travellers, artists, astronomers and ethnographers – royal and common – Islamic civilization was producing renaissance men, complete men, centuries before the term was used in Europe. In them the Islamic ideal was fulfilled. The figure of the complete man plausibly traces its descent from Ali, warrior, scholar and saint. Ali symbolizes the chivalric tradition of Muslim scholarship and war. (See the book of his sayings and traditions, *Nahjal Balagha.*) This chivalric trend would last into the eighteenth century ending abruptly as the sources of patronage ceased with European colonialism. After the colonial period was over the tradition was broken. An entire aspect of Islamic civilization had been lost.

In this section we will consider two Muslim scholars, Al Beruni and Ibn Khaldun. The reason why I have selected these two while touching only cursorily on others – Al Razi, Al Farabi, Ibn Sina, and Al Ghazzali (chapter 3) – whose contributions are considered even greater by many scholars is a simple and parochial one: Al Beruni and Ibn Khaldun laid the foundations of the disciplines within which I work, anthropology and sociology.

Our two scholars come from the ends of the historical Muslim world, Central Asia and the Maghreb. In many important ways they represent the larger Muslim civilizations which provided a reference for their work, Arab and South Asian. Their work illustrates for us the conditions of two distinct, dissimilar periods of Muslim history, the tenth and fourteenth centuries. In the former Muslims are aggressive, expanding and confident; in the latter, the Arab world permanently damaged by the Mongols, they are forlorn and despondent. The scholars have left us a record of their encounters with the supreme conquerors of the time, Mahmud and Taimur. Their personal lives reflect the politics of the age. Both lived and died far from the place of their birth. Al Beruni's was a life of research and academic writing, Ibn Khaldun's an extraordinary combination of action and thought; in current terminology, he is the classic *homme engagé*.

Al Beruni: the first anthropologist

Anthropology is for many social scientists a creation of Western colonialism. With the notable exception of India, the discipline has not flourished in the Third World. This is particularly noticeable in Muslim countries. But Muslims need not reject anthropology as an alien discipline, for it has roots deep in their history. This statement is in direct contradiction to prevailing ideas on the subject.

In this section I wish to introduce Abu Raihan Muhammad Al Beruni (973–1048) to the readers, a man who deserves the title of the first anthropologist. For me the definition of anthropology includes extended participant observation among an 'alien' people, studying their primary texts and learning their language; it also requires that the findings be presented with objectivity and neutrality using, where possible, cross-cultural comparisons.

By contrast with Ibn Khaldun, Al Beruni is little known in the West. Ibn Khaldun, living in North Africa and (eventually) Cairo, has attracted, rightly, the attention of both Western and Arab scholars especially in this century. Al Beruni was born in Khwarizm (or Khiva), lived in the court of Mahmud of Ghazni (Afghanistan) – with whom he had differences – and worked on and in Hindu India. He was not an Arab. The name Al Beruni, the outsider or foreigner, suggests an extra-local background which perhaps sharpened his perception of his own and other societies.

Al Beruni was a many-sided genius in an Islamic age that produced others like him. It was the high noon of Islamic cultural and scientific achievements (chapter 3, section 3). Scientist, mathematician, astronomer and historian, Al Beruni's versatility is unbounded. We are concerned, however, with his famous book on India, popularly known as *Kitab al-Hind* or 'The book of India' (significantly the use of the word investigation in the original title, *Tahqiq ma al-Hind*, 'investigation of India', reflects his own scientific disposition).

The *Kitab* was written after some thirteen years of research between 1017 and 1031. It was translated by Dr E. Sachau into German in 1887 and next year into English as *Al Beruni's India*. Chapter titles reflect modern anthropological interests: 'On the castes, called "colours" (*varna*) and on the classes below them' (9) and 'On the rites and customs which the other castes, besides the Brahmans, practise during their lifetime' (64). Women are also examined: 'On matrimony, the menstrual courses, embryos and childbed' (69).

Al Beruni's methodology is rigorous. 'It is the method of our author not to speak himself, but let the Hindus speak. . . . He presents a picture of Indian civilization as painted by the Hindus themselves', notes the commentary. Al Beruni leans heavily on primary Hindu sources, learning Sanskrit for this purpose: 'I did not spare either trouble or money in collecting Sanskrit books from places where I supposed they were likely to be found.' He was perhaps the first Muslim to study the *Puranas*, the Hindu classical historical texts. In addition secondary sources – translations by Arab and Persian scholars – are consulted. He travels extensively in India and associates with Hindus, especially Brahmans and *yogis*. He emphasizes 'hearsay does not equal eye witness'. Value judgment of other people's customs and cultures is avoided. The anthropologist's task is to 'simply relate without criticizing'.

He is as unsparing to Arabs (when commenting on their pre-Islamic customs) as he is of certain traits of Hindus such as their 'haughtiness'. Terming Hindus 'haughty' may seem like a value judgment but Al Beruni bases his observations on sound evidence. Hindus saw their land, their customs, their food as the best in the world. Perhaps Muslim presence further provoked Hindu 'haughtiness'. The inturned xenophobic pride of the Hindus was to become an essential part of their cultural defence system against the repeated onslaught of Muslims during and after Mahmud's reign.

Al Beruni throws a wide net for comparative purposes, referring to Jews, Christians, Parsis and the ancient Greeks, for whom he has undisguised admiration. And his sympathy for universal mysticism is reflected in the comparison he makes between Sufi, Hindu and Christian mystics.

Al Beruni is as impeccable an anthropologist as he is a Muslim. While referring to the holy Quran to support his statements – his faith in Islam is strong, as is his relief to be born a Muslim – he reflects on the essential oneness of man. Al Beruni's God is the creator of all things and all peoples.

Al Beruni's dispassionate commentary measures up to the most exacting contemporary scientific standards in the social sciences. For me, as an anthropologist, Al Beruni has clearly illustrated the possibility of sustained dispassionate and penetrating analysis of alien cultures within the framework of Islam. Islam has neither hindered the scholar's enterprise nor has his Muslimness been compromised. When Al Beruni wrote, Islam was on the ascendant in world affairs. Yet neither condescension nor contempt mar his work. Al Beruni is a scientist conducting his work scientifically. The recognition of Al Beruni as the first major anthropologist of Islam thus opens theoretical and methodological doors for Muslim social scientists, and raises important questions for them – especially for those working within the Western framework (some of which will be considered in chapter 10).

Almost a thousand years before Western Indianists, such as Louis Dumont and Adrian Mayer, Al Beruni had exhaustively examined, and suggested a methodology for the study of, caste and kinship in India.

Ibn Khaldun: l'homme engagé

Ibn Khaldun's *Kitab al-Ibar*, world history, ranks high in the esteem of scholars. For Arnold Toynbee it is 'undoubtedly the greatest work of its kind that has ever yet been created by any mind in any time or place'. In it the author deploys his knowledge of history, philosophy, logic, dreams, tribal ways, mathematics, and climate from the Arab world and beyond. Arab narrative and interpretative history culminated in the work of Ibn Khaldun. He was jurist, historian, scholar, traveller and statesman, and for us today, the father of sociology, to which he gave the name *Ilm al-imran*, the science of society. Some of the central formulae of the modern age are reflected in Ibn Khaldun's theories: Karl Marx's stages of human history which provide the dynamics for the dialectics of conflict between groups; Max Weber's typology of leadership; Vilfredo Pareto's circulation of elites; Ernest Gellner's pendulum swing theory of Islam, oscillating from an urban, formal, literate tradition to a rural, informal and mystical one.

However, some contemporary Muslim scholars, taking the Islamic argument to its extreme, have criticized Ibn Khaldun for not being Islamic enough in his work. He is attacked for employing 'value-free sociology' (Illyas Ba-Yunus and Farid Ahmad, *Islamic Sociology: An Introduction*, 1985, further referred to in chapter 10).

Ibn Khaldun's life is all the more valuable for us as it records with accuracy and detail the complexity of Muslim society in Spain and North Africa in a certain period of its history. Ibn Khaldun was born in Tunis in 1332. His family, originally from Hadramawt, south Arabia, had migrated a century earlier via Seville to North Africa. Ibn Khaldun's early education included the holy Quran, the *hadith* approved by the Maliki school to which he belonged, law and mysticism. Commentaries on religious treatise, philosophy, history and politics were added later.

Ibn Khaldun's studies were conducted within the frame of the Maliki school, founded in the eighth century by Malik ibn Anas (chapter 3). Emphasizing the 'living tradition' of Madinah, it was essentially a conservative and provincial school which found easy acceptance in North Africa, particularly the Maghreb – the west, from Tripoli to Granada. Restless and ambitious, Ibn Khaldun was eager to put his knowledge to practical use, to locate and influence the Islamic 'philosopher-king'.

When still a young man Ibn Khaldun found employment at Abu Inan's court in Fez. A change of fortune put him in prison for over twenty-two months. In 1362 he left for Granada. Failing in his quest in North Africa, Ibn Khaldun now had high hopes of succeeding in Spain with Muhammad V, the ruler of Granada (1345–91).

Compared to North Africa Muslim Spain was a prosperous and stable civilization, in spite of being attacked by Marinids from North Africa and Christians in Spain. Ibn Al Khatib, first the mentor and later rival of Ibn Khaldun and the powerful chief secretary of the king, has described the grandeur of the cultural life of Granada. He writes of the wealth of its agricultural lands, the high tastes of its citizens and the charms of its women. People were obedient and free of religious fanaticism. Without doubt Muslim Spain was the intellectual and artistic centre of the Maghreb.

In 1364 Ibn Khaldun was sent on a diplomatic mission to Pedro I, the Cruel, king of Castile and Leon (1350–69). The mission revealed to him the weak position of the Muslims in Spain. It was not a peace between two equals, but between a minatory Christian monarch and a frightened Muslim ruler eager to please. Ibn Khaldun saw the writing on the wall for the Muslims of Spain.

Muhammad V was accessible and eager to learn. He sat long hours alone with Ibn Khaldun learning philosophy, mathematics and the fundamentals of religion and law. This access aroused the suspicion and wrath of Ibn Al Khatib, and Ibn Khaldun was forced to leave Granada.

Shortly afterwards, in another twist of fate, he was placed, with pomp and ceremony, in charge of Bijaya, in North Africa, by its ruler. He had thus begun his third venture in practical politics. The ruler's death in battle once again made Ibn Khaldun an exile.

Ibn Khaldun now withdrew for the next decade to research and teach in Baskara and Fez. In 1375 he once again crossed into Muslim Spain. This time, however, he was no longer an ambitious young man but a disillusioned one escaping the turmoil of North Africa.

Muhammad V, too, as predicted by Ibn Al Khatib, had turned into a cruel tyrant. He stripped Ibn Al Khatib of office, expelled him and encouraged his murder. When Muhammad V learned of Ibn Khaldun's attempts to save Ibn Al Khatib he banished him from Granada. Tired and weary of the world, Ibn Khaldun withdrew to the castle of Ibn Salama. There, now in his early forties, he spent four years. His official duties had brought him in contact with many important political actors of Spain and North Africa: kings, ambassadors, tribal chiefs. He now began to work out his ideas. He wished to write a history of western Islam.

Ibn Khaldun began his introduction, *muqaddimah*, in the castle of Ibn Salama. He focussed on the dissimilarities between the Islamic world of the tenth century and, his own, the fourteenth. As a base for the tenth century he selected two scholars, Al Masudi (chapter 3, section 3) and Bakri (d. 1094). Both Al Masudi, the most revered of Muslim historians, and the author of the universal history, *The Meadows of Gold*, and Bakri, author of *Routes and Kingdoms*, used prevalent social and economic conditions in their work.

Not satisfied with simple history, the traditional recounting of dates and dynasties, Ibn Khaldun thought about a new science, the 'science of culture or society', *Ilm al-imran*. He now realized that the scope of his work had to be larger, beyond the confines of the Maghreb. His examples of nomads, for instance, would include Arab, Berber, Turk and Mongol groups.

Another change of fortune in Tunis resulted in an invitation to return to the city of his birth. But by now Ibn Khaldun's attitude to politics had changed completely and he had no wish to be involved in any kind of political activity. In Tunis the favours shown to him roused the envy of other courtiers and once again we find Ibn Khaldun in exile. This time he decided to leave the Maghreb altogether and head for Cairo. Behind him, he left the dark and confused Maghreb and his own frustrated hopes.

In Egypt, where his fame had preceded him, he spent his last years, a quarter of a century. Although he was appointed six times the Malikite Grand Judge and remained active at court he accomplished his purpose of writing his main work.

The last link with the Maghreb was broken when Ibn Khaldun's family, along with his worldly possessions, were shipwrecked near Alexandria. Grief-stricken, he resigned his post and went on pilgrimage to Makkah. His meetings there with scholars and students were not only a diversion from his grief but of assistance to his work.

Ibn Khaldun's knowledge of the tribes, administration and dynasties of North Africa and Muslim Spain were now complemented by the rich civilization of Egypt. It was a civilization that did not entirely meet with his approval.

He found moral corruption and social dissolution. In Egypt he was to remain a stranger, finding it difficult to identify with what he saw as its decadence.

One extraordinary event remains to recount in this, the last phase of Ibn Khaldun's life. In 1401 he met Taimur who had trapped him, along with the Egyptian ruler's army, in Damascus. He stayed in Taimur's camp for thirty-five days and the dialogue between the two is one of the most interesting recorded in history – the one probing with questions implicitly designed to aid the conquest of Cairo and the Maghreb, the other deliberately obfuscating his knowledge with generalizations and theories. Ibn Khaldun's past experience in the courts of North Africa would have stood him in good stead in this encounter.

During the last seven years of his life in Egypt, and up to his sudden death in 1406, Ibn Khaldun remained active as a scholar and judge. He completed his Autobiography, and continued to refine his *History* and accumulate data for it.

Ibn Khaldun's early training, his failures in politics, the long period of reflection on these failures, his investigations into the philosophy of history, his adoption of an academic yet generalized style of writing, and his conservative attitude to life in Egypt all fall into a complex but intelligible pattern. In a sense we may discover the elements of the pattern in his work.

Ibn Khaldun's principal theory may be reduced to one formula – 'Prestige lasts at best four generations in one lineage' – and to one question – 'What keeps society together?' Ibn Khaldun is thus the theorist of social cohesion.

The answer to his central question provides a frame for his theories. Tribesmen, united through *asabyah*, group feelings, cohesion, solidarity, overpower those living in a state of urbanization, *tamaddun*, and who have lost group cohesion. The victory could lead to the creation of a state or dynasty, *dawlah*. In turn, over three to four generations, the urbanized tribesmen must face fresher tribesmen. The cyclical pattern marks Islamic history:

> (The rulers) maintain their hold over the government and their own dynasty with the help, then, either of clients and followers who grew up in the shadow and power of group feelings, or of tribal groups of a different descent who have become their clients.
>
> Something of the sort happened to the Abbasids. The group feeling of the Arabs had been destroyed by the time of the reign of al-Mu'tasim and his son, al-Wathiq. They tried to maintain their hold over the government thereafter with the help of Persian, Turkish, Daylam, Saljuq, and other clients. Then, the (non-Arabs) and their clients gained power over the provinces (of the realm). The influence of the dynasty grew smaller, and

> no longer extended beyond the environs of Baghdad. Eventually, the Daylam closed in upon and took possession of (that area). The caliphs were ruled by them. Then (the Daylam), in turn, lost control. The Saljuqs seized power after the Daylam, and the (caliphs) were ruled by them. Then (the Saljuqs), in turn, lost control. Finally the Tatars closed in. They killed the caliph and wiped out every vestige of the dynasty.

Ibn Khaldun views humanity with a cold sociological eye. He has no sides to take, no lessons to impart. The protagonists – tribesman and townsman, are described with neutrality – reflecting the contempt they feel for each other:

> The Bedouins . . . are alone in the country and remote from militias. They have no walls or gates . . . they provide their own defence and do not entrust it to . . . others. . . . They always carry weapons. . . . Fortitude has become a character quality of theirs, and courage their nature.

Their leaders and chiefs have a difficult time imposing order:

> Because of their savagery, the Bedouins are the least willing of nations to subordinate themselves to each other, as they are rude, proud, ambitious, and eager to be leaders. Their individual aspirations rarely coincide.

Bedouins are 'a savage nation' but more courageous, better, than sedentary people who

> have become used to laziness and ease. They have entrusted the defence of their property and their lives to the governor and ruler who rules them, and to the militia which has the task of guarding them. They find full assurance of safety in the walls that surround them, and the fortifications which protect them. They have become like women and children, who depend upon the master of the house. Eventually, this has come to be a quality of character.

As Ernest Gellner, a fervent admirer of Ibn Khaldun, comments:

> No advice is offered to the social cosmos as to how it should comport itself. Things are as they are. The thinker's job is to understand them, not to change them. Marx's contrary opinion would have astonished Ibn Khaldun. (*Muslim Society*, 1981)

Ibn Khaldun is essentially the sociologist of Islam – the Islam of the arid zone inhabited by tribes and nomads. In these areas temporary dynasties rise as conquering tribes emerge from mountain or desert, and fall never to be heard of again. But a legitimate question may be posed in the context of the theory and categories of Islamic history suggested in this book.

How do we apply Ibn Khaldun's theories to other Islamic systems which are long-lasting and stable with established bureaucracies and written procedures like those of the imperial Ottomans, Saffavids and Mughals, discussed in the last chapter? It is an unfair question as it post-dates Ibn Khaldun, and perhaps he has no satisfactory answer. But it shows that the study of society is a continuing and complex process.

In our time the world of Ibn Khaldun's tribesmen, living in mountain and desert, is changing and shrinking (see chapters 8 and 9). Cities and markets lure the young men; administrators from outside, through taxes and laws, impose their will; the use of superior arms dictates to them and, finally, foreign culture invades the privacy of their homes through the radio, TV, and now the VCR. Nomadic tribesmen are in the process of becoming sedentarized, their values urbanized, without having to leave their lands.

Ibn Khaldun's life is important in another way also. It forms a bridge, a transition, between the distinct phases of Muslim history which we are examining: the Arab dynasties in the tail-end of which – as in Umayyad Spain – he lived, and the great Muslim empires which would develop by the end of the century in which he died. His life also teaches us many things, confirming them for us in our own period: the uncertainty of politics; the fickleness of rulers; the abrupt changes of fortune, in jail one day, honoured the next; and finally, the supremacy of the ideal in the constant, unceasing, search for *ilm*, knowledge, and therefore the ultimate triumph of the human will and intellect against all odds.

6

Islam of the periphery

Muslim societies living on the outskirts of the great Muslim empires, and hence use of the word periphery, are considered in this chapter. We will use the word to denote groups that represent the furthest extension of the critical mass of the mainstream Islamic empires. (I am uncomfortable with the word periphery as, again, the use of it depends on where the user stands: on a lecture tour in Paris I discovered that for French scholars South Asian Islam is '*Islam du périphérie*'.)

1 ON THE PERIPHERY

To categorize these groups is difficult. In cultural terms they are dissimilar. Their societies may be broadly identified as those living in parts of the USSR and China, south of the Sahara in Africa and in South East Asia, including the southern islands of the Philippines, and Indonesia. Their numbers are large. Malay Muslims, spread over the Malay peninsula and Indonesia, are estimated to number about 170 million. Indonesia is the most populous Muslim country in the world. These societies provide the fourth socio-historical category in our construction of an Islamic theory of history.

Although Muslims in this category comprise a significant proportion of the total world Muslim population – between one-fourth and one-third – they are generally ignored in discussions of Islam. The logic is clear. The ideal cannot be attained in a hostile environment, hence Muslimness is compromised. This is not entirely correct nor true as our examination of the three most significant Muslim minorities, in India (chapter 8), where they number about 120 million, the USSR, 45 million, and China, 40 million, will reveal (the last two are discussed in this chapter).

This category of Muslims requires special study, a point emphasized by Professor S. Z. Abedin, editor of the *Journal of the Institute of Muslim Minority Affairs*. He noted:

> How can we live as Muslims in multi-cultural and religiously diverse society? . . . we must discover ways to resolve the duality, the twoness that resides in the minority condition. . . . It needs new categories of thought, a fresh understanding of Islam and a creative capacity for application. (*Muslim Communities in Non-Muslim States*, 1980)

When faced with unbearable majority opposition to their faith Muslims have either fought – *jihad* – or migrated – *hijra*. The Quran pointed to this option – 'He who emigrates in the path of God will find frequent refuge and abundance' (Surah 4, *An Nisa*, Women) and the Prophet's example provided the precedent. It was Usman Dan Fodio who analysed the obligation to emigrate in his work, *Bayan Wujub al-hijrah ala al ibad.* Dan Fodio himself fled persecution to launch a successful *jihad.* But a solution in the seventh – or the nineteenth – century is not always a practical one in the twentieth century. Immigration regulations, visa restrictions, border security make a modern *hijra* difficult. Historically Muslims have cause to be wary of living as a minority; they were banished from Andalusia and Sicily. The twentieth-century emergence of nation-states and minority status have accentuated Muslim problems. Living as a minority in a non-Muslim society in the twentieth century poses special problems: closure or destruction of mosques, lack of religious education, and hostile official policy. It also illustrates the capacity of Muslims to adjust and survive.

Certain characteristics distinguish Muslim societies of the periphery. Because they have remained out of the mainstream of Muslim history they do not have the glamour of the famous Muslim empires or dynasties attached to them. There are no historical Muslim capitals here, no Baghdad, Damascus or Cairo; no towering scholars – Al Ghazzali, Al Beruni, Ibn Khaldun – have worked here, nor mighty emperors – Sulayman, Abbas, Akbar – been born among them. This is not to say that they did not produce people of note. As we shall see, extraordinary Islamic activity is recorded in each area. However, it is marked by a temporary, fitful nature.

Another characteristic of these groups is the lack of communication between each other and with the main Muslim world due to their geographical isolation. However pilgrimages to Makkah and Madinah created links with Muslim centres and Muslim groups.

Most important, Islam in these areas learned to adapt. As its fortunes waxed and waned the customs of Muslim society changed. For most of the time *jihad* was not interpreted as battling against or converting non-Muslim groups, but simply as learning to survive.

Mainstream Islamic tradition brought by Muslims returning from Makkah and Madinah combined with local culture to produce interesting mutations. These are most pronounced in mosque architecture. In Africa the Mali-

Songhai mosques are marked by buttresses, pinnacles and soaring minarets with exposed beams giving a hedgehog effect. In Java and Sumatra mosques are layered and pagoda like. In China they had gabled, tiled roofs which sloped upwards ending in dragon's tails. Chinese mosques did not possess minarets as they were banned by the state. In the interior on one wall were displayed the emperor's tablets before which Muslims were supposed to prostrate themselves.

Muslims had consciously to define and redefine themselves in terms of Islam. Local pre-Islamic customs were not easily excluded. In Africa we have before us the image of King Muhammad Rumfa of Kano symbolically cutting the city's sacred tree by the congregational mosque. Old rituals, animistic practices and taboos revived again and again in the Songhai Kingdom.

In Indonesia the Wayang or shadow theatre, the cycle of plays in the rural areas adapted from stories from the Hindu epics of the *Ramayana* and *Mahabharata*, continued with the introduction of new Islamic characters. Hamzah, the Prophet's uncle, was a favourite. While Islamic characters were introduced in traditional plays pre-Islamic heroes were updated and adjusted to Islam. Tradition among the Tengger of east Java has Ajisaka, famous for his beauty and widsom, visiting the Prophet in Makkah to obtain his spiritual knowledge. But Ajisaka does not become a Muslim. Indeed, impressed by Ajisaka's ability to make himself invisible the Prophet declares: 'You will be my equal . . . when you walk the night, I walk the day.' This division, it is locally interpreted, explains why the islands west of Java are Muslim and east of Java retain their Hindu-Buddhist influences derived from the long dead Majapahit empire.

Another example of the influence of Islam on local culture is provided by the popular dance. Although the traditional forms of dancing remained on the Indonesian islands, now, after Islam, the legs were neither kicked high nor opened wide as shown in the sculptures of Hindu Borobudur.

There is flux and reflux of Islam, growth and decay of Muslim societies, in these areas: the loss of the Niger states to the heathen Bambara; the loss of the Central Asian Khanates to the Russians; the pressures under the Manchu dynasty to convert to Confucianism. But, there are also vigorous attempts at expansion and survival: the three Fullani wars in Africa, culminating in the emergence of Usman Dan Fodio (1754–1817) and the formation of the sultanate of Sokoto; Sultan Agung, the leader of the Padri movement spreading Islamization in Java in the nineteenth century and extending Islam to Sumatra; the Naqshbandi struggle against the Russians and Chinese. Islam was showing remarkable vigour in meeting the challenges which it confronted. The ideal inspired men to action and piety.

By the early years of the twentieth century Islam of the periphery was submerged under different forms of colonial rule. The British colonized

Nigeria, including Sokoto, the French Morocco and the Sahara, while the Italians occupied Libya. The Dutch, and later the Japanese, occupied Indonesia. In Central Asia the USSR continued the policies of the Russian Czars in absorbing the Central Asian Khanates. For many decades after the turn of the century the story of these groups would end like a book shut abruptly.

2 THE MUSLIM MINORITY IN CHINA

Historically there are two main types of Muslim community in China. The older derives from groups of merchants and other travellers who came to China with the advent of Islam in the seventh and eighth centuries. These Muslims integrated into Chinese society while maintaining a special identity as Muslims. They became Sinified through the adoption of Chinese surnames, clothing and food habits. Gradually Chinese dialects replaced Arabic and Persian not only as a means of communication with the Han – the traditional Chinese of the 'Middle Kingdom' – but among the Muslims as well. As a result of this Sinification the Muslims were no longer referred to as 'Arabs', 'barbarians' or 'foreigners', but came to be known as *Hui-hui* or *Hui*. The Hui were seen as a type of 'national' community within China.

The other major type of Muslim community comprises of the Central Asian groups who were brought under Chinese imperial control as a result of the expansion of China in more recent times. These groups were largely concentrated in Sinkiang (Xinjiang) Province and other parts of north-west China and spoke Central Asian languages. Unlike the Hui, they have maintained their ethnic and religious identities virtually intact, despite official policies which aimed to assimilate them.

The oppressive policy of the Manchu dynasty, established in the seventeenth century, aroused many Muslim revolts. Those in Yunnan and Kansu Provinces were the most serious. For more than a decade Muslim leaders like Ma Hualung (d. 1871) were able to control large areas. Similarly, in the far west, Yaqub Beg (1820–77) established a state which received recognition until Chinese imperial control was re-established. As late as 1953 an effort was made to establish an independent Islamic state in Honan.

The new republican regime established in the early twentieth century opened the way for more direct participation of Muslims in Chinese life without direct oppression. The republican government after 1912, for example, formally identified the Muslims in China as one of the 'five great peoples' of China. In this way, the treatment of Muslims as a special community within China predates the establishment of the communist regime.

The People's Republic of China developed a more specified system of recognition. Muslims were not treated as 'one people'. Instead, the particular ethnic groups among the Muslim populations were given direct recognition. This was in line with the general policy of recognition of minority groups of all types within China as 'minority nationalities'.

Muslims were subject to severe repression during the cultural revolution. Punishments involved burning the holy Quran and contact with pigs. In the present climate non-Muslims in Muslim areas are careful not to let their pigs forage freely and are sensitive to the Muslim prohibition against eating pork. The formal recognition of Muslim 'nationalities' has been ensured by constitutional provisions for freedom of belief and also through the creation of special autonomous areas for minority nationalities. These areas in some ways reflect the distribution of Muslims within China. The Hui are found throughout China and there are twelve different Hui autonomous areas in eight different provinces. Most of the other special areas are in north-west China, with the largest being the Uygur autonomous region in Xinjiang. While most affairs are in some way under more central control and Han citizens are important even in the various autonomous areas, the system of minority nationalities provides a basic structure of recognition for the Muslim communities. In Xinjiang, at least, the ethnicity and religion of Muslims are not disturbed. Although repression is still possible and assimilation always likely it appears that fuller autonomy is not an option for Chinese Muslims. Major Chinese Muslim rebellions have not created long-lasting areas of Muslim independence. Similarly, for most Chinese Muslims, emigration, *hijra*, out of China is not a feasible alternative.

3 MUSLIMS IN THE USSR

The relationship of the USSR with its Muslim groups is historical and complex. For the Muslims of Central Asia history follows the rapid rise and slow decline theory. The Mongols – under their great warrior-king Chenghiz Khan and his sons – after destroying the Arab world in a dramatic twist of fate became Muslim. From their heart-lands in Central Asia they went on to conquer Russia. The relationship between Russian and Mongol was bitter; nothing but the sword passed between them.

In another twist of the Central Asian drama, Taimur, a descendant of Chenghiz and himself an avaricious conqueror, in 1395 shattered his kinsmen the Mongols. They were never to recover. Taimur annexed Georgia and Armenia to his domains. Samarkand, Taimur's capital, became a glittering and important Muslim capital. But the Muslims of Central Asia would pay heavily for Taimur's destruction of the Mongols.

Under Ivan the Terrible the Russians launched a successful offensive against the Muslims which would have reverberations for contemporary society. Between 1555 and 1560 St Basil's Cathedral, a popular symbol of Moscow adjacent to the Kremlin, was built to commemorate victory over the Muslims. The rule of the Romanovs, lasting for over 300 years until the Socialist Revolution of 1917, would see the slow, piecemeal incorporation of the Central Asian Muslim states and groups into Russia. One by one they fell, Uzbeg, Tajik and Kazakh. In one sense the contemporary Soviet presence in Afghanistan is a continuation of the same historical momentum.

The story of the northern marches, small lonely groups living hard lives in steppes and desert oases, is one of slow decline and irreversible isolation from the sixteenth century onward. Taimur, who once ruled the world, was long gone and the kingdom of Farghana, which once challenged the Saffavids and the Mughals, was reduced to a few deserted towns and remote tribes. But the Islamic flame, guttering and flickering, was not quite dead. Its flickering would illuminate an age. In the nineteenth century Imam Shamyl is one such Islamic flicker.

Imam Shamyl, ideal Muslim warrior

Imam Shamyl's valiant efforts to create an Islamic state in the face of an expanding Imperial Russia, his correspondence with Queen Victoria – who was interested in stopping the Russian advance to India – and his mention in debates in the House of Commons make him one of the most romantic figures of nineteenth-century Islam. Tolstoy heightened the mystique by writing about Shamyl's area, the Caucasus.

Mystic, warrior and saint, Imam Shamyl lived a hard life in a hard land. He had something of Umar, the second caliph of Islam, about him. He ordered his mother publicly whipped for supplicating on behalf of defaulters; after five lashes he stepped forward to take the remaining lashes on his own back. His little son was sacrificed for freedom. Truly Shamyl believed in his favourite expression: 'This world is a carcass and those who seek it are dogs.'

Imam Shamyl organized and led his followers, called the *Murid*, through what are called the Murid wars. Wearing black, they struck terror in the hearts of the enemy. They assisted the Imam in upholding the laws of the *Shariah*. Underlying the devotion to Islam was the austere, severe Sufism of the Caucasus, Muridism, a branch of the Naqshbandi order. Through severe discipline and by personal example the Imam sought to maintain an Islamic order. This period of history is called 'the time of the *Shariah*' in Daghestan, between the Caspian and Black Seas.

But the Imam was fighting against the clock. He could delay but not stop the Russian advance. In the end he was overpowered. He spent his last years in Makkah and Madinah, dying there in 1871. The last word he uttered was 'Allah'.

The last Muslim areas incorporated by Imperial Russia were Transoxiana, which included the historical cities of Bukhara and Samarkand. But incorporation was not without problems.

Muslims in the early days of the USSR

When the Naqshbandi revolts in the Caucasus died down after Imam Shamyl, a number of revolts among Turkish groups in Central Asia began. They reached a climax during the First World War. Of these the Basmachi revolt in Turkestan immediately after the establishment of the Bolshevik government in 1917 is the most significant.

The Basmachi revolt came closest to success in opposing a major communist regime and is therefore worth examining more closely. Initially, most Muslims in Central Asia had supported the overthrow of the Czarist regime. Russian suppression of the Turkestan revolts during the First World War had been severe and many Muslims believed that the Russian Revolution would mean that Muslims would achieve freedom to rule themselves. However, following the establishment of the Bolshevik government, friction developed in Central Asia which led in varying stages to the outbreak of fresh revolts against central control.

For almost a decade these revolts opposed the extension of communist control. They received support from modern, educated Muslim Central Asians as well as the more traditional groups of tribal leaders and *ulema*. This general cluster of opposition movements came to be called the Basmachi or 'Freemen's Movement'. Although at times there was a region-wide co-ordination, usually the Basmachi revolt was a scattering of groups which had the same goal of opposition to centralized Russian communist control. There was little long-lasting co-ordination of efforts. For a brief period of time in 1921–2, especially under the leadership of Enver Pasha, a former leader in the Ottoman empire, the movement achieved a more effective unification, but this did not last long.

The Basmachi movement was finally defeated but it left behind a legacy, a memory of revolt, for the Muslims of Soviet Central Asia. Even though there were many different Muslim groups in Central Asia with different understandings of Islam, all elements of Turkestani society were agreed on one, and possibly only one, issue: Islam and Turkestan were unquestionably linked. Even if the understanding of what Islam was varied, religion was a fundamental part of the self-identity of Turkestan. Thus, at the beginning of the Muslim experience of being a minority within the Soviet Union, there was a clear linkage, at least in the Central Asian communities, between territorial and national identity and Islamic faith.

Even before the Russian Revolution the *jadid* – modern – movement among Turkish Muslims fought for modernist reform. The Jadids wished for reforms within the frame of the Russian Empire. After the Revolution some Muslims wished to synthesize Muslim identity and communist ideology. One of their most important leaders was Mir Sayyed Sultan Ali Oghlu or Sultan Galiev. He fell victim to Stalin's purges in the 1920s for 'nationalist deviationism'.

Contemporary Muslim society in the USSR

The importance of Islam in the Soviet Union today has come to be associated with the fortunes of the nationalities whose special identities are in some ways tied to Islam. The most important of these are represented in the separate republics of Kazakhistan, Kirghizistan, Tajikistan, Turkmenistan and Uzbekistan.

In recent years there appears to be a steady increase in the influence and power of the non-Russian nationalities in the Muslim areas. This may be related to the growing educational level of the various national groups in Central Asia and also to developments in population composition. A recent study concludes that in Kazakhistan and Central Asia

> the indigenous nationalities are increasing their level of educational attainment and increasingly assume a leading role in the economy and the administration of their republics. In part, this process is the indirect result of general economic and social development, modernization and changing demographic relationships, but it is also linked to deliberate policies both of the native populations themselves and the Soviet authorities. (R. Karklins, 'Nationality power in Soviet Republics', in *Studies in Comparative Communism*, 1981)

Some scholars argue that even though certain Muslim practices like recitation of prayers after a meal continue, they 'have lost their religious significance. It would be a mistake to consider them the continuation of Muslim practices. People view them as a part of traditional life, an ethnic heritage that may protect them from the onslaught of modern ways' (I. Basgoz, 'Religion and ethnic consciousness among Turks in the Soviet Union', in *Islam in the Contemporary World*, ed. C.K. Pullapilly, 1980). Others believe that the continuation of Islamic customs presents a clear continuation of the importance of being a Muslim in communist society. Practices associated with the major life events of birth, marriage and death emphasize the Islamic character of life. In the USSR circumcision takes on an obvious meaning. It implies that the young Muslim is a member of an overall community, the *ummah*, which he shares with his brethren and which is the world of Islam.

The growing strength of national identity among the Muslim people in the Soviet Union can be and is interpreted in a wide variety of ways. Some scholars see the growing national feelings as potential threats to the general Soviet system. One scholar, for example, believes that 'national and autonomous strivings . . . in Kazakhistan and Central Asia are very likely to grow' and that 'illustrations of increasing native power in the Muslim republics went beyond cadre selection, education, and demography, and included the growth of native assertiveness and pride' (Karklins, *op. cit.*).

Other scholars see the emergence of national identities as reflecting the adjustment of non-Russian peoples to the Soviet system (for example, Basgoz *op. cit.*). In specific terms, the particular national groupings that have emerged with real strength are smaller groups that have adapted themselves to existence within the Soviet system.

In particular, Sufi orders and centres have been historically a source of strength to Muslims and this continues to be the case. Professor V. N. Basilov, a leading Soviet anthropologist, has established the continuing strength of traditional custom and ritual among Central Asian groups ('Honour groups in traditional Turkmenian society' in *Islam in Tribal Societies: From the Atlas to the Indus*, eds A.S. Ahmed and D. Hart, 1984). D'Encausse writes that 'Soviet Moslems, having repeated to their foreign Moslem brothers for more than twenty years that Islam is able to accommodate itself very well with Communism, have gone on to blend Islam and Communism into an astonishing syncretism' (H. Carrère d' Encausse, *Decline of an Empire*, 1981).

In the contemporary Soviet Union, Muslim preachers work on defining a progressive Islamic socialism:

> Soviet Moslem sermons pick up this general theme of Islamic-socialist compatibility by finding predictions of the Soviet state in the Koran, by referring to the building of communism as the 'great earthly ideal of the Prophet Muhammad', and by proclaiming that the articles of the 1977 constitution of the USSR 'correspond fully to the teaching of the Holy Koran and the utterance of the Prophet Muhammad'. (B.L. Larson, 'The Moslems of Soviet Central Asia', PhD thesis, University of Minnesota, 1983)

While the reasoning and conclusions may not be in accord with the orthodox interpretations of Islam nor in agreement with what non-Muslim scholars may think Muslim teachers should be saying in the Soviet Union or China, the adherence of these Muslim preachers both to Islam and to living in communist societies appears to be authentic.

My own brief visit to the mosque in Moscow confirmed this. The mosque was well-kept and well attended. Muslims sat on the thick prayer carpets, lost in meditation, turning beads. Decorum was not allowed to be forgotten. An old Uzbeg lady walked up to our party and vociferously protested to our guide, a Russian professor, for not covering his head. The same professor had been upbraided earlier by another old lady, this time in a Russian Orthodox church, for laughing in a place of worship. It was my fault. When he lit a candle as a mark of respect for the ritual in process, it fell. I whispered, 'God cannot accept offerings from atheists.' He laughed, provoking anger in the worshippers. Later, people suggested that the authorities had staged the incidents to illustrate the freedom of worship enjoyed in the USSR. Perhaps. But as I requested the visit to the mosque and the church at the last minute, *en route* to another programme, I think not.

None the less the demographic argument worries Russians. Muslims are multiplying three times faster than them. By the year 2000 they may number between one-quarter to one-third of the population. But the authorities can do little about these statistics.

The conclusion cannot be escaped that Muslims in the USSR and China have neither been crushed out of existence nor assimilated beyond recognition. Reports from both countries indicate the vigour of faith and practice among millions of Muslims. The conclusion is critical for Islam: it is possible for Muslims to survive as a minority without *jihad* or having to migrate. A new, twentieth-century answer is in the process of forming to a problem that dates back to the seventh century.

Sometimes Muslim, sometimes Christian, sometimes Buddhist and sometimes pagan, the story of the Muslims of the periphery is an agonising tale of a religious civilization appearing to run fitfully to ground. It makes harrowing reading. But it is also uplifting in its record of renewal; a confirmation of the vitality of faith through heroic individual endeavour and the struggle to reach towards the ideal in spite of unfavourable circumstances.

7

Under European rule: the colonial impact on Muslim society

Colonial rule for Muslims was an unmitigated disaster. No arguments about Europe providing railways and the telegraph, or maintaining law and order, can conceal or assuage this fact. Colonization affected the Islamic ideal by contorting and smothering it. During the colonial century Muslims would wage a desperate battle to salvage the ideal. The costs would be heavy, and Muslims are still paying them.

Europe – England, France, Germany, Spain, Portugal, Italy – insatiably swallowed Muslim lands; Russia displayed a similar appetite for the Muslim Central Asian states. One by one, kingdoms and states, large and petty, fell. The Europeans were able to subjugate what had been established and complex civilizations. Colonial rule paralysed Muslim societies, congealed thought and froze their history. European notions of race and class entered and became part of Muslim society. Worse, the colonial period destroyed Muslim confidence, creating in them and of them an image of childlike helplessness.

In Europe's advance towards technology and industry, Muslims found themselves bound in shackles. In this phase of history European armies, backed by industrial force, colonized Muslim societies despite their valiant efforts to resist. Muslims were finding it difficult to reconcile themselves with what was rapidly becoming the European phase of world history, and in their failure and anger they rejected the symbols of modernity. It was easy to fall back to old, pre- or non-Islamic, superstitions and beliefs. Muslim leaders would successfully convince their followers from Sudan to Swat to face European bullets with sticks and lances. They had blessed Muslim weapons, bestowed on them magical powers which would prevent injury to the true believers. Beliefs such as these assisted the Europeans in consolidating their hold. It was a complete dissolution, an Islamic collapse. The nightmare of colonization had begun.

What is notable in the turbulence of the nineteenth century and in the face of advancing Europe is the visible, potent presence of the ideal. The greater the abyss into which the Muslim world would fall the greater the emphasis on the ideal. Across Africa and Asia men of learning and leadership clung to the Quran and *Shariah* as imperial European forces closed in: the Sanusi and Mahdi orders fighting Europeans in Africa; Imam Shamyl in the Caucasus struggling against Russians; the Naqshbandi Khojas, dressed in green, resisting Chinese central authority; Ummar Tal Al Haji whose theocratic state the French eventually absorbed; Muhammad Abdul Hassan in Somalia, Abdul Qadir in Algeria, the Akhund of Swat and Sayyed Ahmad Barelvi in north India, and Haji Shariatullah in Bengal – all fought the enemies of Islam. However, by the time the century turned the Muslim world was still smouldering but it was subdued.

1 THE DISINTEGRATION OF SOCIETY

The undisguised voices of the colonial masters jar on our modern post-independence sensibilities. An unrelieved strain of racist vulgarity and religious prejudice runs through them. We are astonished at their crassness. But at that time and in that place these were the authentic voices of Europe.

Colonial perceptions

Let us hear them, the builders and governors of empire, hailed in their time as the good and the great. For Lord Clive, the conqueror of India, the 'typical' Indians 'are servile, mean, submissive and humble. In superior stations, they are luxurious, effeminate, tyrannical, treacherous, venal, cruel.' 'A Persian is a coward at the best of times,' concluded Lord Curzon, Viceroy of India, and imperial expert on Persia. Lord Macaulay, the President of the Indian Law Commission whose Minute on Education would affect Muslim society profoundly, dismissed Indian learning thus: 'medical doctrines which would disgrace an English farrier, astronomy which would move laughter in the girls at an English boarding school – history, abounding with kings thirty feet high and reigns thirty thousand years long; and geography made up of seas of treacle and seas of butter.' Lord Cromer of Egypt describes the Egyptian mind, making comparisons with Europeans:

> Sir Alfred Lyall once said to me: 'Accuracy is abhorrent to the Oriental mind. Every Anglo-Indian should always remember that maxim.' Want of accuracy, which easily degenerates into untruthfulness, is in fact the main characteristic of the Oriental mind. The European is a close reasoner; his statements of fact are devoid of any ambiguity; he is a natural logician, albeit he may not have studied logic; he is by nature sceptical and requires proof before he can accept the truth of any proposition; his trained

> intelligence works like a piece of mechanism. The mind of the Oriental, on the other hand, like his picturesque streets, is eminently wanting in symmetry. His reasoning is of the most slipshod description. Although the ancient Arabs acquired in a somewhat higher degree the science of dialectics, their descendants are singularly deficient in the logical faculty. They are often incapable of drawing the most obvious conclusions from any simple premises of which they may admit the truth. Endeavour to elicit a plain statement of facts from any ordinary Egyptian. His explanation will generally be lengthy, and wanting in lucidity. He will probably contradict himself half-a-dozen times before he has finished his story. He will often break down under the mildest process of cross-examination.

European artists and writers reinforced the picture of the 'decadent' Orient in the minds of their administrators. This picture was exaggerated and often wildly inaccurate. It sometimes reflected the urges and instincts of its creator more than the reality. Here is the famous French writer Flaubert on Cairo:

> To amuse the crowd, Muhammad Ali's jester took a woman in a Cairo bazaar one day, set her on the counter of a shop, and coupled with her publicly while the shopkeeper calmly smoked his pipe.
>
> On the road from Cairo to Shubra some time ago a young fellow had himself publicly buggered by a large monkey – as in the story above, to create a good opinion of himself and make people laugh.
>
> A marabout died a while ago – an idiot – who had long passed as a saint marked by God; all the Moslem women came to see him and masturbated him – in the end he died of exhaustion – from morning to night it was a perpetual jacking-off. . . .
>
> *Quid dicis* of the following fact: some time ago a *santon* (ascetic priest) used to walk through the streets of Cairo completely naked except for a cap on his head and another on his prick. To piss he would doff the prick-cap, and sterile women who wanted children would run up, put themselves under the parabola of his urine and rub themselves with it.

Public sex, animal buggery, communal masturbation – it was European fantasy running riot in an imagined Orient; a fantasy imposed on the colonized.

Society fragmented

Draconian punishment and savage reprisals met signs of rebellion among Muslims. It crushed their spirit and fragmented their society. Like debased children natives were to be administered severe punishment when naughty. India in 1857, when large parts of the countryside and the natives enlisted in the colonial army rose against the British, gives us many examples. The following account about rebelling soldiers, not far removed from the peasantry to which they belonged, was written by a Deputy Commissioner of Amritsar, Mr F. Cooper, a man in charge of a district, the *mai-baap*, mother-father, of South Asian peasants:

> The 1st of August was the anniversary of the great Mohammedan sacrificial festival of the Bukra Eed. A capital excuse was thus afforded to permit the Hindoostanee (sic) Mussulman horsemen to return to celebrate it at Umritsir (sic) while the single Christian, unembarrassed by their presence, and aided by the faithful Seiks (sic), might perform a ceremonial sacrifice of a different nature. . . . As fortune would have it, again favouring audacity, a deep dry well was discovered within one hundred yards of the police-station, and its presence furnished a convenient solution as to the one remaining difficulty which was of sanitary consideration – the disposal of the corpses of the dishonoured soldiers.

Pinioned, the prisoners were brought out in batches to be shot:

> About 150 having been thus executed, one of the executioners swooned away (he was the oldest of the firing-party), and a little respite was allowed. Then proceeding, the number had arrived at 237; when the district officer was informed that the remainder refused to come out of the bastion, where they had been imprisoned temporarily, a few hours before. . . . The doors were opened, and, behold! Unconsciously the tragedy of Holwell's Black Hole had been re-enacted. . . . Forty-five bodies, dead from fright, exhaustion, fatigue, heat, and partial suffocation, were dragged into light.

These, dead and dying, along with their murdered comrades, were thrown by the village sweepers into the well. Cooper continues:

> The above account, written by the principal actor in the scene himself, might read strangely at home: a single Anglo-Saxon, supported by a section of Asiatics, undertaking so tremendous a responsibility, and coldly presiding over so memorable an execution, without the excitement of battle, or a sense of individual injury, to imbue the proceedings with the faintest hue of vindictiveness. The Governors of the Punjab are of the true English stamp and mould, and knew that England expected every man to do his duty, and that duty done, thanks them warmly for doing it.

Indeed, the Governor of the Punjab, Lawrence – after whom one of Lahore's main gardens and other main features are named – applauded his subordinate:

> Lahore, 2nd August, 1857.
>
> My dear Cooper, I congratulate you on your success against the 26th

> N.I. You and your police acted with much energy and spirit, and deserve well of the State. I trust the fate of these sepoys will operate as a warning to others. Every effort should be exerted to glean up all who are yet at large.

Robert Montgomery, whose name honoured a major Punjab district, now Sahiwal, and who succeeded Lawrence as Lieutenant-Governor of the Punjab, also wrote to Cooper:

> Sunday: 9 a.m.
>
> My dear Cooper, All honour for what you have done; and right well you did it. There was no hesitation, or delay, or drawing back. It will be a feather in your cap as long as you live. . . . The other three regiments here were very shaky yesterday; but I hardly think they will now go. I wish they would, as they are a nuisance; and not a man would escape if they do.

A short while later Montgomery wrote to Hodson, congratulating him on a deed which has found few defenders, even among the British. Hodson had brutally shot the male members of the family of the king of Delhi, the frail and old poet, Bahadur Shah Zafar, the last of the Mughals (see chapter 4, section 1):

> My dear Hodson, All honour to you (and to your 'Horse') for catching the king and slaying his sons. I hope you will bag many more.
>
> In haste, ever yours,
> R. Montgomery.

No remorse, no pain is contained in the correspondence; it is all killing and punishing. Europeans at their best were paternalistic, stern Victorians who always knew best. Kipling created for us in his poems the stereotypes of the African and Asian in imperial eyes. He is the 'big black boundin' beggar' ('Fuzzy-Wuzzy'); the women, 'Funny an' yellow' ('The ladies'); the 'natives' are a 'blackfaced crew' ('Gunga Din'), 'Half devil and half child' ('The White Man's Burden').

The negative images and the savage punishments formed a psychological pressure on the colonized, and created grief and anguish in them. A letter written shortly after 1857 by Mirza Ghalib in Delhi, once the mighty and flourishing capital of the Mughals, captures the mood in sociological detail. For families, for groups, for individuals, their lives had disintegrated:

> At two separate points in your letter yesterday I see that you have written that Delhi is a big city and there must be plenty of people with all sorts of qualifications there. Alas, my dear boy, this is not the Delhi in which you were born, not the Delhi in which you got your schooling, not the Delhi in which you used to come to your lessons with me to Shaban Beg's

> mansion, not the Delhi in which I have passed fifty-one years of my life. It is a camp. The only Muslims here are artisans or servants of the British authorities. All the rest are Hindus. The male descendants of the deposed King – such as survived the sword – draw allowances of five rupees a month. The female descendants, if old, are bawds, and if young, prostitutes. Count the number of Muslim nobles who are dead: Hassan Ali Khan, the son of a very great father, who had once drawn an allowance of a hundred rupees a day, died in despair, his pension reduced to a hundred rupees a month. Mir Nasir-ud Din, descended on his father's side from a line of *pirs* (saints) and on his mother's from a line of nobles, was unjustly put to death. Agha Sultan, son of Paymaster Muhammad Ali Khan, who has himself held the rank of Paymaster, fell ill; without medicine, without food, at last he died. Your uncle provided for his shroud and his burial. Then let me tell you of my friends: Nazir Husain Mirza, whose elder brother was numbered among the slain, is left penniless – not a farthing comes in. He has been granted a house to live in, but let us see whether he is left in possession or whether it will again be confiscated. Buddhe Sahib sold off all his property, lived on the proceeds while they lasted, and has now gone empty-handed to Bharatpur. Ziya-ud-din had properties returned to him that brought in a rent of five hundred rupees a month, but they have again been seized.

And so it goes on, a depressing account of a society falling apart.

The very definition of Muslim is altered, perception of Muslimness by Muslims affected. In the following passage Hali, himself a noted Urdu poet, describes an incident in Delhi after the events of 1857 involving Ghalib:

> I have heard that when Ghalib came before Colonel Brown (Burn) he was wearing a tall Turkish-style head-dress. The Colonel looked at this strange fashion and asked in broken Urdu, 'Well? You Muslim.' 'Half,' said Ghalib. 'What does that mean?' asked the Colonel. 'I drink wine, but I don't eat pork,' said Ghalib. The Colonel laughed, and Ghalib then showed him the letter which he had received from the Minister for India (sic) in acknowledgement of the ode to Her Majesty the Queen which Ghalib had sent. The Colonel said, 'After the victory of the Government forces why did you not present yourself at the Ridge?' Ghalib replied, 'My rank required that I should have four palanquin-bearers, but all four of them ran away and left me, so I could not come.' The Colonel then dismissed him and all his companions with every courtesy.

Ghalib, perceptive and shrewd, was making a point. His Muslimness had been damaged, diluted. The times were inauspicious; it was easier to wallow in pathos, to avoid reality, to somehow survive, than confront the powerful new forces.

The themes of pathos, tragedy, loss are reflected in the verses of the Urdu poets. Dr Aziz in Forster's *A Passage to India* reflects this quality faithfully in the Indian Muslim. Dr Aziz is ill in bed and surrounded by sympathetic Muslim companions:

> he held up his hand, palm outward, his eyes began to glow, his heart to fill with tenderness. Issuing still farther from his quilt, he recited a poem by Ghalib. It had no connexion with any thing that had gone before but it came from his heart and spoke to theirs. They were overwhelmed by its pathos; pathos, they agreed, is the highest quality in art.

In not so subtle ways the British ridiculed the leaders of Islam, its kings and saints. Rulers such as Siraj-ud-Daulah (of the Black Hole of Calcutta fame) and Shah Shuja-ul-Mulk became 'Sir Roger Dowler' and 'Cha, Sugar and Milk' respectively. The Akhund of Swat was the subject of Edward Lear's poem, with the refrain, 'Who or why, or which or what, is the Akond of Swat?' And, of course, those religious leaders leading revolts against the British across the Muslim world were simply dubbed and dismissed as the 'Mad Mullah'.

Islamic titles were deliberately employed in a manner calculated to humiliate Muslims. Khalifa – caliph – the highest political authority in Islam, and *Khansama* – one of the highest officials in Mughal India – were bestowed on the lowest functionaries of the British administrative structure: the barber, bouncer at the dens for drugs and a junior field clerk became *khalifa*, the cook became *khansama*. These titles have remained in common usage, Muslims unaware of their recent associations and origins.

While ridiculing Islamic customs Europeans encouraged natives to behave like them. Sometimes with comical results as the following story related by Wilfred Blunt illustrates:

> The Mufti's brother had gone in an evil moment to a ball given by the Khedive in Cairo. What the Mufti's brother expected to find in the ballroom is not recorded. What he did find he described to the Englishman as follows:
>
> 'I went with two friends, men like myself in the legal profession, and we arrived among the first, none of us ever having been at such an entertainment before. As we were depositing our coats and umbrellas, for it had rained, suddenly I saw in a mirror a sight reflected such as I had never in my life beheld, two women were standing behind me, naked nearly to the waist. I thought it must have been some illusion connected with my illness, and I was very much frightened. Their faces and arms and everything were displayed without any covering, and I thought I should have fallen to the ground. I asked what it meant and whether perhaps we had not come to the right house, and they told me "these are the wives of

> some of our English officials". "And their husbands," I asked, "do they permit them to go out at night, like this?" "Their husbands", they answered, "are here," and they pointed out to me Mr Royle, the Judge of Appeal, before whom I had often pleaded, a serious man and very stern, as the husband of one of them. This judge I saw dancing with one of these naked ladies, gay and smiling and shameless, like a young man. "And he is here," I said, "to see his wife thus unclothed? and he dances with her publicly?" "That," they answered, "is not his wife, it is the wife of another".'

Horror is piled upon horror, until the Mufti's brother flees; he can, he says, understand everything except that the husbands did not send their wives home.

At the height of their glory and power the Mughals had encouraged marriage with Rajputs; the mothers of many Mughal princes and emperors were Rajput princesses. However, a marriage between the British Viceroy and a Rajput or Muslim princess would have been unthinkable. However high his social position a native remained lower than the lowest of the British. For example, the prince of Berar, son and heir of His Exalted Highness the Nizam of Hyderabad (next chapter, section 2) complained to Somerset Maugham that he was not allowed to set foot at the fashionable Yacht Clubs of Bombay and Calcutta. Gandhi's son was refused admission to a European restaurant in Shillong. Nehru was almost thrown out of a first-class train compartment usually reserved for the British. And Muslim society, too, was affected by class and caste.

Professor Imtiaz Ahmad, in Delhi, has documented the growth of caste-like structures among Muslims in numerous academic papers. He shows how *ashraf* – Sayyeds, Pukhtuns – considered themselves superior to the *ajlaf*, recently converted Muslims. But these divisions are not to be taken too seriously; note the recently self-elevated sheikh in the proverb calculating if crops are good again next year he will become a Sayyed. However it is significant that traditional leadership after the collapse of the Mughal empire in India was provided by the *ashraf*. Sayyeds are conspicuous among the leaders: Shah Waliullah, Sayyed Ahmad Barelvi, Sir Sayyed Ahmad, Sayyed Amir Ali. The men of the sword, defeated by Maratha and Sikh and later the British, were in disarray; they would emerge, a century later, and after independence, to rule as colonels and generals.

Divide and rule

The nature of British policy reflected to an extent the social order of Britain. This included a relatively stable agricultural gentry, a growing merchant class and a generally acceptable monarchy. It was a society divided into distinct classes. An equally significant feature was the perception of racial difference between the English, Scots, Welsh and Irish. It created in the English an island mentality, a dislike of and contempt for foreigners. Sometimes the definition of foreigner for the English would include the dominated Welsh and Irish.

Such notions of race and class fitted comfortably into African and Asian social structure. And where chiefs did not exist they were created. An entire administrative philosophy, Indirect Rule, was based on this approach. The policy was successful in places like Nigeria and Baluchistan where chiefs existed in society, but failed where there were no chiefs as in the North-West Frontier Province of India. Entire British regiments were raised on the basis of caste and race. The north Indian races, the Pukhtuns and Punjabis in particular, were designated 'the martial races'. Bengalis were considered 'inferior material' for the army – a myth finally laid to rest in 1971 when Bengalis achieved independence after armed struggle with the Pakistani army dominated by 'the martial races'.

In India in the last century the British went one step further along the caste road of the Hindus. They created a wholly new agricultural society, based on a different kind of caste, 'the canal colonies' of the Punjab. A model province was ordered for South Asia. Virgin land was provided to settlers in the Punjab. The village scheme reflected the South Asian caste structure. The *chaudhry* – or *lambardar* – headed the village. Beneath him were members of the dominant *baradari* or *qom* (lineage or tribe). At the bottom of the ladder were the *kammis* – the occupational groups – the barbers and carpenters. The mullah, the religious functionary who led the Muslim prayers in the mosque, and who symbolizes Islamic function in village society, was deliberately included among the *kammis* as a sign of humiliation (for a contrast of their role with that of religious leaders refusing to submit passively see chapter 3, section 6). It was made explicit that Muslim rule was over.

The mullah was clearly subordinated to the *chaudhry* or the *lambardar* of the village appointed by the British. Perhaps the harshness was due to British inability to deal with another, altogether different, type of mullah, the one who led revolts throughout the empire among tribal groups. The British dismissed the leaders of Islamic revolts against them as mere fanatics. The 'Mad Mullah' was a handy imperial label to explain away Muslim leaders whether in Africa or Asia. Until today the mullah has not entirely shaken off his association with the *kammis* of the village. In the revenue records, the *jamabandi*, he is still described as *kammi*. In this phase of history the mullah had become a metaphor for Islam, his place in the village hierarchy a reflection of his destiny and that of his religion.

Administration from Nigeria to Malaysia rested on one simple philosophy: the maintenance of law and order. This justified everything else – the colonial presence, the draconian laws, the paralysis of social life, the policy of divide and rule. Administration thus tended to be static, discouraging change. This same inertia still characterizes the former British colonies. Ethnic conflict is particularly brutal and vicious wherever the British ruled: Pakistan breaking apart in 1971 in an ethnic revolt led by the Bengalis, the Biafrans failing in theirs in Nigeria; in Zimbabwe, Shonas and Ndebeles fighting each other; in Sri Lanka, Tamils and Sinhalese at each others' throats; and in what was the jewel in the crown, India, Kashmiris, Punjabis and Assamese in an ethnically venomous free for all.

Macaulay's Minute and Muslim society

The British ruled with a languid economy of organization and effort. There was a certain neat logic in British colonial philosophy. If all their subjects could not be elevated to British standards, embraced by their civilization, at least a class, the upper layer, could be salvaged. The colonized had to simply become as much as possible like their masters.

Lord Macaulay's 'Minute on Education' in 1835 established English as the medium of instruction in India. With this one step he aimed to create a social class, a buffer, between the British elite and the rural masses:

> We must at present do our best to form a class who may be interpreters between us and the millions whom we govern; a class of persons, Indian in blood and colour, but English in taste, in opinions, in morals, and in intellect.

Macaulay's Minute would produce native Englishmen, black sahibs but still sahibs.

When English replaced Persian, the court language of the Mughals, Muslims found themselves at a crippling disadvantage. A reluctance, a mental block, to speak or learn English grew among them.

The Indian generation after Macaulay, 'English in taste' would be mainly Hindus. Schools, colleges and service in the army and civil administration assisted in this process. Among the Muslims the man who advocated and effected the synthesis was Sir Sayyed Ahmad, 'Loyal servant of the Crown'.

Sir Sayyed was creating a third type of Muslim leadership, one drawing its inspiration from British culture. Liberal, modern, rational and nationalist ideas jostled with Islamic ones in the thought of these Muslims. The mixture would be as heady in the promise it held as it would be frustrating for its lack of form and clarity. This type would be distinct from the earlier two, orthodox, formal, legalistic and syncretic, mystical, informal, discussed in chapter 4. Sir Sayyed would dismiss the former as fanatics and condemn the latter as charlatans.

Reflecting the European intellectual fashions of his time, Sir Sayyed was something of a scientific rationalist: 'Reason is the instrument that offers knowledge of every reality.' If Muslims continued to shut out modern – by which he meant British – civilization they would be reduced to *khansamas* (cooks) and *khidmatgars* (attendants). The Muslim tendency to wallow in past glory was therefore a dangerous opiate. The bluntly expressed views outraged religious circles. For them 'The Aligarh movement revived the rational theology of the neo-Mutazilites . . . Islamic Sharia, according to them, was incomplete unless Greek philosophy and logic were incorporated into its system' (Syed N. Nadvi, 'The Aligarh movement and its educational policies: a critique', *Muslim Education Quarterly*, vol. 4, no. 1, 1986). 'The Mutazilite approach was . . . developed as a result of an inferiority complex.' Muslims had to be protected from the ideas of Sir Sayyed. He was called a heretic, even a Christian. Sixty *ulema* circulated a declaration condemning him as an apostate, *kafir*. The Mufti of Madinah condemned him to death. A century later the *ulema* are still reproving: 'It is generally agreed that Sir Sayyed failed in his mission' concludes Syed Nadvi (1986).

In *The Loyal Muhammadans of India*, Sir Sayyed defended Muslim loyalty to the British. Muslims, he argued, were as loyal as the most faithful Hindus. The college that he founded at Aligarh in 1875 was called the Muhammadan Anglo-Oriental College, its very name illustrating the synthesis he wished to effect. In his mind were Oxford and Cambridge. Resigning from government service in 1876 Sir Sayyed lived in Aligarh promoting the college until his death in 1898. His success affected the future course of events in India.

The seeds of the partition of British India into two, Hindu and Muslim, were sown by Sir Sayyed. After Aligarh he abandoned his position as an ambassador of Hindu-Muslim amity – something M.A. Jinnah, the creator of Pakistan, would do two generations later: 'Now, suppose all the English were to leave India – then who would be the rulers of India? It is necessary that one of them – Mohammedans and Hindus – should conquer the other and thrust it down. To hope that both could remain equal is to desire the impossible and inconceivable' (*The Times*, London, 16 January 1888).

Macaulay's vision and Sir Sayyed's ethos would bear triumphant fruit in one of the most influential and popular books written on Islam, Justice Sayyed Amir Ali's *The Spirit of Islam*. Translated into numerous languages, including Arabic and Turkish, it was written in English. *The Spirit of Islam* is an excellent example of Islamic apologetics. Amir Ali conducts a vigorous debate with Christianity, especially its scholars. But the voice is over-eager, too keen to convince. It has the ring of someone establishing credentials for membership to an exclusive club: in spite of our black appearance we both belong together (Semites), our values are the same (liberal), don't misunderstand us (we are loyal citizens of the British crown) and not such bad chaps. The familiar polemics – the Prophet's marriages, for instance – are explained in this light. Even the terminology and spellings are Anglicized, without the least consciousness of the implications – 'Church of Mohammed', 'Sunni Church', 'Saracens', 'Lower Race', etc.

The author was a successful lawyer who would rise to the highest rungs of his profession in British India. 'Liberal' in his views, he married an English woman of 'some position'. But the Anglo-Indian social climate did not encourage synthesis and was unsparing. 'The English solicitors looked upon me as an interloper; the Hindus frankly disliked me; whilst the Muslims considered me a renegade because of the English method of life I had acquired,' Amir Ali wrote in his *Memoirs*.

At least two generations of Muslims, in the first half of the century, would be influenced by *The Spirit of Islam*. Thinking and behaving like English gentlemen they would none the less be proud of their Islamic identity. There is a naive confidence in their posture:

> A young Muslim fashionably dressed, sits with his friends in the Lahore Coffee House and talks, in English, of Marx or tennis. He has perhaps never studied the Quran . . . yet intensely conscious about being a Muslim, he insists that he and his co religionists in India are a nation, and he is, he says, ready to fight to establish for them a free country. (W.C. Smith, *Islam in Modern History*, 1957)

Among Amir Ali's admirers were Mr M.A. Jinnah and Iqbal, whose vision of a Muslim homeland, a Pakistan, was influenced by his work. Mr Jinnah wanted Amir Ali to become President of the All-India Congress, before he broke with the party. Iqbal, a contemporary at Cambridge, helped prepare the index of *The Spirit of Islam*. For Professor Anne Marie Schimmel it was a key book in her study of Islam. On the other hand, Maryam Jamilah, an American Muslim, would write: 'If the Ulema had been alive to their duty instead of sleeping the contents of this book (*The Spirit of Islam*) should have been denounced as heretical' (*Islam and Modernism*, Lahore, 1968).

The next generations of Muslim leadership, influenced by the writings of Sir Sayyed and Sayyed Amir Ali, would come from Aligarh. They would provide leadership in the campaign for Pakistan.

The movement for Pakistan was led by Mr M.A, Jinnah who, like Sayyed Amir Ali, represented the synthesis between South Asian and British culture. If Sir Sayyed was cast as a scientific rationalist, in European terminology, Jinnah was an English liberal. Trained as a lawyer in London, he possessed a superb command of English in which he spoke and thought. His almost English aloofness and bearing – elegant suit, spats, hat, watch-chain and cigar – appeared to confirm his reputation as a person of impeccable integrity and with high notions of justice and what was right. Like Sir Sayyed before him he was called a *kafir* by many of the *ulema;* but the ground swell for Pakistan, which gathered swiftly and became irresistible by 1947, drowned their voices.

On the surface an unlikely Muslim hero, he was to stir the Muslims of South Asia as no leader has done before or since. For those in Pakistan he would be Quaid-e-Azam, the Great Leader. Among his most devoted and active workers would be the students of Aligarh.

In Pakistan the men from Aligarh would form an influential network of generals, civil servants, politicians and businessmen. One of them was Ayub Khan, President of Pakistan. Even as a politician, forced to appeal for votes, Ayub Khan never quite managed to shake off the values and change the behavioural patterns he acquired at the Royal Military Academy, Sandhurst, and in the Indian Army. His impressive physical bearing, clipped moustache and haircut, and his pastimes – shooting grouse on the demesnes of Scottish lords, the golf course, whisky in the evening – reflected an Anglicized lifestyle and social values. This was mimicry, but mimicry of the highest order.

Ayub Khan ruled Pakistan as a benevolent dictator, a stern but sympathetic headmaster. His views are candidly expressed in his autobiography *Friends not Masters* (1967). The title, with its 'come back all is forgiven' message to the West, sums up the author's social and political philosophy.

As Aurangzeb and Dara Shikoh are example figures of two types of Muslim leadership in South Asia, Ayub Khan represents the third. Aurangzeb to him would be a religious bigot, in British Indian army slang 'a damn mullah, a bloody fanatic', and Dara Shikoh an Oriental mystery. In him Macaulay stood vindicated, Sir Sayyed triumphant.

You, my father

The results of Macaulay's experiment – and Sir Sayyed's efforts – were, at best, mixed as we see in the following poem for my father, a civil servant of the British Raj, a man with Aligarh associations. 'You, my father', was written by me in 1970 when I was 27 years old. In it I perceived my father as representing his generation. Looking at it now with the perspective of years, it contained the ideas of a young man. It was not good poetry, being ready to reduce to caricature, parodying what was already a parody. But it attempted to express something that was important to me. My father, his life simplified by the Raj, frozen by imperial fiat, was not faced with the agony of choices, the pain of transition in the same measure as I. Through him I was tied to a past, one I could not repudiate nor own.

I saw in those forgotten files
a photograph
a fading daguerreotype
of you, my father
now so gentle
white and near

you, my father
half-seen in the yellowing solar topee
knee-long shorts and the Imperial stance
the faithful servant of the Raj
that strode a world
so secure and warm
under the never-sinking pink sun;
misted autumnal khaki world
cricket flannels, Simla summers
polo and pith helmets
sherbet and shikar
Indian heat and the gymkhana retreat;
Olympian security
felt
not always shared
and the distant tread of Gandhian
feet naked in the night.
Yours a simple wardrobe:
the other native mask
inturned, cloth-spun, clay-made
that looked over your shoulder
to a favourite Mughal,
to some Ghalib,
Aligarh
and even Iqbal.
Inside: lapped about
in the sure susurrant waves
in the ocean of shared Muslim cultures,
ruffled by the deeds of dead Muslim heroes.
Outside: basked in the warmth
of an Empire at high noon.

My father did not like the poem either. The following lines were particularly offensive:

You stood to attention when your father
entered
(or an Englishman)
you walked your morning constitutionals
(or played tennis if the *sahib* so wished)
you fought to pull up *babu* standards
(and to strive up to the *bara sahib*'s).

The poem concludes by contrasting the external calm of my father's generation to the confusion facing mine, growing in the post-colonial phase of Muslim history. The paradox is clear: independence from the colonial powers presents us not with too few choices but too many:

But that misted subliminal stance
on the two stocky legs
of security and confidence
I lack.
In my repertoire:
the Mao book, the American scheme
the English tweed, the Indian dream
the Mughal drug, the Muslim scream
and I rest bewildered
weary-legged and stooped in youth
the forest is thick
the night black
and the sky-lights too many
and the sky-lights too bright.

Not unnaturally the poem ends with mixed emotions:

I put back the gray daguerreotype
with
a little atavistic nostalgia
a little admiration
and some envy.

The choices remain open and the dilemmas unresolved – Aurangzeb, Dara Shikoh and, with the coming of the British, Sir Sayyed and Ayub Khan. Yet it is worth repeating that the distinctions between them are not absolute, not water-tight. In my father I saw the piety of Aurangzeb, the tolerance of Dara Shikoh, and the wish to live in the here and now, the world of today, of Ayub Khan. But the conflict they presupposed was left latent, perhaps unrecognized; not possessing the power to make choices that was sensible. Hence my father's life was in harmony.

It was easy to yearn for a recent colonial past which promised a kind of stability by negating the capacity to think for oneself. Years after I wrote the poem, and after my father's death, I began to understand why he did not like the poem. What was damaged was his sense of self, what was hurt was his pride, wounds which he kept to himself. And in the middle of his life and career he had made one momentous, all-changing decision: to opt for Pakistan when offered a choice in 1947 (see 'Connecting' in chapter 11). The migration meant a severance with the past, an act of blind faith in the Muslim nation.

Perhaps it was an act of atonement; life under the British in India for the servants of the Raj was not as free of disharmony as I had imagined.

But there were also native groups who evoked in the European a kind of affection bordering on respect. Away from the courts and cities, in remote valleys and barren hills, the European located the 'noble savage'. In the following section we reflect on this interesting aspect of the colonial encounter.

2 THE MYTH OF THE NOBLE SAVAGE: MUSLIM TRIBESMAN

If European colonization was a debilitating encounter for Islam it was an unprecedented calamity for its tribes. Away from the cities, the courts of law and the centres of learning the tribesman was isolated by the colonial authorities. Travel to and from the tribal areas was discouraged. The colonial period froze their particular customs, substituting them for wider laws, and administratively restricted them to areas defined as 'tribal'. Tribesmen themselves differentiated, as in North Africa, between their areas – *bled s-siba*, the land of dissidence – and those controlled by central authority – *bled l-makhzan*. Worst of all, because its subtle influences still permeate tribal society, the European myth of the tribesman as the noble savage is perpetuated.

The European vision of the noble savage

The concept of primitive man, free from the trammels of corrupting civilization, was an attractive one in a Europe faced with the social problems accompanying its industrial revolution in the eighteenth century. Exploitation of women and children for labour, alcoholism, disease and illiteracy were common in the industrial areas. The age of the machine, heavy, sinister and uncomprehending, had begun; that of honour and chivalry ended. Even on the threshold of the industrial revolution earlier times were viewed in a romantic and nostalgic light. European philosophers were revolting against the dehumanizing tendencies of the machine age.

Rousseau's noble savage embodied the innocence and purity that man had lost in his transition to the industrial era. Irrevocably lost at home, the idea would find its expression in the imagination of Europeans as they administered and wrote of remote tribes in Africa and Asia in the next century. The tribesman also reflected and embodied some of the idealized virtues of the Victorian gentleman. Across the two colonized continents the groups that best symbolized the noble savage were Muslim tribesmen, the Berbers, the Bedouin and the Pukhtuns (chapters 8 and 9 comment on contemporary Bedouin and Pukhtun societies respectively).

To the Berbers in north-west Africa, the Bedouin along the North African littoral and in the Arabian peninsula and the Pukhtuns in the North-West

Frontier Province of what is now Pakistan and Afghanistan colonization usually meant destruction – destroyed villages, water-tanks and grain-stores and frequent 'butcher and bolt' raids. It was an almost total failure in communication between two systems. Nevertheless, a miasma of romance and mystification enveloped the colonial encounter.

The romance was most pronounced in Morocco for the imperial French and India for the British, the jewels in the crown. The history, customs and languages of both societies were explored by colonial scholars and administrators. Although Morocco was incorporated in 1912 the 'civilizing mission' of France began in the last century. By 1904 the *mission scientifique au Maroc* was founded in Tangier. Its members spoke Arabic and Berber and helped to train colonial administrators. The study of Indian languages and history had begun more than a century earlier with the establishment of Calcutta.

In their search for the noble savage Europeans imagined they had located racially superior Africans and Asians among these tribal groups. For the British Afridis, the masters of the Khyber Pass, were descended from Alexander's Greek troops: blue eyes and blond hair were cited as proof. The difficult and inaccessible mountains among which these tribes lived supported the myth. They were cool in summer and cold in winter, reminding Europeans of home. Snow in the Atlas mountains in Morocco and the Pukhtun mountain ranges in north India made Europeans nostalgic:

> 'There was among the Pathans [Anglo-Indian for Pukhtun] something that called to the Englishman or the Scotsman – partly that the people looked you straight in the eye, that there was no equivocation and that you couldn't browbeat them even if you wished to. When we crossed the bridge at Attock we felt we'd come home.' (Charles Allen, *Plain Tales from the Raj*, 1977)

The inaccessibility of the mountains ensured that the groups were 'lost', cut off, from larger cultures and therefore had preserved their racial purity. No matter that North Africa, where the Berbers and Bedouins live, and the northern passes of India, straddled by the Pukhtuns, have been invaded, and with each invasion re-settled, for the last thousand years.

The tribesmen we are considering in this section were incorporated into the colonial frame at a comparatively late period, the turn of the century. The later period was marked by greater understanding of the natives and a higher degree of tolerance for them by the Europeans. The plains lay subdued and the cities subjugated. In India memories of the uprisings of 1857 had already faded. There were no new worlds to conquer. The minor skirmishes with the tribesmen were little more: minor crises on the periphery of empire.

These colonies attracted the brightest and best imperial administrators and scholars, those who saw themselves as a special breed. They represented a different generation of Europe and a different mood. After the 1857 uprisings India became a colony of the crown and no longer the concern of a commercial company. Earning profits was thus not the key to service in the colonies. A better educated – almost entirely at Oxford and Cambridge – and more prosperous officer, usually with a socially middle-class background, came to India. These officers were motivated in their zeal by various factors, which included the making of a name, the study of the tribes they administered, improving their conditions, or, reflecting Rousseau's concept, escaping a Europe which they saw as decadent and thereby discovering a nobler, purer life and people.

Younger than their predecessors, fresh from élite schools, the administrators set about their task with energy and imagination. Many would die young in the prime of their lives and on duty. Burnes killed in Kabul and Nicholson while recapturing Delhi provided the prototype of this breed of officer for the British empire.

Life as an extension of the public school

Life in the tribal areas was an extension of, a metaphor for, the public school. The empire secure, its lines demarcated, the new breed of officers were bored and craved excitement; it was the wish to break or bend the school rules in an innocent adventure. And the Berber or Bedouin or Pukhtun was the most likely person to provide the excitement. He was someone not at your school but none the less a fellow of spirit and adventure, someone who could take a beating in the boxing ring or mauling on the rugger field and not complain. Most important, he was someone who could give as good as he got. Naturally enough, Flashman, the likeable rogue of Rugby, first plunges into his adventures in Afghanistan among the Pukhtun.

Public school idiom translated easily into tribal vocabulary. 'Sportsmanship', 'scouts' honour', 'gentlemanly', 'winning fairly or losing honourably' reflected tribal concepts of 'honour', 'courage' and 'word'. One of the most celebrated of tribal codes, Pukhtunwali – the code of the Pukhtuns – was an embodiment of these concepts. An Indian administrator, Philip Woodruff records:

> Frontier officers were a rather special breed of the British and they were sometimes almost converted to the Pathan's sense of honour and usually to his sense of humour; it did not often happen the other way round. The same kind of stories recur whenever people talk about the Frontier; they remember, for instance, the Zakka Khel men in 1908 crowding round Roos-Keppel, once their Political Agent, when the expedition against them was successful and fighting over. 'Did we fight well?' they asked and he replied: 'I wouldn't have shaken hands with you if you hadn't.'

The titles of Woodruff's books reflect the theme of this section: *A Matter of Honour* (1976) and *The Men who Ruled India: The Founders* and *The Guardians* (1965) – the last two titles derived from Plato.

The colonial encounter was reduced to the nature of a cricket match – it was 'our chaps' versus 'your chaps'. Many writers have actually used the game analogy for the British encounter with the Pukhtun:

> It is a game – a contest with rules in which men kill without compunction and will die in order to win, in which kinship and friendship count less than winning – but in which there is no malice when the whistle blows and the game is over. And the transfer of an important player may be arranged at half-time while the lemons are being sucked. (from Woodruff)

Even the sordid business of bombing tribesmen was cast in a 'sportsman-like' mould and a proper 'warning notice' issued before air-raids. Otherwise it would simply not be cricket:

> Whereas *lashkars* [war parties] have collected to attack Gandab [Mohmand Agency in the Frontier Province] and are to this end concentrated in your villages and lands, you are hereby warned that the area lying between Khapak-Nahakki line and the line Mullah Killi-Sam Chakai will be bombed on the morning of [date] beginning at 7 a.m. and daily till further notice.
>
> You are hereby warned to remove all persons from all the villages named and from the area lying between them and the Khapak and Nahakki Passes and not to return till further written notice is sent to you, Any person who returns before receiving such further written notice will do so at his own risk.
>
> Signed Griffith – Governor [of the N.W. Frontier Province], dated 4th September 1933.

The absence of colonial women in these tribal areas heightened the public-school flavour of life. Whether in the interior of Morocco in the Berber areas or in the tribal areas of the Frontier Province women were strictly discouraged. The stations were officially designated as 'no family stations'. Rumours of homosexuality, deeds of physical courage and honourable escapades, one side of public-school life, marked the encounters between Europeans and the tribesmen.

The scholar-administrator

Immersing themselves in tribal custom and language, many of the officers left behind detailed ethnographic notes of distinction. Our post-colonial knowledge exposes the racism evident in the writing but the quality of research is impressive. A present-day sociologist or anthropologist would have to work hard to match it. The following are the best known accounts, recognized as classics in the field, covering the span of the Muslim world from the Berbers at one end to the Pukhtun at the other: Robert Montagne's *The Berbers: Their Social and Political Organization* (1931), Richard Burton's *A Personal Narrative of a Pilgrimage to al-Madinah and Meccah* (1855), T.E. Lawrence's *Seven Pillars of Wisdom* (1962), E.E. Evans-Pritchard's *The Sanusi of Cyrenaica* (1949), Olaf Caroe's *The Pathans* (1965) and Evelyn Howell's *Mizh: A Monograph on Government's Relations with the Mahsud Tribe* (1931). The authors are imperial military or civil officers. Their lives spanned a century of colonial administration – a hundred years separate the books of Burton and Caroe. Their work reflected and popularized the concept of the noble savage.

Sir Evelyn Howell's introduction in 1905 to the Pukhtun Mahsud tribe, the subject of his little classic, *Mizh*, was as dramatic as the land and people he writes of. It followed the murder of the previous Political Agent and Howell's subsequent posting out of turn at the young age of twenty-seven as acting Political Agent, South Waziristan Agency. I met him, sixty years after his arrival in the land of the Mahsuds, at Cambridge, where he lived opposite my college, Selwyn. He was mentally alert and spoke with lively memory of past days on the Frontier. He was preparing for a discourse on Khushal Khan Khattak, the Pukhto poet, whose poems he had translated with his friend Olaf Caroe. He died a few years later at the age of ninety-four. All his life he maintained a warm affection for the Muslim groups he had administered. My appointment as Political Agent, South Waziristan, allowed me to pay tribute to Howell. Retrieving a copy of *Mizh*, a confidential British Indian report, I persuaded Oxford University Press to republish it in their Oxford In Asia Historical Reprint Series (1979). Caroe wrote to me from his home in Sussex, England, and was delighted. The myth of the noble savage and its perpetuation by European administrators are amply reflected in Howell's preface:

> I spoke above of political officers as the custodians of civilization dealing with barbarians. Against this definition, if he were to hear it, I am sure that Mehr Dar, or any other intelligent Mahsud malik, would emphatically protest. Their argument, which is not altogether in a sub-conscious plane, may be stated thus – 'A civilization has no other end than to produce a fine type of man. Judged by this standard the social system in which the Mahsud has been evolved must be allowed immeasurably to surpass all others. Therefore let us keep our independence and have none of your *qanun* [law] and your other institutions which have wrought such havoc in British India, but stick to our own *riwaj* [custom] and be men like our fathers before us.' After prolonged and intimate dealings with the Mahsuds I am not at all sure that, with reservations, I do not subscribe to their plea.

The romance of the Frontier was to reach its literary apogee with Rudyard

Kipling, troubadour of empire. His most popular stories feature Pukhtun characters like Mahboob Ali in *Kim* and, an obvious caricature, the character attributed to the tiger Shere Khan in *The Jungle Book*. Kipling reflects sympathy for the underdog and his ethnic references are perhaps not wilfully malicious. None the less the African and the Asian are 'The White Man's Burden' (as we saw in the last section). Contrasting strongly in theme and tone of address is the encounter between the Pukhtun, in this case an Afridi outlaw, and the Britisher in perhaps the best known of his imperial poems, 'The Ballad of East and West'. The theme and literary tone are grand and imperial, they manifestly transcend colour and race. Here is a meeting of two races on equal footing reflecting a mutual admiration and acceptance of each other's ways:

> But there is neither East nor West, Border, nor Breed, nor Birth,
> When two strong men stand face to face, though they come from the ends of the earth!

By the end of the poem the 'two strong men' have come to terms:

> They have taken the Oath of the Brother-in-Blood on fire and fresh-cut sod,
> On the hilt and the haft of the Khyber knife, and the Wondrous names of God.

A certain respect for the rough and wild tribesmen emerges that contrasts with the open and general contempt for other natives in the empire. It is the Pukhtun in the Pass who forces questions about the 'Arithmetic on the Frontier' where

> Two thousand pounds of education drops to a ten rupee jezail.

There was also a more serious purpose than schoolboy fun and games and an expression of male chauvinism in propagating the myth of the noble savage. It suited imperial strategy to divide Muslim society. In north west India the tribal areas of the British and in Morocco the Berbère Dahir of the French drew boundaries around tribal groups, cutting them off from those living in the more settled areas. Racial – ethnic – differences between the groups were underlined to further widen the gap. It was the imperial maxim – divide and rule.

Although not in the romantic vein the tradition of an impressive standard of scholarship in studying these tribal groups continues into the post-colonial period. Notable examples in the social sciences include Ernest Gellner, Clifford Geertz and David Hart for the Berbers, I.M. Lewis and Donald Cole for the Bedouin, and Fredrik Barth for the Pukhtun.

Perpetuating the romance: the Islamic ideal perverted

A generation after the European colonists went home the romance of the colonial encounter is perpetuated through Western films and novels. But the romance is Narcissistic, depicting an exotic European hero in love with himself. And this trend continues in the face of the bitterness and ambiguity among Muslim tribesmen regarding the colonial powers after the Second World War, Israel and its wars with the Arabs, and the public posture of the newly independent nations.

Costly and popular films reflect the Narcissistic romance: Sean Connery as a Berber chief in *The Wind and the Lion*, Peter O'Toole as T.E. Lawrence in *Lawrence of Arabia*, and the recent TV series, *The Far Pavilions*, which included Pukhtun history, characters and areas. Hollywood had discovered the romance of the desert sheikh early in its history. Valentino had made the role popular. The Hollywood images of the lone hero in flowing robes, astride a camel, silhouetted against the red glow of the evening sky, were not new. They lay embedded in the countless adventures and stories of the heroes of empire, the soldiers, travellers and scholars.

On the Frontier today the romance engendered by the colonial encounter is still preserved. It began with the Independence of Pakistan when Sir George Cunningham, an ex-Governor of the North-West Frontier Province, was recalled from Glasgow by Mr M.A. Jinnah, the Governor-General of Pakistan, to become the first Governor of the Province. The billiard room in the North Waziristan Scouts' Mess, Miran Shah, is still dominated by the portrait of Captain G. Meynell VC, Guides Frontier Force, and 'killed in action Mohmand operations – 29 September 1935'. Lt-Colonel Harman (immortalized by Howell's account of him in Caroe's book) stares from a painting in the dining room of the Wana Mess in South Waziristan. A note in T. E. Lawrence's hand thanking the South Waziristan Scouts for their hospitality is enshrined in a glass box in the Wana Mess library. The 'Gate of Khyber' at Jamrud, the mouth of the Pass, built by Pakistan, quotes Kipling's lines from 'Arithmetic on the Frontier' on a marble slab.

It is important to note that the symbols of the romance of the Frontier are maintained by the political and military administration. Most writing on the Frontier in Pakistan is in a romantic vein. Articles on the Frontier in magazines and newspapers have titles such as 'The Romance of Tribal Customs, Traditions'. Perpetuation of tradition is itself part of the romance. No such symbols of Frontier romance or nostalgia are visible among the tribes themselves. It is a one-way nostalgia. The romantic gloss does not change the savagery or determination of the colonial encounter: barbed wires enclosing tribesmen and the bombing of their settlements did not win friends for the Europeans. In any case the myth of the noble savage, the affection and respect for him, is partly false.

The European scholars and administrators took Muslim names – Richard Burton's was 'Mirza Abdullah', John Burckhardt's 'Shaykh Ibrahim', that of Snouck Hurgronje, who took the first photograph of the Kaaba in 1884, was 'Abd al-Ghaffar' – and adopted Muslim manners and dress. But it is significant that they did not convert to Islam. Their flirtation with Islam was incomplete, their understanding of it tendentious. Their studies served the empire, their theatricals personal egos. In their colonial careers they were acting a part; their adventures were mimicry.

Racism is never far from the surface; it permeates the work of colonial officers. Burton, who was viewed suspiciously by British contemporaries as having crossed the limits of civilized decency and gone quite native, frequently refers to the 'orient' as 'barbarism'. Racial and intellectual arrogance colour his judgment. His advice to travellers in the 'orient': 'The more haughty and offensive [the traveller] is to the people, the more they respect him; a decided advantage to the traveller of choleric temperament' (*A Personal Narrative of a Pilgrimage to al-Madinah and Meccah*, 1855). The 'oriental' officials can only be dealt with 'by bribe, by bullying or by bothering them'. Burton concedes the Baluchi tribesman 'has his own ideas of honour, despises cowardice as much as any belted knight in the dark ages' but is none the less 'violent, treacherous and revengeful, addicted to every description of debauchery, dirty in person, rough and rude in manners' (*Sindh and the Races that Inhabit the Valley of the Indus*, 1851). The Sindhi is several degrees worse, 'cowardly' and 'debauched', and the women 'remarkable for their disregard of decency and morality'. The Arab 'is the mirror of chivalry' but also 'a mere barbarian who has not forgotten the savage'. The Arab's 'crass and self-satisfied ignorance makes him glorify the most ignoble superstitions, while acts of revolting savagery are the natural results of a malignant fanaticism and a furious hatred of every creed beyond the pale of Al-Islam' ('Terminal Essay' in *Arabian Nights*, 1886).

The strain of racial contempt which runs alongside the affection for the tribesmen escapes those who perpetuate the romance of the encounter. The very victims of the myth, the tribesmen, are those most enraptured by it.

The Muslim tribesman confronted and rejected the colonial forces, acquitting himself with honour. For him the encounter was *jihad*, a Muslim duty, without romance. After the colonial era, and because his world was changing with bewildering speed, his identity being defined in terms of the freshly formed nationalism, he leaned on the myth of the noble savage for support. But the myth is posture and self-deception ('Afghan refugees: displacement and despair' in chapter 9).

Long after the Europeans have gone home the tribesman cites Montagne or Lawrence or Caroe for references to his glory and virtues. He employs their ideas and their categories, in Morocco *bled s-siba* and *bled l-makhzan*, in

Pakistan 'tribal areas' and 'settled areas', innocent of the original purpose they served. Not quite aware that such European divisions helped to weaken him by separating him from other groups, he perpetuates alien ideas.

Drawing firm tribal lines around himself the tribesman wishes to preserve his exclusive identity. The Prophet's warning that there is no Bedouinism in Islam is forgotten. The outside world is rejected. Schools are discouraged for they are seen as an attempt to wean him away from his culture. Illiteracy, supersitition and ignorance are the costs. The Islamic ideal, dimly understood, is perverted.

Imperial expansionism worked in two opposing directions within tribal society. External pressure created homogeneity within the tribe which ensured safeguarding and preservation of tribal cultural values. An aspect of this pressure had the opposite effect: allowances, estates and titles exacerbated and deepened internal conflict based on tribal rivalry. External history is seen locally as unending sequences to aggrandize, interfere or encapsulate. This explains suspicion regarding official schemes sponsored by the government. A legacy of suspicion against central authority still haunts the successor states in the tribal areas of the Muslim world.

The Muslim tribesman was neither wholly noble nor completely savage; in parts, in certain aspects of his behaviour, he was both noble and savage. Now stripped of his tribal lifestyle and confidence, not adjusted to the modern ways, the tribesman is vulnerable and his life fragmented. The conflict between Islamic law and tribal custom creates ambiguity in society (examples relating to women are discussed in chapter 9, section 2). The tribesman faces the difficult and complex task of reconciling his Islamic faith to tribal customs and behaviour. The European myth of the noble savage, because it was imported and partly false, adds to the difficulty. The endeavour to locate his identity within Islam while preserving what is of value in the tribe must begin by confronting, assessing and rejecting the myth of the noble savage. If the tribal past is not mastered through inquiry and scholarship it will pervert the future.

PART TWO

Contemporary Muslim Society

8

Princes and paupers: Muslim societies in Saudi Arabia and south India

The colonial masters have gone; Muslims are free again. But the Europeans have left behind a great deal of damage. Muslim society has been turned inside out. Muslims are discovering that to be independent and rich – at least in some parts – is not to be free of difficulties. Here in Part Two, we consider some of the major problems which create concern in contemporary Muslim society, our final socio-historical category. This may be simply viewed as falling into three broad divisions: tribal, peasant-agriculturalist and urban. The taxonomy of Muslim society is neither complete nor sequential. The exercise is merely a starting point for a sociological discussion. In some important ways the first, tribal, provides us with clues to the other kinds of society. The three kinds of society interact and overlap, adding to the complexity of contemporary Muslim society. Muslim tribes, peasants or city-dwellers have one thing in common: they are not immune from the pressures of the contemporary world.

Juxtaposing different Muslim societies in this chapter allows us to appreciate the subtlety and richness of the ideal. Muslims focus on different aspects of it in differing social situations. It is the holy Book which inspires Saudi society. It is the Prophet for south Indian Muslims, who emphasize the gentle, contemplative, side of his character. In Saudi society the ideal is confident and aggressive, in south India different aspects of the ideal, humility and gentleness, are prominent. Many of the characteristics of Saudi society, and some of its dilemmas, are reflected in other societies on the Arabian peninsula; those of the United Arab Emirates are discussed in the next chapter.

1 SAUDI ARABIA: THE REAWAKENING OF THE PENINSULA

There is no better way to discover Islam than climbing Mount Hira, I said earlier. The climb also tells us something about Saudi society.

Wahabi doctrine, which dominates Saudi Arabia, places no special significance on holy sites. Visits to them are said to degenerate into worship of the place rather than of God. No special religious value, therefore, attaches to Mount Hira. Still it is a popular place for Muslim visitors – except perhaps for the rich and powerful; helicopters cannot land on the peak and the climb is steep.

Mount Hira is in a state of deliberate neglect. The path through steep boulders and loose rocks is dangerous in parts and unmarked. Coca-Cola and Fanta cans are strewn about. Pakistanis, Egyptians and Iranians, judging by their names and addresses, have scribbled their identity around the cave. Also hand painted, just above the cave, are the actual first words revealed to the Prophet.

The group of Pakistanis from rural Punjab who seemed to appear from nowhere on the peak, and just as abruptly disappeared, were indignant at the neglected condition of Mount Hira. 'What do these pleasure-loving Bedu know of Islam?' they offered, ethnicity clearly dominating religion (for the interaction between Arab and South Asian ethnicity see chapter 9, section 1). For these Pakistanis Mount Hira is miraculous double proof of their faith: because of the shape of the cave the prayers point to the Kaaba (before the revelation which changed the direction from Jerusalem to Makkah), and because of the visibility of the *haram sharif* which houses the Kaaba. But few complaints can be made about the two holiest places of Islam, the Kaaba in Makkah – the house of God – and the Prophet's mosque in Madinah and, in it, his burial place.

As Richard Burton, disguised as a Pukthun doctor, noted in the last century, the experience of seeing the Kaaba for the first time creates ecstasy in non-believers. It reduces believers to tears. Standing majestically, a solemn, gigantic mystery shrouded in dark heavy cloth, amidst an eternal flow of humanity circling its base, it is the holiest of holies for Muslims. Its religious and historical associations make it the core point of the faith.

The wonder is the *haram sharif* on which some 2 million pilgrims descend annually for the *haj*. Latest technology has been employed for the comfort of the pilgrim. The marble floors, chemically treated, are cool in summer, warm in winter. Once the pilgrim's feet were lacerated by scorching stones and pebbles. Fans, continually in motion, provide a breeze; containers, constantly replenished, water. Powerful arc lights, like those used in stadiums and at airports, convert night into day. Attendants – mostly non-locals, about 1,500

Pakistanis – care for the comforts of the pilgrims. Here everything – the arrogance of Saudi bureaucracy, the bad manners of the hotel staff – is forgotten. Even death here is welcome. It is the short cut to paradise. Indeed many old and ailing pilgrims come with this thought in mind. The heat, the crowds, the exertion take a toll of one to two thousand lives during *haj*.

Watching the worshippers, murmuring incessant prayers like the distant therapeutic sounds of flowing water, two facts stand out: the egalitarian nature of Islam and its universalism. Stripped to the regulation dress, two unstitched pieces of white cloth worn in a specific manner, no jewellery allowed, princes and paupers, presidents and pick-pockets jostle and are jostled anonymously in the unending crowds. The different colours, heights and sizes of Muslims reflect the diversity of Muslim society; and here all barriers of caste, class and colour are removed. Overweight, pale, Egyptian scholars, tall, lean, black Sudanese, blue-eyed blonds from Europe, small, brown, slant-eyed Malays – all creatures of God, Muslims, are one in the house of God. All are pilgrims – some scurrying from prayer site to site, greedily adding up merit; others lost in meditation, suspended in some dream-like world; still others unconsciously weeping tears of ecstasy. The live dynamism and power of a world religion are here amply displayed.

The second most holy mosque in Islam, after Makkah, is the Masjid an-Nabawi, the mosque of the Prophet, in Madinah. It is presently undergoing rapid development and extension. When complete the complex will boast underground parking, gardens, six new minarets – in addition to the present four – and a capacity for 250,000 worshippers. After the power and passion of Kaaba the city of Madinah comes as a soothing emotional anti-climax. The people are friendly, languid and hospitable. They pride themselves on belonging to the city the Prophet chose as his home and where he lies buried. Places, mosques, lanes evoke the Prophet's life, his triumphs, his personal tragedies and his presence. For the Muslim it is like coming home.

Photographs of Makkah and Madinah taken less than a generation ago show mud huts, wooden homes, dusty streets, impoverished vistas (see the coffee-table book, *Mecca the Blessed, Madinah the Radiant*, Esin, 1963). That has changed. In its place are sleek fly-overs, well-constructed tunnels for vehicular traffic, luxurious hotels and ambitious expansion plans. In one generation over a thousand years are changing. But the past is still visible in the architecture: the 500 bulbous domes in the courtyard around the Kaaba built by Sinan, the Turkish architect sent by Sulayman; the Byzantine influences (window motif, cupolas, foliage painted in purple) in the Madinah mosque. Both cities are sacrosanct, signs proclaim that non-Muslim visitors are prohibited from entering. The king of Saudi Arabia takes pride in his title – and job – of Khadim al Haramain, the servant of the holy places. His patronage ensures funds for their development and attention for their problems.

Contemporary Muslim areas
(shown shaded)
Canada
United States
Mexico
Atlantic Ocean
Pacific Ocean
Peru
Brazil
Argentina
United Kingdom
France
Spain
Morocco
Algeria
Mauritania
Mali
Senegal
The Gambia
Guinea-Bissau
Guinea
Sierra Leone
Liberia
Ivory Coast
4

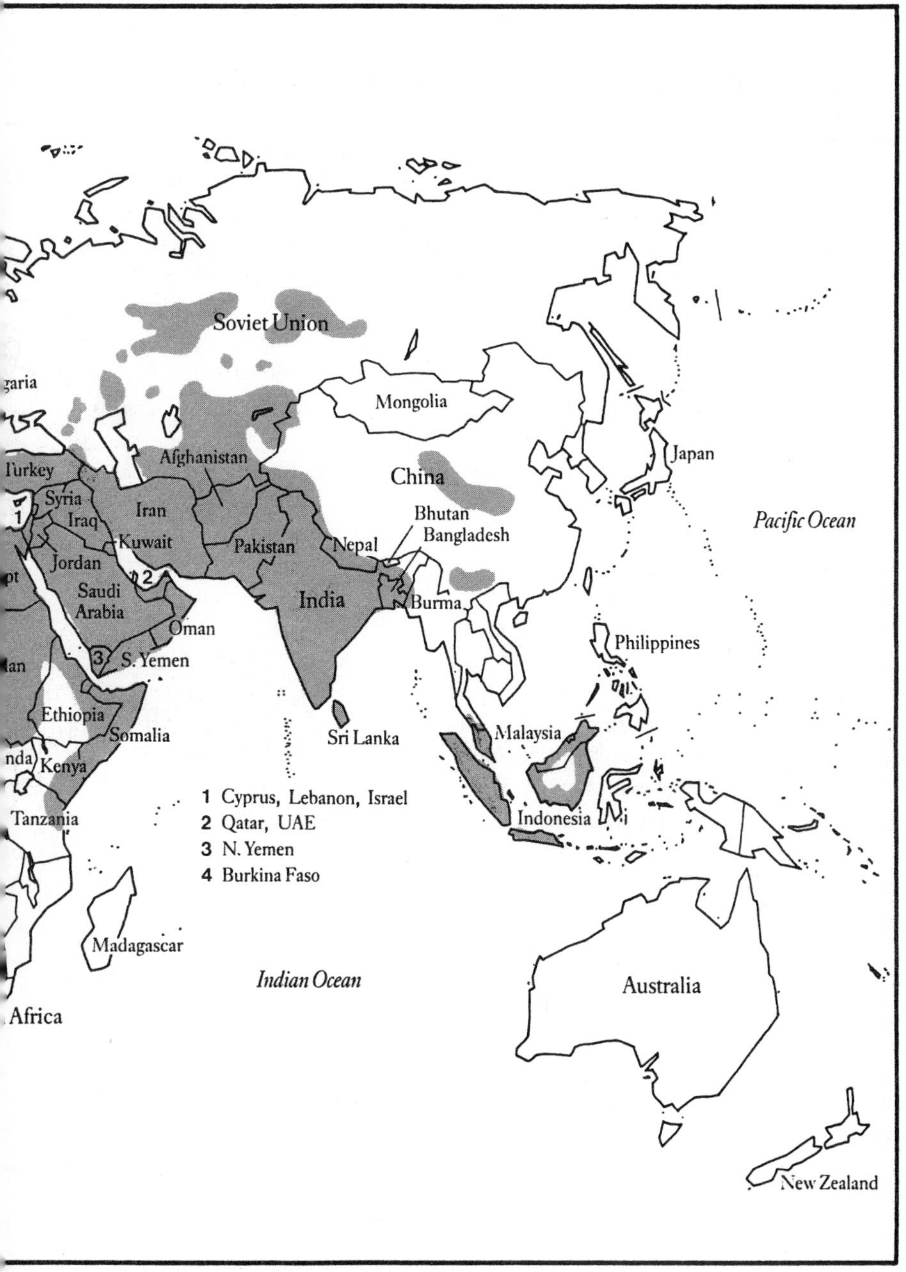
Soviet Union
Mongolia
China
Japan
Pacific Ocean
Afghanistan
Turkey
Syria
Iraq
Iran
Kuwait
Pakistan
Nepal
Bhutan
Bangladesh
Jordan
Saudi Arabia
India
Burma
Oman
S. Yemen
Philippines
Ethiopia
Somalia
Sri Lanka
Malaysia
Kenya
Tanzania
Indonesia
1 Cyprus, Lebanon, Israel
2 Qatar, UAE
3 N. Yemen
4 Burkina Faso
Madagascar
Indian Ocean
Australia
Africa
New Zealand

Religious government

The history of the Arabian peninsula followed a pattern: a thousand years of oblivion and then, briefly, with Islam, world attention; another thousand years of darkness and again, recently, this time with oil, world attention. The first time round the Arabs became masters of fabulous wealth and power, as we saw in the earlier chapters. But that was outside the peninsula. This time the wealth would be available on their doorsteps. It would test them severely.

In a sense Saudi Arabia is attempting the key question of our times: how Islamic must a Muslim government be? The answer was solved neatly in eighteenth-century Arabia. Religion and government fused when Sheikh Muhammad Wahab gave his daughter to Muhammad ibn Saud, a petty chief, in Darryah, near Riyadh, the capital of the Najd. An alliance which would stand the test of time was formed. Division of labour was demarcated between the two, the sheikh would provide religious direction, Saud exercise political authority.

Sheikh Muhammad Wahab drew inspiration from the ideas of Imam Hanbal as interpreted by Ibn Taymiyah (see chapter 3). About five centuries separate Wahab from Taymiyah, and Taymiyah from Hanbal. But the fervour is not dimmed over the thousand years. Ibn Taymiyah spoke against innovation (*bida*), saint worship and pilgrimages to shrines. The followers of Sheikh Wahab would translate his words into action. In 1801 they sacked Karbala and destroyed Hussain's tomb, thereby incurring the eternal wrath of the Shia. They captured Makkah in 1803 and Madinah the following year, destroying venerated tombs and purging the cities of all that savoured of idolatry. The tomb of the Prophet was one of their main targets. Muslims, especially outside the peninsula, condemned these actions, derisively calling the followers of Sheikh Wahab, the Wahabis. The Ottomans, with Egyptian forces, destroyed their power in 1818, razing Darryah to the ground. But the doctrine would not die and its message would continue to reverberate across the Muslim world.

Islam for Sheikh Wahab was earnest piety; his Saudi followers reduced it to its bare essentials, to plain faith and simple rituals. In particular it was shorn of the excess, ecstasy and magic that characterized Sufism (chapter 5). Indeed, it would act as a useful corrective, a reference point, to the aberrations and accretions formed around Islam, examples of which we saw in chapter 6. On the Saudis it would exert unceasing pressure, directing them towards its vision of the world.

In the late nineteenth century, the Saudi clan, backed by the followers of Sheikh Wahab produced one of the most extraordinary Muslim leaders of modern time, Abd-al-Aziz Ibn Saud (1880–1953). In 1902, when he was twenty-one, Abd-al-Aziz led a daring night raid with forty followers and captured Masmak, the fort of Riyadh. Masmak is today preserved, notwithstanding Wahabi doctrine, as a national monument. It is a small mud fort. One of the world's mightiest economic empires was won cheaply; no Qadsya or Panipat, no slaughter of thousands and armies of hundreds of thousands.

Organizing his followers, especially the hard core of dedicated idealist warriors, the Ikhwan – the Muslim Brothers – Abd-al-Aziz spread his rule over the peninsula. The Ikhwan encouraged extreme asceticism, in places beating women who wore silk or men who were late for prayers. Left alone by Western powers still recovering from the First World War, Abd-al-Aziz captured Hijaz and imposed Wahabi views on Makkah and Madinah by 1925. He now had both Najd, the base of his power, and Hijaz, containing the holiest places of Islam. Little was left for him but to change the name of the peninsula in 1932 to Saudi Arabia, after his family, the Al Saud.

With the establishment of Abd-al-Aziz's rule the Ikhwan became a threat to him. They resisted the introduction of innovation in any form, including motor-cars and telephones. In the battle of Sabila in 1929 Abd-al-Aziz destroyed them.

With the creation of Saudi Arabia the concept of a nation grew among the Arabs. Before then people belonged to a particular clan and, more, generally, tribe. Some, the literate, were aware of a larger entity called the *ummah*, the brotherhood of Islam. But not all Muslim brothers were liked. Abd-al-Aziz wrote in a letter in 1913 about the Turks, who had until recently ruled most of the peninsula as part of the Ottoman empire: 'a people who, calling themselves Musalmans, had for years neglected their faith, oppressed their subjects, embezzled religious endowments, broken every ordinance of the Quran and subverted the Khalifat.'

The country was vast, over half the size of India, and under-populated – about 1½ million when it was created (an estimated 6 to 7 million now). By the time of his death Abd-al-Aziz had sired 300 sons and an unknown number of daughters; his links cut across clan and tribe.

Almana, one of Abd-al-Aziz's assistants, has written an account of those early days (*Arabia Unified*, 1982). Until the 1920s the capital, Riyadh, had no electricity, drainage or plumbing. Living conditions were appalling. Oil was discovered in 1938. From one of the poorest areas on earth the country would become one of the richest within one generation. Henceforth the remote, inaccessible peninsula would attract the attention of the world.

Things moved swiftly for Saudi Arabia after the discovery of oil. By 1964 when Faisal, a son of Abd-al-Aziz, replaced Saud, his bumbling brother, as king, the state was an economic giant. But it was almost bankrupt due to mismanagement; the treasury contained 300 riyals. Fecundity had been the only talent of Faisal's brother: he had 53 sons and 54 daughters. Faisal was austere and a committed Muslim; he was the only son of Abd-al-Aziz who ruled with the blood, from his mother, of Sheikh Wahab in his veins.

Faisal attempted to live up to ideal Islam. For instance, he bought the last 4,000 slaves in the kingdom at £1,000 each and gave them their freedom. When Henry Kissinger warned him that Saudi oil wells might be captured and blown up Faisal, it is widely believed, replied: 'We will go back to living in the desert and off our date trees.' There is little doubt that he meant it.

Education, communication, defence and development flourished under Faisal. But more than that, in a few brilliant, diplomatic strokes he provided direction to the Muslim nations. Faisal's significance is that when other Muslim Afro-Asian leaders talked of Russian and Chinese socialism or Westernized democracy, he espoused Islam.

Faisal pushed Muslim heads of state to meet in Rabat in 1969, after the fire in the Al-Aqsa mosque in Jerusalem. In 1972 he goaded Anwar Sadat into throwing the Russians out of Egypt. Next year he backed Sadat's October war against Israel. More important, he launched the movement to use oil – more correctly, oil prices – as a strategic weapon. Prices went up and money now poured into Saudi Arabia. Next year he was the star of another conference of Muslim heads of state in Lahore. From a marginal player in world politics Saudi Arabia was emerging as a central superstar. Faisal was not only changing Arab destiny but the world.

In 1975 Faisal was assassinated by a nephew educated in America. His death created a credibility gap for the house of Saud and the state lost the sense of direction he had provided.

Change in society comes in different forms. In some cases it is structural, where an entire society is turned upside down, as in Iran. Alternatively, bringing in another kind of change, the rulers, the élite, set the pace, as with the Saudis.

Fortunately for their subjects the Saudi family is collectively guided by its wiser elements. The Saudi family – there are estimated to be about 5,000 princes – share the Saudi cake with the poorest camel owner in the kingdom. A camel brings in twenty riyals as subsistence allowance. Saudi Arabia is the rare, truly welfare state providing the entire range of human needs – from education to medicine – for its citizens.

The statistics of growth are impressive. Take education. The adult literacy rate – about 30 per cent – is not unimpressive considering that in 1915 there were only two basic schools, one in Makkah and the other in Jeddah. Now there are 6,000, with 50,000 teachers, teaching a million students. The university in Riyadh has the biggest campus in Asia. Only a decade ago there was no university for women, but women now constitute 25 per cent of all university students. However, they still attend classes on a separate campus and listen to the lectures of male professors over closed-circuit TV. For them a beginning has been made in the workforce, too, where they number about 5 per cent. King Abd-al-Aziz University in Jeddah, the country's leading university, contains some bright sparks and some well-equipped departments. When I presented parts of this book as a seminar there a stimulating and open-minded discussion followed (see interview by M.A. Khan in *Saudi Gazette*, 13 April, 1985). Muslim academics and technologists grapple with practical problems employing modern knowledge. For example, at the Haj Research Centre, Jeddah, the annual problem of storing meat, organizing tents and transport during *haj* is being researched. Auguring well for the future, a small group of earnest, qualified Saudi professionals in their forties with Western PhDs furiously work to implement the Islamic vision based on the ideal. Islamic endeavour – building of schools, universities and mosques, organizing seminars and conferences – is actively supported. In this sphere of activity commitment to Islam, not race or colour, is what matters. Dr Abdullah Naseef is an eminent example of the scholar-activist. An American-educated geologist, Naseef was until recently the active Rector of the King Abd-al-Aziz University. He is presently head of the Rabita-al-alam-al-Islam which oversees Islamic religious and educational activity throughout the world. He is constantly on the move, one day in Chicago, the next in Islamabad, where he heads the Islamic University.

It is in physical growth that the achievements are noteworthy. Take the main cities. Jeddah is a unique port: it is clean. No part of it symbolizes this better than the Corniche. This is a 40–50 mile long six-lane highway along the Red Sea. Placed at every few yards are attractive experimental sculptures, triangles and circles, their monotony broken by sayings from the Quran. Jeddah also boasts the world's largest airport. Its *haj* terminal receives a million pilgrims annually. In 1950 Jeddah was under 1 square kilometre in size and kept itself alive selling fish to pilgrims. Its construction area nowadays covers 150 square kilometres. Riyadh, also less than 1 square kilometre in 1950, spreads over 100 square kilometres. Its airport, built for 3½ billion dollars, is probably the cleanest in the world. Its 2,000 acre diplomatic enclave boasts sports clubs with swimming pools that can create surf and are a modern miracle amidst the sands.

The Saudi Arabian Basic Industries Corporation (SABIC) is causing the desert to bloom. At Jubail and Yanbu 10 billion dollars worth of petrochemical plant has been installed, increasing world petrochemical capacity by 5 per cent. At Jubail a 20 billion dollar city is being constructed. By the end of the century the population of Jubail is expected to grow tenfold, to 300,000.

But it is the aspects of religion, again and again, which are notable. The mosques are clean, full, attended by prosperous-looking worshippers, their cup running over. Islam permeates Saudi Arabia; Islam as theology, as food, as clothes. And now – with the Saudis – Islam as politics. Saudi Arabia, observed Al Farsy, a Saudi intellectual, was 'the only nation to use a sacred scripture, namely the Quran, as a constitution' (*Saudi Arabia: A Case Study in Development*, 1980). The tax on camels (and now on trucks), the weekly *majlis* (audience) with the rulers, the consultative role of the *al-Shura*, the respect for religious scholars, were all based on Islamic custom and faith.

Sheikh Abdul Bin Baz is probably the most influential religious scholar in the land; he is also something of an institution. His advanced age and learning underscore the reputation of wisdom; his blindness and austerity enhance it. The sheikh has become famous by sticking to basic Islam, to its fundamentals. In a land ruled by fundamentalists this appears to be the easy thing to do. 'I would destroy the *haram sharif* as it detracts from worship of God,' he is attributed – incorrectly – as saying. But in the public eye the rulers had moved on to bend, subvert and change the rules to suit their needs, and by remaining a fundamentalist in spite of official honours the sheikh ensured his status and position. He was officially the President of the Dawah and Ifta – Islamic research and propagation – Ministry. Unofficially, I was told by admirers, if it were possible he would be elevated to the ranks of the Companions of the Prophet. It is the highest status possible for a Muslim.

The oil, and the power it brought to Saudi Arabia, is reflected in the sheikh's large block of offices. It also allows him extraordinary authority. Here is no scholar isolated in an ivory tower. Three or four secretaries, taking down his words, help to provide an ambience of temporal power as he replies to letters and dictates notes. He answers varied questions, theoretical and practical, sends out thousands of copies of the holy Quran, and non-Muslims find it felicitous to accept Islam as their faith in his presence. When I visited, Filipino girls, their hair wrapped in scarves, were accepting Islam.

Indeed, the sheikh's selfless devotion to Islam had become a legend. To obtain his blessing was to obtain true benediction. Presidents and kings made public obeisance and sought his assistance. My friend, a prince of the house of Saud, recalls as a child his uncle, King Faisal, kissing the sheikh's hand in a rare public gesture of reverence. President Zia sent his men to obtain the sheikh's approval for the new laws on Islam in Pakistan, but they have no answer yet. This is shrewd – the sheikh must conserve his blessing, also his energy. He told me he has not yet visited Pakistan, where he has many admirers. The sheikh's commitment, austerity and knowledge have made him into the personification of the ideal Muslim.

Saudi Arabia's Islamic posture and wealth gave it considerable leverage in those Muslim countries actively engaged in Islamization such as Sudan, Pakistan and Malaysia. But there is the other side of the coin. The enormous wealth of the Saudis has attracted envy and comment.

The romantic glow surrounding the raggedy, bone-poor but noble Arab, discussed in the last chapter, evaporated with his wealth. In place of the desert hero, relegated to Western films and novels, emerged a different kind of Arab, one neither Burton nor Lawrence would understand – or recognize – easily. In his robes and Rolls Royce the Arab became the cartoonist's delight, little more than a caricature. In the West, whether as the rapacious controller of oil prices or the neurotic hijacker, the Arab is now a favourite villain. He replaces the Russian and Chinese villains who were once favoured in Western popular literature. Heroes like James Bond had frustrated them in countless adventures. In the 1980s a new villain has emerged. Of sinister appearance, with dark glasses and beard, wearing headdress and robes, he is easy to identify. On television and in the media, serious or popular, the caricature is perpetuated. The villain in the *Star Trek* film *Wrath of Khan* looks suspiciously like a Muslim tribal chief in dress and appearance. *Jihad*, Geoffrey Clarkson's new novel, makes explicit the menace of Islam; on the cover: 'Islam in a Holy War against the West: The weapon – our money!' (1981).

For the West the wayward Arab elite in the casinos of London and Paris are debauched wastrels; for many Muslims they symbolize the gap between the ideal Islam they claim to patronize and actual behaviour which is un-Islamic. The British TV documentary *Death of a Princess* – purportedly about the life of the Princess Mishail – and the diplomatic furore it created typified the Saudi response to criticism. In a huff Ambassadors were recalled. Authors and books viewed as unfriendly, a term used in the broadest sense, are banned. Blacking or tearing out offensive bits in a journal are common practice by the censors. For the Saudis, intensely private, their society obsessively closed, the world's curiosity and interest in them created severe pressures. They were discovering that to be enormously wealthy was not to be free of problems.

Saudi society

Those who plan for Saudi Arabia appear to respect Ibn Khaldun. One of the main streets in Makkah is named after him. But they do not seem to have understood his main theory regarding integration and cohesion, *asabyah*, among tribesmen. Official policy encourages urbanization of nomads. 'In recent times the trend has been towards further urbanization and away from nomadism, a trend encouraged by the Government,' noted Al Farsy (*op. cit.*). *Al-din hadari*, faith is sedentary, say the Arabs. But by providing free apartments, and suggesting sedentarization through generous hand-outs – any Saudi receives a loan of 300,000 riyals for a house – they are destroying the *asabyah* which, Ibn Khaldun argued, kept the tribe together. It is a terrible paradox.

Saudi society is tribal. Islam overlays and influences but does not entirely erase tribalism. Take the name of the country, Saudi Arabia – the Arabia of the family or tribe of Saud. Position on the family tree often determines position in government. Sometimes the two are synonymous. Key jobs – defence, governorships – are held by members of the family. Of course there are exceptions. Some men of talent and energy find their way to the top; Sheikh Yamani, the oil minister, providing a high-profile example. But their lineage, as lesser people, is clearly identified. The unceremonious dismissal of our example, Yamani, in late 1986 illustrates the point. For the Saudis tribal identity is still the key to their rule. My friend recounted easily, without once tripping, his relationship to Saud, the founder of the dynasty. But the Prophet's Islamic revolution was aimed precisely at mitigating tribalism, as his denial of Bedouinism in Islam underlines.

At the bottom of the Saudi hierarchy are the people who have come looking for employment, poor Arabs like the Egyptians and Palestinians and poorer Pakistanis and Indians. Egyptians and Pakistanis view each other as competition, ethnicity negating religious bonds. According to official statistics there were 100,000 Egyptians, 70,000 Yemenis, 60,000 Pakistanis and 50,000 South Koreans – the new trend in labour – in the Kingdom (Al Farsy, *op. cit.*). But according to officials in the Pakistan Embassy there could be ten times that number of Pakistanis and most of them illegal imigrants. Riyadh is Pakistan's biggest embassy in the world after London. However, by the mid–1980s the Saudi boom was over. In 1985 some 40 to 50,000 Pakistanis were sent home. This belies the reality. Many returned using illegal routes and methods. Most manage to elude the authorities by keeping out of sight and on the move, like some of the Pakistanis we met earlier in this chapter on Mount Hira.

Saudis call the South Asian Muslim – in particular the numerous Pakistanis – *maskeen*, destitute, poor; or sarcastically, *rafiq*, friend. The *Arab News* carried a lengthy correspondence on this in 1985. Pakistanis, in turn, with equal nuances address Saudis as *Sheikh* – or, surreptitiously, Bedu, dismissing them as illiterate camel-owners. The narrow vision is frustrating for those who are not Saudi, including other Arabs like the Egyptians, and who are in Saudi Arabia to serve the Islamic vision.

The closed nature of Saudi society encourages the outsider to believe that Saudis possess a phlegmatic temperament and do not feel the impact of change. An Arabic novel published in Lebanon, *The Cities of Salt: Diaspora*, by a Saudi, dispels this belief. The hefty novel, 600 pages, is in the form of an allegory. It describes an integrated, idyllic tribal community living around an oasis. Oil is discovered, Americans appear, first as friends, later as masters. The community begins to disintegrate; sons kill and become insane. Life is beginning to imitate art. Depression, paranoia, drugs, recently even AIDS – one face of modern life – may be glimpsed in Saudi society.

Social scientists in the kingdom are concerned about the society within which they must live; a society unfortunately with little time for their diagnosis. In sample studies they estimated that Saudi society had the highest VCR rate (per set per person) in the world. The impact on the closed society of Saudi Arabia of the films – many of them of the blue kind – and their values can only be imagined.

If Saudi self-criticism is muted, other Muslims have begun to comment on Saudi society. Recently, critical items dealing with the themes of ethnic discrimination and corruption have been prominently published in Pakistan (notably in the *Herald*, Karachi, and *The Muslim*, Islamabad). The October 1985 issue of the *Herald* contained a piece, 'Unholy terror', describing the lusty attack of a Saudi on a Pakistani officer's wife. The *Star*, Karachi's popular 'evening' paper, in its issue of 20 February 1986, carried an article, 'Of oil gents and oil gluttons'. Akbar Hussein, the author, confessed, 'I remember how my blood boiled at reading how an oil-sheikh blew a million dollars at the roulette tables of Monte Carlo in a single night, or some minor princeling bequeathed a million pounds to a barmaid because he had a satisfactory one-night stand with her.' The article concluded: 'So now that oil prices threaten to fall through the floor, I gleefully echo a character from Burroughs's book *The Naked Lunch*. How I would love to be around when the Arabs ran out of oil.' The high expectations – and subsequent disappointment – of many non-Arabs who see the Saudis as guardians, custodians, of Islam partly explains the sharpness of the criticism.

Out of the waste land of the Arab desert had come Islam. That was the wonder. For Arabs, this was the proof of their superiority for all time. Non-Arabs see it otherwise: 'The greatest Prophet had to be sent here because they are the worst people.' It is a simple, tribal society spoilt by wealth. High-rise blocks of flats are empty because Bedouin find them cramped and, in any case, cannot carry their goats up the staircases. Deserted modern towers stand throughout the kingdom as evidence of Bedouin reluctance to change.

The bounties of wealth, the power of Islam – in Saudi Arabia the ideas are fused, even support each other. But the two are separate and irreconcilable because they assert opposed philosophies of life. Indeed, Islamic history may be simply constructed correlating excessive wealth with a decline in Muslim morality and therefore power. 'Stay away from the men of wealth and power,' the Prophet had warned.

The lessons of Islam that power and wealth corrupt are in danger of being forgotten. The ultimate reality – the dividing statistic, the final factor – is income per capita in dollars. The Saudis claim figures between 22,000 and 25,000. The contrasts with the other brethren of the Muslim *ummah* are dramatic: 350 for Pakistanis, about 150 for Bangla Desh. The endless examples of wealth are crude. A simple graduation earns 50,000 riyals from the Treasury; a satisfied Saudi will tip a Rolls Royce (in England) or Mercedes Benz (in Pakistan) after a successful hunting trip. It is a society that is in danger of losing its head.

Wealth in this abundance created in the tribesmen a vice they did not possess: indiscretion. With wealth they could now translate every whim, every fantasy, into reality. In the process they would antagonize non-Muslims, and humiliate Muslims – both seeking business transactions. The Arabs are paying for such enormous wealth. The great and sudden wealth was a terrible test, one easy to fail. It is doubtful if many Saudis can now live up to Faisal's boast to Kissinger.

For a land that produces so little there is so much consumption; and the consumption is so extravagant. In the luxurious hotels – Hyatt, Sheraton, Inter Continental – and the shopping malls every conceivable food, every item, is available in large, almost vulgar, quantities. The gourmet's cornucopia sharpens images of starving Africans in Somalia and Ethiopia, not far from here, just across a short strip of water. But there was no public response to the African catastrophe from Saudi Arabia, no urgent relief programmes. It was, as commentators noted, 'Alice in Wonderland.'

Lunching at the opulent Marriott at Riyadh, after visiting Darryah, I asked a Saudi friend, bright and sensitive, what would happen if Sheikh Muhammad Wahab were to walk into the hotel. 'He would chase us out asking if this was indeed his land,' he replied with a note of sorrow in his voice. His answer encapsulated the Saudi dilemma.

The pious Saudis, those who strive for the ideal, are aware of the dangers of affluence and easy living. They know that Saudi society may be damaged in the process of growth and transition. They must strive, run – *jihad* – harder. These Saudis are also concerned at their country's dearth of leaders, intellectuals and artists. Society is reduced to a people on the make, on the look-out for easy and quick money; a people pampered and spoilt. The men of piety are critical of the men of wealth who rotate beads ceaselessly, mechanically, recounting the names of God, but whose thoughts are on material objects – import permits, property, sex. Their spirituality is depleted, their morality corrupted. Religion for the men of wealth is no longer a vision, it is simply transparent strategy. Islam has become a parody of the Saudi vision of religion.

The *mutawa*, those who consider themselves the active guardians of morality, are still known to beat the exposed legs of European women and slap the tardy Muslim late for prayer. But their energy is wasted. Society responds to them with mock seriousness. In Riyadh they are fast becoming anachronistic, in Jeddah almost a thing of the past.

The excessive wealth has engendered a society of consumers, of parasites. There is no pain of creation, no yearning for perfection, no agony of achievement in society, just effortless purchase. The effeminate mincing walk, the time spent adjusting the headdress in front of a mirror, speak of a life of ease among the young; pale skins, pot bellies, thin limbs, reflect a lifestyle of tinned foods, white bread and darkened air-conditioned rooms for the elders. It is two generations since Masmak. 'The well-padded forms who flop into the armchairs at the Riyadh camel races are scarcely the desert panthers who created the kingdom,' wrote Robert Lacey in *The Kingdom* (1982).

This is a crisis of transition of which Saudis are aware. Safeya Binzagr, an artist, writes: 'Intellectual activity is no longer dominated by a school curriculum heavily laden with religious studies but rather by the limited horizons of such television programmes as *Star Trek, Baretta* and *Disney World*' (*Saudi Arabia: An Artist's View of the Past*, 1979).

The imported Western systems – of education, technology, communications – are imperfectly understood and poorly translated. The core of the tribal code – kinship ties interpreted as nepotism – negates the very essence of the open, Western system based on competitive merit. Ideas are borrowed, swallowed whole. So are concepts, turn-key projects, high-tech programmes. Riyadh, expanding and growing in leaps and bounds, reflects the Saudi eclecticism in its architecture which is Moroccan (Maghreb), Mughal (South Asian) and Western. The capital has still to determine its identity.

Saudi Arabia can be a nightmare of misapplied technology. Reservation enquiries are answered by Saudia, the national airline, in American accents but the simplest problem – a change of route – ensures a collapse of communication. A jet airliner, with all passengers on board, burned on the runway while the airport, with equipment worth millions of dollars, watched in helpless despair. Abandoned cars, like discarded toys, are littered along the highways, expressing the exhaustion of the owners' will in the encounter with the twentieth century. Few people were so ill-equipped for the modern world, yet few people are embracing it with the fervour of the Saudis.

Nothing illustrates the dilemmas facing the Saudis better than their response to the attempt of Juhaiman, a student of Bin Baz, to seize the Kaaba in 1979. Dissatisfied with their society Juhaiman and his well armed companions were prepared to die in an effort to restore ideal Islam in it. If the Saudis acted swiftly critics would complain of ill-planned hastiness, if cautiously of faint-heartedness. Too much force would have been read as a sign of weakness, too little as one of carelessness. To hurl in foreign commandos would be criticized as violating the sanctity of the *haram sharif*, to rely entirely on Saudis would perhaps risk a messier ending. And all this while the attention of the Muslim world, in acute suspense and feeding on wild rumours, was riveted on Makkah. The crisis showed how vulnerable a government is in such cases in spite of huge amounts spent on internal defence (one-third of total government spending, about 18 billion dollars in 1985, was spent by the Saudis on defence and internal security). 'It is a power of astonishing fragility,' calculated Lacey.

The pace of change underscores the unanswered nature of a fundamental question: how is the latest twentieth-century technology to be grafted to seventh-century Islam? The conflict between Allah and Mammon in society is not resolved. At least some of the answers lie in the swiftness and drama of the Saudi story. It has not even been a century since Abd-al-Aziz took Masmak.

Yet in the midst of the oil, the wealth, the power, the growth – and the arrogance and corruption they generate – the ideal is visible. Different aspects of it are expressed in different sections of society by Faisal the king, Bin Baz the religious figure, Naseef the scholar-activist, and Juhaiman the young rebel and idealist. This indeed is the Saudi miracle; the Saudi vindication of faith.

The Protestant work ethic

Perhaps another test awaits the Saudis. A dramatic turn in events is taking shape. The word is out: oil is down, from 10 million barrels a day a few years ago to less than 4 million. Oil prices too are falling and consequently oil earnings – from 113 billion dollars in 1981 to 28 in 1985.

The impact is felt across the board: pay, allowances, perks. A quiet panic appears to grip those in society accustomed to the recent wealth. The élite have made their plans for the future. In 1977 Saudis are said to have bought 75,000 houses in Britain alone. Others fall back on the comforting, familiar thought that they are Allah's favourites and so will be provided for. 'When the oil runs out in those hills,' said friends, pointing at the hills around Makkah, 'Allah will produce gold and silver in them.' In one important way they are right. As Sheikh Yamani said to Lacey, 'One day even we will run out of oil. But we will never run out of Makkah and Madinah.'

Max Weber had underlined the role of the Protestant ethic in the success story of modern capitalism. Work for its own sake, combined with thrift and austerity, laid the foundations of the Western capitalist economy and society. But in parts of the Muslim world, as in Saudi Arabia, the discovery of oil has abruptly brought new and untold riches. In other cases, such as Pakistan, income has been augmented through the remittances of migrant labour. In both cases wealth has been generated by forces that are not internal to the structure of society. Society is being transformed as a result of economic changes which remain external to it. Unless social scientists analyse the social situation and the leaders of society utilize their knowledge the consequent problems will be seriously disruptive. Saudis are being tested by excessive power and wealth. We now turn to a society being tested just as severely because it has little of either, the Muslims of southern India.

2 THE ANDALUS SYNDROME IN SOUTH INDIA: *À LA RECHERCHE DU TEMPS PERDU*

Juxtaposing the Muslims of Hyderabad in India with those in Saudi Arabia creates unsettling emotions. The contrast in terms of the power and wealth Muslims enjoy is dramatic; as Saudis must strive to achieve the ideal in spite of them, the Muslims of India must learn to do so without them.

Muslim society in the south of India raises fundamental questions relating to Muslim societies throughout the world. Can Muslims with memories of political domination live as a minority group with honour and in security in a larger non-Muslim society? Or must Muslims be in the majority to order their lives satisfactorily? Although the answers are of immediate concern to Muslims in India, the USSR and China, they may raise serious issues for Muslim societies elsewhere ('Islam of the periphery', chapter 6). Indian Muslims would tend to answer the first question in the affirmative. Pakistan, on the other hand, was created by Muslims who said 'yes' to the second question.

Muslim society and history in South Asia are generally viewed from a north Indian perspective. The Indian dynasties – the slave kings, Tughlaks, Mughals – fascinate us; their architecture – the Taj Mahal in Agra, the Red Fort in Delhi, the Badshahi Mosque in Lahore, the gardens in Kashmir – dazzles us; their almost mythical personal affairs – Razia fighting in a man's world to maintain her rule, Muhammad bin Tughlak brilliantly but erratically defining his role as a Muslim king in a Hindu land, Akbar groping towards a synthesis of religions, Shah Jahan inconsolable at the death of Mumtaz, Aurangzeb enforcing his vision of Islam on a crumbling empire – distract us and form the legends of Indian history. The south is thought of, if at all, as an appendix, an incidental extension, of the north.

A visit to the south, however, changes the perspective, for the achievements of the Muslims of south India stand favourable comparison not only with those in the north but anywhere in the Muslim world.

It is almost a thousand miles from Delhi to Hyderabad. Here the ruling Muslims had to make serious efforts to live with the majority Hindus or face extinction. There was no going back. Their boats were burned when they crossed into the south.

And the south is a different world. We are no longer in the shadow of mighty mountain ranges and by powerful rivers – the homes of divine spirits – but on anonymous plains and plateaus. The weather is mild, the landscape gentle. No longer Aryan, we are in Dravidian land. Telugu, 'the Italian of the East', and Tamil, not Hindi, are spoken here. The issues in Hindu society are different. Muslims do not form a central obsession. The Brahmans do, against whom there are strong feelings and movements inconceivable in the north. The threat in the south was not seen in communal, Hindu-Muslim, terms but in that of militant northern empires wishing to extend their borders.

There is a gentleness, a softness, of speech and bearing in the south which contrasts with the aggressive manners of north Indian groups. The growth of the recent communal violence in the south is widely explained as one of the unsavoury imports, an aspect of north Indian society and politics. Historical or social precedence does not exist for it in the south. However, Muslim society is diverse and complex, evoking different responses in different places. The one emotion that is aroused in all Muslims is a nostalgia for the past.

Muslims confronting the glories of their history feel a sense of loss. The nostalgia for past greatness is rooted in the Arab view of history. It is a legitimate perception. After the destruction of Baghdad by the Mongols Arab history would never be the same again. The past, therefore, became a crutch, an anodyne. And for Muslims in South Asia never more so as than in what was once the Muslim Deccan, the kingdom of Golkonda, and its successor, the state of Hyderabad.

Here Muslims suffer from what we are calling the Andalus syndrome. Andalusia, as we know, once formed the great Muslim civilization in the Iberian peninsula and what is now Spain. Interesting conceptual similarities are discernible between the Andalusian and Hyderabad civilizations, although there is a gap of 500 years between the times they came to an end, and three continents separate them.

An Umayyad started the dynasty in Andalusia when the Umayyad dynasty and empire had collapsed in Damascus, the capital; in Hyderabad, a Mughal governor sent from Delhi, the capital of the Mughal empire, established the dynasty which was to shine long after the Mughal empire was dead. A synthesis of religious cultures is recorded in Hyderabad between Hindus and Muslims and in Andalusia between Christians, Jews and Muslims. The synthesis stimulated a flourishing of art, architecture and literature. Muslims were never quite masters of the Iberian nor the Indian peninsula. The civilizations of Hyderabad and Andalusia ended abruptly, in mid-air, leaving a permanent trauma, a sense of bewilderment, in their societies.

A forlorn nostalgia, a pain, an emotion sometimes too deep for words, haunts these societies. Andalusians in Morocco prominently displayed the keys of their former homes as symbols of the lost land. Hyderabadis in Karachi continue to eat Hyderabadi food and wear Hyderabadi clothes on special occasions, preserved as a part of their lost, cherished civilization. The Andalus syndrome creates a neurosis, a perplexity, in society. It is a yearning for a past that is dead but will not be buried, a fear of an unreliable future which is still to be born.

Hyderabad: Muslim glory in south India

The history of Muslim rule in south India may be refracted through Ibn Khaldunian eyes. Fresh groups, from the north in our case, overpower established dynasties and, their energy depleted after a few generations, themselves fall victim to fresher conquerors. In south India the cycle is repeated every seven generations, about two hundred years, the average age of the Muslim dynasties. Thus the Bahmani sultans overcoming Hindu kings ruled for two centuries. Their territory was then split into five Muslim sultanates. One of these was the Qutub Shahi kingdom of Golkonda.

Seven Qutub Shahi kings ruled for just under two centuries. They were enthusiastic builders and tolerant rulers. The city of Hyderabad, the Char

Minar tower – a symbol of the city – the Makkah Masjid, the royal tombs and the Golkonda fort are their monuments. Their Shiaism was pronounced – Hyderabad derives from Hyder, a name of Ali, and the Char Minar is in the shape of a *tazya*, symbolic of Karbala. Historians suggest their Shia fervour roused the orthodox fury of the Mughal Emperor Aurangzeb. The emperor destroyed the last Qutub Shahi king, moving south from Delhi for the purpose. From the line of his governor, Mir Qamarud-din, came the Nizams, who ruled for over two centuries. The seventh Nizam, in turn, was defeated by armies from the north, from Delhi again, when his state was occupied and merged with the Indian Republic in 1948.

The vacuum created by the destruction of the Muslim states in the south by Aurangzeb was to be filled by the state of Hyderabad. For the next hundred years the action in India would be in the Deccan. First the wars of Aurangzeb, then, in the eighteenth century, the rivalry between the French and the English, and the rise – Hyderabad – and fall – Mysore – of states would occupy history. Clive, Sivaji, Wellesley, Hastings, Haider Ali, Tipu, the Nizams, were the central actors in the Indian drama; and they all played their part in the south. Only in the nineteenth century would the centre of gravity shift to the north of India.

From the middle of the nineteenth century, when the British saw Muslims as the main culprits for the uprisings of 1857 and discriminated against them, to the middle of the twentieth century was a period of despair for Muslims in South Asia. At a time when Muslim fortunes were at a low ebb Muslim civilization in Hyderabad shone brightly. It is thus doubly significant.

Little did Mir Qamarud-din, the Mughal Viceroy in the Deccan, realize that his dynasty would one day hold the torch for Muslim civilization in South Asia when he assumed the title of Asif Jah in 1724 and declared virtual independence from Delhi. His state, Hyderabad, was assuming the mantle of succession to the Bahmanis, Vijayanagar and the Muslim sultanates.

Seven Nizams – Asif Jah I to VII – ruled Hyderabad. All except the last are buried in Makkah Masjid. With considerable skill they steered the state away from the turbulence of south Indian politics in those turbulent centuries and thereby created and maintained an island mentality for their subjects. In the late eighteenth century the Nizam remained loyal to the British against his fellow Muslim, Tipu Sultan, and also, in the next century, during the uprisings in 1857. In 1918 the British conferred on Nizam Mir Osman Ali Khan the highest title in India, 'His Exalted Highness'. The Nizams were patrons of art and learning. Many were accomplished artists themselves. Perhaps the greatest patron was the last Nizam, Osman Ali.

Although Muslims only accounted for about 15 per cent of the population their rule was benign; during the early period of crisis their Hindu subjects neither allied with the Hindu Marathas nor with the Europeans. Key officials, like the Diwan, were Hindus. So were many of the feudal lords, the *jagirdars*. A sense of Hyderabadi identity was created in the concept of *mulki*, native of Hyderabad, irrespective of religion.

The area of Hyderabad, although fluctuating with the expansion and designs of British power, was just over 82,000 square miles when the state was finally absorbed into India in 1948. The state had its own railways, army, post and currency. The administration was headed by a prime minister, notably those furnished by the Salar Jangs. Splendid parks and well-stocked museums graced its capital city, Hyderabad. Indeed, many people like E. M. Forster considered, 'Hyderabad the only pleasant great Indian city' (*The Hill of Devi and Other Indian writings*, 1983).

The centres of learning received the Nizam's lavish patronage and attention. The central institutions – the medical colleges, the High Courts, the legislative Council – were housed in large, imposing buildings in what is locally termed Indo-Saracenic architecture. Their arches and domes could compete with north Indian Mughal architecture in splendour. But the pride of the Nizam was surely the Osmania University.

Founded in 1918 with an initial enrolment of 225 students the Osmania University spread over 2,000 acres (now reduced to 1,600 by the demands of more recent academic institutions). Within ten years of its birth the academic standards of its engineering and medical faculties were acknowledged in India. A university college was started for women in 1926, well before other Muslims in India were prepared to allow this development in their areas. The Osmania was the first university in India to use a native language, Urdu, as a medium of instruction. In 1938 the magnificent arts college building was constructed. Its architecture was a conscious synthesis between Hindu and Muslim cultures: pillars in the Ajanta style on the ground floor and Muslim arches on the first floor around the building. Osmania's library was one of the best stocked in India and today has about half a million books.

In nineteenth-century India Sir Sayyed Ahmad and Sir Salar Jang I, Prime Minister of Hyderabad, were famed for their efforts in education for, and their vision of, Muslim society. During 1857 both demonstrated their loyalty to the British. In the terrible aftermath this allowed them to provide shelter to Muslims, to salvage and attempt to rebuild Muslim society. Sir Sayyed encouraged Muslims from other parts of India to work with his close friend Salar Jang and live in Hyderabad. Many Muslims from Hyderabad rose to heights. Two, Mohsin-ul-Mulk and Waqar-ul-Mulk, in turn succeeded Sir Sayyed as Secretary of Aligarh University.

In 1888 was founded the *Dairatul-Maarif-it-Osmania*, an institution which promoted the collection of rare and original Arabic manuscripts and their translation into Urdu. Famous works of literature were translated into Urdu by a vigorous department, the *Darul Tarjumah*. These translations provided a legitimate scientific and intellectual base for the language.

Urdu writers like Zafar Ali Khan and Maulvi Abdul Haq, *Babai Urdu*, the father of Urdu, came to work in Hyderabad. The Nizam patronized the *Anjuman-i-Taraqi-Urdu* which had its headquarters in his state. He continued to support the Anjuman when it shifted to Delhi. A beginning was made in Urdu theatre which would flower later in Pakistan. But the Nizam was not an Urdu chauvinist.

One of the lasting contributions of the Nizam is his patronage of the translation of the holy Quran made by Marmaduke Pickthall, an English Muslim, into English. Published in numerous editions as a Mentor Classic it is dedicated 'to his exalted highness the Nizam'. Native sons, too, excelled in English. Imad-ul-Mulk was considered one of the best English writers of his time. He wrote the petition submitted by the delegation whose leader was the Aga Khan to Lord Minto, Viceroy of India, in 1906. The petition sowed the seeds for the Muslim League and the idea of Pakistan.

Indeed, the Nizam gathered together in Hyderabad the best talent that money could attract, with a healthy eclecticism. Sir Ross Masood, the grandson of Sir Sayyed Ahmad, was his Director of Education – he later became Vice-Chancellor of Aligarh University; Professor von Fürer Haimendorf was advisor on tribal affairs, and later became Professor of Anthropology in London University.

A market in Hyderabad, still known as Madinah market, donated its earnings to the people of Madinah in a gesture of Islamic brotherhood. A generation later the discovery of oil in Saudi Arabia and the loss of Hyderabad state would reverse the economic situation of the two societies in a poignant twist of history.

Jagirdars, feudal lords, owned 30 per cent of the land in Hyderabad, covering 6,500 villages; by 1949 there were 1,167 *jagirdars*. About 10 per cent of the land was *sarf-i-khas*, the Nizam's direct estate, the rest, about 60 per cent, was under the land revenue system. The Nizam was reputed to be the richest man in the world.

For the élite it was a life of leisure and grace. In a letter from Hyderabad dated 12 November 1921, E. M. Forster portrays this life:

> 'I am having a lovely time here and enjoying every moment of it. [Ross] Masood in such good form, the weather perfect and exhilarating, beautiful things to look at, interesting people to talk to, delicious food, romantic walks, pretty birds in the garden'. (Forster, *op. cit.*)

The Hyderabad high culture produced a characteristic Hyderabadi cuisine (*bagharey began*, *kat*, *khattee dal*), cut of clothes (*khara dopatta*, *kurta choli*, *chow hashia*), and manner of speech (*khey* for *key* and *qaaf*, easily noticed in conversation, and mocked by those who speak Urdu in the north). The culture is perhaps best illustrated in that unique collection now housed in the Salar Jang Museum of Hyderabad. Among private collections the museum is the 'richest in the world', boasts the guide book.

The museum is a private collection of the Salar Jangs, the prime ministers of the state. Most of the items were collected by Salar Jang III. He remained a bachelor, devoting his energy to the collection. Idealized paintings of Salar Jang III depict the different stages of his life, dashing in army uniforms designed by European tailors and more accurate, crueller, photographs showing a man with heavy-lidded eyes, sagging jowls and large ears. It is a trajectory of indulgence and affluence.

The museum is an Allahdin's cave of treasures collected from all over the world. From ancient Egypt, China, Japan and Europe, stones, paintings and statues adorn the museum. Erotica and religious manuscripts, the rare and the vulgar, are gathered with equal enthusiasm. Illustrated manuscripts from Bukhara and Golkonda, the autograph and hunting knife – decorated with emeralds and other precious stones – of the Emperor Jahangir, the fruit knife of his empress, Noor Jahan, are all on display. There are also one of the oldest fragments of the holy Quran in the Kufic script, from the ninth century; the oldest dated manuscript, Al Ghazzali's *Tahafat-ul-Falasifah*, dated 1113, two years after the author's death; and what the guide book claims is 'the earliest specimen of Islamic jade not only in India but in the whole world', a book-stand in white jade with the owner's name, Shamshudin Iltutmish, the slave sultan of Delhi, dated 1209–10. There are 8,856 Urdu, 3,226 Persian and 2,110 Arabic volumes in the museum. Here it is difficult to relate the grandeur of the not-so-distant past of Hyderabad civilization to the wretched condition of its inheritors today.

The Hyderabad civilization was rapidly reaching its climax, in a burst of fresh creativity, when it was terminated at that point. In the early twentieth century when India was beginning to demand first greater participation in government, and later independence from the British, Hyderabad, maintaining its island mentality, remained isolated from the mainstream of politics. This artificial isolation created a hot-house atmosphere in the state, explaining its brilliant growth – reaching a peak at the time India achieved independence in 1947 – and also its abrupt downfall.

Makkah Masjid, Madinah market, Saracenic arches, the Arabic language – here was an attempt made by its rulers to create a society which drew inspiration from outside, non-local, sources. The foundations of society were thus weak. Grand titles, elegant clothes, sophisticated cuisine, patronage of arts – Hyderabad civilization reflected leisure, wealth and security. But beneath the brilliance was the reality of a highly feudal order, an exclusive language, an imported religion surrounded by a vast non-Muslim majority. A small but active communist movement merged with that of the Congress to demand change and assisted in the demise of the Nizam's state. Hyderabad was a house built on sand. An artificial creation, it would collapse easily.

Contemporary Hyderabad Society: *dil toot gia*

Becoming aware too late, too slowly, of the movements for independence in British India, the Nizam in 1947 found himself isolated, figuratively and literally, from both the Congress and Muslim League. The unreal politics of the *Majlis-i-Ittehad-i-Muslimeen*, the local Muslim party, in attempting to turn the clock back, further isolated Hyderabad. These factors would cost the Muslims dearly.

Matters were worsened by the Nizam's feeble and ambiguous attempts to establish an independent state, and vaguer sentiments about joining Pakistan, with which he had no borders. The ambiguity provided a golden opportunity for the Indian government, directed by Patel, and insatiably absorbing Indian states, to order troops into Hyderabad. Delhi, with a wary eye towards Pakistan, took the precaution of ordering the action the day after its founder, Mr M. A. Jinnah, the only man whose wrath mattered, died in September 1948. The conquest of Hyderabad was a walk-over as the ill-disciplined Hyderabad force, the Razakars, scattered before the Indian army. There was no match between the units of the India Army, fresh from winning laurels in the Second World War, and Hyderabad troops who had not fought a serious war in centuries. After the success of what is officially called the Police Action of 1948 Hyderabad became part of the Indian Republic.

The manner of Hyderabad's incorporation into the Indian union left unpleasant memories, creating a base for future communal problems: outsiders seeing their role as conquerors, the *mulki* as victims. There was exaggerated talk in Hyderabad of *zulm*, injustice, women dishonoured, men humiliated.

When the Indians entered Hyderabad, Muslim society was divided into three categories: a small, aristocratic élite, mostly relatives of the Nizam and *jagirdars*, a growing middle class of doctors, academics and service people, and the majority who were generally poor – domestic servants, labourers on the land, shop assistants. While the upper and lower classes remained behind in India, dazed, baffled and doubtful, many of the middle class migrated to Pakistan.

In Pakistan this class did well. Professor Raziuddin Siddiqui, Vice-Chancellor of Osmania in 1948, became Vice-Chancellor of the Islamabad University, Professor Hashmey its Dean. Sibte Hassan, Ibrahim Jalees and Khawaja Mueenuddin contributed to Urdu literature. Sibte Hassan founded the illustrated weekly *Laila Nahar*. The two plays of Khawaja Mueenuddin, *Lal Qila se Lalu Khet Tak* and *Mirza Ghalib Bandar Road Par*, popularized Urdu drama while discussing serious themes. Two Hyderabadis played major roles in politics. Ghulam Muhammad, ethnically a Punjabi, became Governor-General while Maulana Abul Mawdoodi founded the Jamaat-i-Islami, the orthodox Islamic party, with a vigorous and dedicated membership. Others left South Asia altogether. Professor Aziz Ahmad was Director of an Islamic Centre in Canada when he died a few years ago and Dr Hameedullah, self-exiled from the 1948 days, lives in Paris (see also chapter 10). Both made international names in Islamic studies.

The abrupt removal of the middle class, the most dynamic components of society, ensured its collapse in Hyderabad. It is a collapse which is evident today.

The remnants of the middle class who did not migrate to Pakistan camoufl-aged themselves. Religious customs were altered – 'Hello' was substituted for *salaam*, 'goodbye' for *khuda hafiz* – and symbols – beards for men, *burkha* for women – were dropped. Hindu symbolism was adopted, for instance the *bindi*, the circle on the forehead, by women. In some cases names, the final tell-tale, were changed altogether or disguised. Becoming invisible, many Muslims did well. They became business executives and civil servants. Their invisibility was a cause and consequence of their success.

With the migration of Muslims out of Hyderabad after independence other social processes were taking place, affecting its communal balance. First, a large-scale shift of Muslims from remote villages into Hyderabad district, where they form 15 per cent of the population, and in particular into Hyderabad city, where they are almost 40 per cent in number, and second, some years later, an influx of Hindus from outside into what was the state of Hyderabad. The outsiders found an isolated community. S. C. Dube, three years after the Police Action, interviewed villagers just outside Hyderabad who had never heard of Gandhi and Nehru and had no idea of the Congress struggle against the British for independence (*An Indian Village*, 1955).

Many of the new settlers had little sympathy for *mulkis*, records Zahir Ahmad, a distinguished Hyderabadi, once the Indian Ambassador to Saudi Arabia:

> Their culture, based upon exploitation, was confined to a few hundred families in the cities only, mind you, and so fragile was it that it was shattered at the first impact of change. What was their past, may I ask? Historically: naked conquest and holding on to power, the purpose of which was nothing but idleness and a life of ease. (*Dusk and Dawn in Village India*, 1980)

For these settlers Hyderabad civilization was isolated from mainstream Indian life. By clinging to the old ways Hyderabadis were rejecting modern India.

Overnight, therefore, Hyderabad civilization – dress, food, language –

became obsolete, redundant, a thing of the past. In 1948 Urdu ceased to be the medium of instruction at the Osmania University and the *jagirdari* system was abolished; in 1956 the name of the state, Hyderabad, disappeared from the map and its territories were merged with three neighbouring states. The state, from over 80,000 square miles, was literally cut down to size and reduced to the district of Hyderabad, just over 5,000 square miles. It name and its identity were gone; the story of the state of Hyderabad was over.

For Muslims there was now the price to pay for the years of domination and rule. Professor Ratna Naidu of Hyderabad University, studying communal violence, has concluded:

> The Hindu has for decades stored within his unconscious rages against the Muslims for humiliating memories they evoke for their conquering role in Indian history, for their role in dividing the subcontinent, for their special status today as a political pawn during elections, and the pseudo-privileges which these generate, such as the retention of their personal laws. ('The communal edge to plural societies', Ghurye Award speech, ICSSR, 1982)

The figures since independence suggest the difficulty Muslims are finding in restoring their position in society. At best the graph over the last three decades showing their representation in various walks of life is static (R.Reddy, 'Politics of accommodation: the case of Andhra Pradesh', unpublished paper, 1982). Although forming 8 per cent of Andhra Pradesh's 45 million population, they are generally under-represented: 1 Muslim out of a total of 77 is registered as an owner of a major or medium industry in the state; 11 Muslim and Christian candidates out of 300 in 1957 and 11 out of 294 in 1983 were members of parliament; about 7 per cent Muslims in 1956 and the same percentage in 1983 were in the Andhra Pradesh cabinet; 3 Muslims and Christians out of 43 in 1951–2 and 1 out of 42 in 1980 were Lok Sabah members from Andhra Pradesh. Their general poverty – Muslims are rick-shaw-pullers and servants – and low literacy rate – about 25 per cent, also the average for the state – traps them. Muslims are in danger of becoming not only a backward but an invisible minority.

Few Muslims from Hyderabad have successfully overcome the sense of loss, the Andalus syndrome, to make a mark on contemporary Indian life. The exceptions are Professors A. M. Khusro, Member, Planning Commission, and Bashirudin, Director, Centre for Study of Developing Societies, Delhi. In India today perhaps the best known Muslim from Hyderabad is Azharuddin, the star batsman of the Indian cricket team (for scoring centuries in each of his first three Tests against England he is in *The Guinness Book of Records*, 1986). There are only 3 Muslims in the 83 entries in the 'Who's Who' section of the *Andhra Pradesh Year Book* (1980).

In spite of – or perhaps because of – these statistics of despair, Muslims cling to their language, Urdu, and customs tenaciously: Urdu signs on Muslim shops; spirited, though small Urdu dailies; women in *burkhas;* men in *achkan-sherwani* and Muslim beards are the evidence. The *Majlis-i-Ittehad-i-Muslimeen* capitalizes on such sentiment and has established a strong following in the city among Muslims. Unfortunately its vision is restricted to Muslims and it cannot, therefore, provide universal answers or appeal. Its politics are strident, its policies sterile. It therefore perpetuates the very condition it wishes to abolish.

The Majlis in a sense symbolizes the Muslim community. It has been out of step with larger developments from the start. Earlier, when Congress represented the freedom movement, it opposed the party and as a result suffered. Its present support of the Congress has isolated it from the emergent and triumphant local parties, in particular the Telugu Desam.

The Majlis kind of politics reinforces the isolation of the Muslims in the south. In contrast, since independence, Muslims in the north remained in the main-stream of life, many rising to high positions, including that of the President of India. They played an active part in the drama of independence, many contributing to the politics of Congress. Their language, Urdu, and culture, though associated with them was not exclusively their preserve. In the south Urdu was always a minority and élite language. In Andhra Pradesh there are only 7 per cent who speak Urdu compared to 86 per cent who claim Telugu as their mother tongue. Another recent cultural development which further reinforces the sense of Muslim isolation is wide-spread and energetic Hindu revivalism.

Hindu revivalism is not directly related to Muslims; nevertheless, it makes life uncomfortable for them. In Andhra Pradesh the revival is a combination of various factors. In part it is a reassertion of Telugu language and culture; in part a political statement against the domination of Delhi represented by the Congress – the historical revolt of the south against the north. The man who symbolizes the revival is N. T. Rama Rao, the Chief Minister of Andhra Pradesh.

Rama Rao made his name and fortune playing divine and mythical characters in Telugu films. He believes he has a divine mission to purify society. What is more important, people, especially in the villages, believe in his divinity. To them he is god incarnate, possessing miraculous powers. 'He is *bhagwan*, god, divine', I heard educated people in Hyderabad say of him without a hint of self-consciousness. Rama Rao may appear comical in the eyes of the Delhi or Bombay intellectual but, like Ronald Reagan in the USA, he is a reflection of popular culture, its authentic theatrical expression. Both seek to locate the roots of society, to capture its most basic ideology, and to translate these into easily understood politics.

Gods, kings, saints – where does the role of one end and the other begin? Miracles and divine justice in daily life, it was difficult to tell where fantasy ended and reality began. We were back to the flying chariots, demonic giants, talking animals and god-like heroes of the ancient scriptures. Society was not reverting to the past, the time of the Vedas; Vedic times were invading the present.

Religious revivalism easily converts to communal violence; it is the facile translation, the corruption, of faith. The figures for violence indicate that the problem is a growing one. In two extended articles on communal violence published by the *Economic and Political Weekly* in January 1985, Gopal Krishna concluded: 'The scale of communal violence has increased over the years . . . a semi-permanent group warfare . . . at the end leaves everyone injured, impoverished, embittered and confirmed in their hostilities.'

Gopal Krishna's figures show notable increases in communal violence. In 1961 there were 153 rural incidents and 286 urban ones; in 1970 rural incidents had increased to 403 and urban ones to 526. In 1961, as a result of communal violence 139 people were killed and 755 injured; in 1970, 297 were killed and 1,676 injured. In these statistics Muslims lose heavily in lives and property, as the guardians of the law, the police, are notorious for their partisan attitudes.

Hyderabad was 'noted' for recent communal violence by Krishna. But this kind of violence is relatively new. During his fieldwork in 1951–2 Dube observed that Hyderabad had 'a fairly honourable record of communal harmony' (*An Indian Village*, 1955), this in spite of the stereotypes. Muslims found Hindus 'cowardly and mean'. Hindus complained: 'The Muslims are good in only two things – they eat and copulate like beasts.' Muslim claims to social superiority were dismissed: 'A Hindu untouchable of yesterday becomes a Muslim today; and tomorrow he will start proclaiming that his forefathers lived in Arabia.'

In 1967 there were 510 incidents spread over 6 days and in 1968 the riots lasted 36 days: 'Hyderabad emerges as the single major centre of communal trouble in Andhra Pradesh.' Krishna suggests two reasons why this is so: 'There was a considerable Arya Samaj activity in the city over a long period.' Along with this Hyderabad faced the problem of the collapse of Muslim society: 'It has a large Muslim population, a part of which has experienced reverse social mobility.' The communal riot in 1984 was the worst. Knives dipped in cyanide, it was rumoured, were used to inflict maximum pain on the enemy.

Muslims in Andhra Pradesh are crowded in Hyderabad city, where they form a large percentage of its population. Professor Ratna Naidu described what she called their 'ghetto' mentality. Poverty, overcrowding, lack of facilities such as water, and the constant communal pressure make life difficult for them. In any case the noise, pollution and anarchy of traffic make Hyderabad a difficult city to live in. Their history only appears to worsen matters for Muslims. The past grandeur, the splendid buildings, appear to mock their contemporary situation.

An avenue of escape was provided for Muslims by employment opportunities in Arab countries. Unfortunately this does not always result in a satisfactory social conclusion. The visible signs of affluence – a radio, perhaps television – among Muslims arouse jealousy in neighbours. The underlying anger expresses itself in open resentment when the migrant workers return to Hyderabad. A moral argument is also employed. Rumours circulate of unscrupulous Muslims who employ – or marry – women from Hyderabad but abuse them sexually by loaning their favours to rich clients in the Arab states. The theme of poor Hyderabadi girls being married off to outsiders who make their fortunes in Arab lands was explored with melancholy brilliance in the Indian film *Bazaar*.

Perhaps the loose identification of those Muslims who go abroad with the larger world of Islam, currently aggressive and vigorous, also antagonizes the majority. The importance of 'Allah' on a necklace or rosary is exaggerated. There is also the Pakistan factor.

Pakistan remains a symbol of fear and hate, a menace, for non-Muslim Indians. It is a convenient lightning rod. If it did not exist it would have had to be invented. It is also, perhaps indirectly, unconsciously, employed to apply pressure on Muslims. A Muslim vociferous on the question of rights for his community can provoke the devastating accusation: 'You are pro-Pakistan.' The charge can be carried to absurd limits. One of India's best known actors, Dilip Kumar, having been accused of being overly popular with Pakistanis is now wary of meeting them.

Pakistan was negatively associated with almost every major national crisis in the press during the short period I was visiting Hyderabad. These were discussed daily, sometimes hysterically: the Sikh problem, the spy scandal in Delhi, Indira's assassination, military conflict in Gilgit, religious clashes in Kashmir. An editorial in the *Deccan Chronicle*, pointing a finger at Pakistan for its alleged complicity in India's problems, greeted me on my arrival in Hyderabad ('Pak-trained extremists', 29 January 1985). The *Blitz* carried an illustrated article on Pakistan's drug war – smuggling drugs through the Rann of Kutch to corrupt Indian youth. The disorientation in society, the paper argued, would pave the way for a regular military invasion. In an atmosphere of suspicion rumours assume credibility. Comic-book villains, painted black, roamed the land and comic-book plots were hatched to damage India. In the general hysteria the critical faculty was suspended.

The increasing incidence of communal violence, therefore, has many explanations: a minor revivalism dramatized by Arab money and coinciding with a major Hindu revival, Pakistan, the politics of India, the 'ghetto' mentality, poverty, illiteracy. And shot through all these is the sense of loss, the yearning for a past.

For those of the old Muslim élite who are still alive affectionate memories of the past mingle with the realities of today. Zahir Ahmad reflected on this bitter-sweet theme with the consciousness of an exiled Andalusian grandee: 'There was something like a magic dream clinging to everything I saw, yet deep down in my heart there was a feeling of being an alien in my own home' (*Dusk and Dawn in Village India*, 1980); and on the malaise of the Muslim: 'It was not so much the loss of wealth that mattered to him as the loss of faith in the life in which he had been brought up.'

In his comfortable home in Banjara hills Zahir Ahmad contrasted 'the grandeur of the past and the splendour of the present confusion'. Mourning for the past, suffering from anorexia, the élite has failed to provide leadership to the community. They appear to have little to offer apart from nostalgia and self-pity.

The view of nostalgia for the past and sorrow for its passing is not exclusive to Zahir Ahmad's class. At the Hyderabad airport I stood in line, waiting for the customs' check, when the man next to me, shown to be a Muslim by the presence of his veiled wife, a labourer to the Arab states by his appearance, asked me a question: 'Saudi?' 'Pakistani,' I replied. On my answer he observed that although many Hyderabadis were in Pakistan they never returned. I asked why. '*Dil toot gia*,' he said in Urdu, forlorn, far-away, almost to himself: the heart was broken. 'Theirs and ours.' We parted company on that note. He could neither annul the past, nor recreate it. Worse, I had nothing to offer in his pain, his loss of self.

The emerging realities, the emerging relationship between Hindu and Muslim, are symbolized by the Lord Venkateswara temple. Popularly called the Birla temple, after its builders, and situated on a hillock, it dominates Hyderabad. It is made of a thousand tons of marble brought from Rajasthan by artisans who, it is believed, are descendants of the makers of the Taj Mahal. Bright lights shine on it at night making it visible for miles. Like the Sacré Coeur in Paris, which it resembles in the night from a distance, the temple commands the city. In contrast the Char Minar tower, once the heart of the city, survives amidst the noise, bustle and traffic more as an archaeological wonder, a tourist attraction, than a live monument. The only signs of recent investment are in the Hindu temple, attached to its base and providing another source of communal friction. The contrast is symbolic of dominant Hindu and decaying Muslim society.

But reversal of social position is only one of the problems facing contemporary Muslim society. Ethnicity, the role of women, refugees, all create problems and thwart the move to the ideal, as we will see in the next chapter.

9

Muslim society turned inside out: ethnicity, women and refugees

Excessive wealth in Muslim society on the one hand, and deprivation of power and privilege on the other, thwart the move to the ideal, we saw in the last chapter. Other contemporary problems which distract from the ideal are discussed in this chapter. The excess of wealth in society creates the need for re-definitions among Muslims, employer and employee, local and non-local, nourishing the concept of ethnicity. Risking a certain amount of repetition we deploy data from Arab society – this time the UAE – to analyse ethnicity. Also discussed will be the unsatisfactory situations of Muslim women – far removed from the ideal – and Afghan refugees.

1 *'DUBAI CHALO'*: ETHNIC ENCOUNTERS BETWEEN MIDDLE EASTERN AND SOUTH ASIAN MUSLIM SOCIETIES

Social scientists believe that ethnicity – language, food, folk art, dress, custom, the rubric which we may define as local culture – is created within and by society during the passage of time; it is therefore particular to that society. Religion, it is argued on the other hand, is something introduced into, or superimposed upon, society from outside. This is especially true of the world's universalistic religions. In certain specified situations a contradiction may develop between a strong, particularistic, local ethnic tradition and a universalistic religion. Islam, born in a tribal society, confronted this problem from the beginning. We saw how the Prophet, aware of the fissiparous dangers of ethnicity and tribalism, decried these in his saying 'there is no Bedouinism in Islam'. His was a universal message transcending race and tribe. But in spite of the Prophet's warning ethnicity remained to identify, and separate, groups within Islam.

The mechanism whereby boundaries are defined and maintained between groups has always interested sociologists and anthropologists. Anthropologists have concerned themselves with tribal boundaries and maintenance of ethnicity, usually involving neighbouring tribes or ethnic groups. Important issues have been raised as to how ethnicity is maintained. In this section are examined two major Asian ethnic groups interacting intimately with and learning to adjust to each other.

The UAE and Pakistan

When two ethnic groups with developed cultural traditions interact in an unequal relationship within the frame of one religion the problem of ethnicity becomes complex and interesting. The United Arab Emirates provide us – as did Saudi Arabia – with a contemporary example in which Muslim ethnic groups interact intimately and unequally with each other. Although there are many non-Arab Muslim groups in the UAE we will concern ourselves here with the Pakistanis. Arabs, speaking the Arabic language, proud of Arab history, conscious of their Arab genealogies and their local origins, define themselves as *watani*, or natives. In contrast their employees the Pakistanis (mostly) speak Urdu, the national language, are conscious of their South Asian origin, and belong to diverse cultural and ethnic backgrounds – Punjabi, Baluch and Pukhtun. Added to this is the fact that sudden wealth, a lot of it for the Arabs and relative increase for Pakistanis, has shaken the cultural kaleidoscope out of the pattern of the past for both groups.

As Islam is not the issue – both groups being Muslims of the same sect, Sunni – ethnicity becomes important in definitions within and between the groups. This is further exacerbated by the employer-employee nature of the relationship.

The saying *Dubai chalo*, 'let us go to Dubai', which is the equivalent of the expression 'Westward ho!' in Western tradition, has become part of Pakistani culture: popular films around this theme are *Dubai Chalo* in Urdu and *Visa Dubai da* – 'visa for Dubai' – in Punjabi. It signifies the possibility of gathering relatively quick, legitimate, and huge amounts of wealth in the Arab states. Dubai therefore has come to mean in Pakistan a modern-day El Dorado or Shangri-La. For many Pakistanis *Dubai chalo* has indeed proved a fortunate slogan.

There are estimated to be over 2 million Pakistanis in the Arab Gulf States sending home about 3 billion dollars annually. The figure is almost half of the country's entire foreign exchange earnings. Indeed, Pakistan's economy from the 1970s has come to depend heavily on this source of foreign exchange. The government of Pakistan has a fully-fledged Overseas Employment and Manpower Division to deal with migrant labour. The Pakistan International Airlines manager in Dubai informed me that the highest number of operations in landing and taking off and the second highest revenues (after Jeddah) for the airline were in Dubai. However, there has been a price to pay. This has been called the 'Dubai syndrome' by psychologists in Pakistan, and will be discussed later in this section.

The contrast between the UAE and Pakistan is striking. The UAE is sparsely populated with 1½ million people while Pakistan's population is about 100 million. The per capita income of the former is in the highest bracket in the world, 34,000 dollars, and Pakistan's among the lower ones, about 350. However, Pakistan has a basic infrastructure of education, civil and defence services which is one of the best in the region and which the UAE lacked, but is fast acquiring. The people of the UAE speak Arabic and are culturally part of the Arab world; Pakistanis speak Urdu, a language of South Asia, although with a significant percentage of borrowed Arabic and Persian vocabulary, and are part of South Asia. The UAE has remained on the periphery of Arab history and culture. Pakistan – or its putative ancestors, the Muslims of north India – have been in the mainstream of South Asian politics and culture. Its culture includes the poetry of Mirza Ghalib, its architecture the wonder of the Taj Mahal. Complex bureaucracy, irrigation networks and revenue systems were, and are, its features.

The UAE is mainly a tribal society; Pakistan society is a mixture of tribesmen, agricultural peasants and city-dwellers. Since independence the UAE has been ruled by tribal chiefs, wearing tribal clothes, living tribal lives and speaking Arabic. Pakistan was the creation of a barrister educated in London and has been ruled for the most part by Sandhurst-trained generals or Oxford and Cambridge educated politicians, speaking English. The official language in the UAE is Arabic, while in the official files of Pakistan it is still English. In the UAE offices, where an instant civil service corps has come into being, the young officers wearing immaculate Arab dress, clean white robes and smelling faintly of expensive perfumes, conduct office procedure in Arabic. In Pakistan the dusty files, tacky furniture and weary bureaucrats portray a decrepit and run-down administrative machine.

In spite of these differences Pakistan has always had a special relationship with the UAE. Both are self-consciously Islamic in their political and social stances. Pakistan was the first to acknowledge the independence of the UAE by establishing its embassy there in 1971. It provides a wide range of services to the UAE, from advisers to the rulers to humble construction workers. When the Pakistani community wished to open their own cultural centre in Abu Dhabi the Sheikh donated 1.5 million dollars. The grateful Pakistanis called their school after the Sheikh's son. Many citizens of the UAE own property in Pakistan. Karachi, in particular, attracts wealthy UAE Arabs. In turn, many of the wealthy business families, the Haroons from Karachi and the Saigols from Lahore, have invested in the UAE. Conscious of the need to expand into the Gulf are Pakistanis like the editors of the *Pakistan Economist*, who changed the name of their journal to the *Pakistan and Gulf Economist*. According to certain Pakistani writers these editors are not alone in casting an avaricious eye on Gulf dollars. Pakistani banks have been accused of providing armies of prostitutes – as many as 10,000 – to satisfy Arab appetites (Tariq Ali, *Can Pakistan Survive? The Death of a State*, 1983).

Life in the UAE

The vital factor which makes the UAE, in which are located the main emirates and towns, Abu Dhabi and Dubai, important in the region is its oil. Its successes and its failures both stem from its oil revenues. In 1982 the federal budget for the UAE was 6.1 billion dollars. Abu Dhabi, which is the dominant partner in the UAE, showed an income of 8.3 billion dollars. UAE 'allowables' were fixed at 750,000 barrels per day compared to 1,195,000 in 1981. As a consequence, the income per capita of the UAE is probably the highest in the world at 34,000 dollars – a fact helped by the quadrupling of oil prices in ten years. Of the total population of about 1½ million 85 per cent are expatriates. Abu Dhabi is the largest emirate, about 26,000 square miles, and forms 80 per cent of the UAE. Dubai, once a dependency of Abu Dhabi, has an area of 100 square miles and a population of about 60,000 living mainly in Dubai.

With such huge revenues and sparse populations the rulers of the UAE can afford to build lavishly and dream ambitiously. Abu Dhabi is building a sports complex costing 225 million dollars. It will house a future world Olympics and will possess a football stadium with a seating capacity of 100,000. The airport, patterned after the Charles de Gaulle airport in Paris, is costing 200 millon dollars. The headquarters of the Bank of Credit and Commerce International boasts the most sophisticated banking technology in the world. But in spite of this enormous wealth Abu Dhabi has not lost its head. It is the cultural and political capital of the UAE, and it is rather self-consciously dignified and sober.

Dubai, in contrast, is the commercial and fun capital of the area; a place for 'buccaneers', according to Linda Blandford in her controversial book, *Oil Sheikhs* (1978). The turquoise waters and excellent beaches of the Gulf attract women in bikinis notwithstanding the Islamic revivalism in the region. Not to be outdone by the capital, Dubai is building a sports complex, complete with an ice rink, for 130 million dollars. It is also engaged in constructing one of the biggest dock complexes in the world with the latest equipment to service the biggest tankers. Another dock complex is under construction at Jabal Ali.

The main roads of Dubai and Abu Dhabi, with neat green islands in between, are models of symmetry and engineering. Only the best roads in North America or Western Europe could compare with them. Along the roads I noticed the neon lights after dark, in flower designs with four tubes each on every electric pole, on all night, each bulb glowing. It was the comfortable warm glow of opulence, steady and bright. In contrast I thought of the erratic electricity of Pakistan, of the constant 'load-shedding', especially in the hot summer months. Abu Dhabi is not like the other capitals of Islam, Karachi or Cairo, where the lights and voltage fluctuate and telephones are out of order for much of the time.

Luxury is on ample display, and the world's entrepreneurs compete to outdo one another in promoting their goods. Recently a French perfume was introduced to the world by gushing forth from fountains and into pools in a Dubai hotel. Marie Antoinette in Dubai, where drinking water is scarce, would have approved an injunction to 'give them perfume instead'. In any case drinking water, like almost every thing else, is imported (from Italy). Water for Abu Dhabi – some 9 million gallons daily – is extracted from recently installed foreign plants. Entire plays with their casts are flown in from New York and London for a few days' performance. During my stay, in the summer of 1982, *Gulf News* announced the arrival of Lulu. Like the French perfume, sometimes new plays are first introduced to the world in the UAE.

Ice skating, Kentucky fried chicken, Olympics stadium, cartoon strips including Andy Capp, Blondie and Garfield (in the *Gulf News*) – it is all happening in the Gulf. The Hyatt hotel in Dubai is surely the centre of the UAE wonderland. Situated by the shore it overlooks the clear waters of the Gulf. The hotel's luxury rooms, and swimming pool on the 30th floor, cater for every jet-set need. Its ice rink is a marvel. The Arabs who come to skate, many in their traditional robes, to the latest Western pop-music on the loud-speaker, have come a long way from the tribesmen we saw in chapter 7.

In the port cities on the Arabian peninsula, among the affluent, tribal ideas and ways are disintegrating. A dangerous void is forming. The contemporary Bedouin has neither mastered the new world nor forgotten the old. Worse, he cannot handle his new wealth. The Bedouin attitude to money is that it came easily and it is spent easily. Courtesy to strangers, part of the natural code of the tribesmen, was lost in the transition from camel to Cadillac.

The bankruptcy of ideas is compensated by energy. Banks, sex, property, the Arabs are buying them up with a blind frenzy. But the energy is without direction; it confirms the bankruptcy. In place of vision there is imported technology, in place of concepts, instruction manuals. Statistics have become a substitute for excellence. The only yardstick is the one which gives the largest 'cut', the biggest percentage. It is the price for moving in the space of one generation from desert to luxury apartments, from a rest stop in the sand dunes to luxury bathrooms with gold plated toilet seats.

Like societies everywhere Arab society has its particular strengths and weaknesses. But Arab weaknesses are reduced to caricature by Westerners. Many feel a sense of humiliation at having to accept jobs and favours from the Arabs.

Perhaps there is also the envy for Arab wealth. For Westerners the UAE is an 'instant' civilization, built on sand, which will suddenly vanish. They see it creating paranoia and neurosis in its inhabitants and also in those who come into contact with it. The UAE diplomats abroad, Blandford claimed, all possessed PhDs, the letters, according to her, standing for prostitution, hashish and drugs. The chapter in her book on the UAE was titled 'Nutty present, dotty past'. Lurid stories and lewd doings are hinted at.

The cover of his novel *Dubai* (1977) by R. Moore, the author of *The French Connection*, sports a dashing Western hero with a machine gun in his hand. Alongside him is pictured a half-naked, obviously sensual, dusky female – vintage Orientalism. In the background is a minaret. The three parts of the book, called respectively, 'gold', 'oil' and 'insurgency', reflect the three ingredients which to the West constitute the modern Arab state. In *Arabia: A Journey through the Labyrinth* (1979) J. Raban noted that 'Plato's ideal city-state had its base in a slave class and so did Abu Dhabi'. The Pakistanis, for Raban, constitute the latter class. Other writers talk of the Western inheritance 'east of Suez' and argue for the need to control the Gulf directly and militarily (J. B. Kelly, *Arabia, the Gulf and the West*, 1980). They argue that, left to themselves, the Arabs will destroy each other in tribal fashion, thereby inviting Soviet intervention. The sheikhs are not to be trusted to stand and fight in the region, they argue. Most of them have ensured their positions by buying property in the West. They will fly out when the first shot is fired.

Islam in UAE society

Islam came early to the region. The Sheikh of Abu Dhabi is said to have in his possession a letter written by the Prophet inviting the leaders of the region to accept Islam. Traditional tribal structure and organization adapted themselves to Islam and therefore survived. Both are clearly visible in the social and political life of the area. The mosque, the symbol and focal point of Muslim society, is everywhere. There are estimated to be 1,400 mosques in the UAE.

The rulers of the Emirates are tribal chiefs leading their tribe on the basis of loyalty and past history. Abu Dhabi itself was founded by the grandson of Nahayyan, the direct ancestor of the present ruler, Sheikh Zayd Nahayyan, in 1761. Nahayyan claimed descent from the Prophet, and origin from Najd in Saudi Arabia. The tribe of Nahayyan historically dominated the area and, on the basis of this domination, has a monopoly of power and therefore access to the recent wealth. Its sixty-seven tribal sections and sub-sections form the core of government. Non-tribesmen, settlers, expatriates, overseas employees, all remain outsiders in the most profound sense. The name Galadari, for example, is displayed in neon on many shops and buildings but the owners, because they are of Iranian descent, remain outsiders.

Women, too, in Islamic tribal fashion play a prominent role in political affairs especially in dynastic matters, although this role is contrary to the popular image of tribal Muslim women. When Sheikh Zayd deposed his brother Sheikh Shakhbut and became ruler he honoured his promise to his mother, Sheikha Salma. She had made her sons swear to remain united and never to kill each other. Sheikh Zayd's wife, Sheikha Fatimah, plays a leading role in business enterprises and women's development schemes. Her influence at court is widespread.

Life in the UAE is not all jet-set frivolity and material values. Consider the United Arab Emirate University at Al-Ain. The university, the first and major institution of its kind, was begun in 1977. The faculty has a staff of over 400, which includes Egyptians and Pakistanis. Art, Science, Agriculture and *Shariah* are taught. The language of instruction is Arabic, but English is used in Science. By 1981 some 400 students had graduated. Of its 4,000 students almost half are women. Women are educated on a separate campus and are taught up to graduation. The Pakistani professor of English informed me that his female students were more hard-working and promising than the males. But the question he raised about their future is an important one. Will their talents be allowed to expand so that they will contribute to the development of the nation or will they be married off and locked in homes to supervise domestic chores?

In an interview with Professor Ezzedin Ibrahim, an eminent Egyptian scholar and the president of the university, I was informed of the aim to make the university one of the best in the region and the Islamic world (reported in the *Gulf News*, 17 September 1982). Professor Ibrahim is also an adviser to the Sheikh, and both are keen to develop links within the Muslim world, especially with Pakistan. The Sheikh has already donated money for three Islamic centres in Pakistan. He and the professor were in close touch with Pakistanis concerned with education. They were following closely the attempts in Pakistan to 'Islamize' life.

It is at this level that the power and significance of Islamic brotherhood are most notable. There is mutual understanding and respect between Muslim academics regardless of ethnic backgrounds. These men are striving to set and reach Islamic ideals. They are no longer Egyptians or Arabs or Pakistanis but Muslims tied together by the bonds of Islam.

The rulers of the UAE are brave men, rushing their countries in the span of one generation through historical sequences which often take three to four lifetimes. Fortunately they are also mostly wise men, ruling as concerned chiefs, caring for their people and ensuring distribution of wealth. The vast wealth, tight tribal organization and small population allow the system to function smoothly. However, there are structural flaws in society. The major weakness is society's dependency on foreign labour. Let us examine the consequences of this in encounters between Arabs and Pakistanis in the UAE.

Dubai chalo

Expatriate labour – some 200,000 Pakistanis and about 250,000 Indians – make the wheels of the UAE go round. They contribute on all levels of life. At the bottom of the social ladder South Asians sweep UAE streets, clean UAE houses and man UAE taxis. At the middle level are medical doctors, bankers, engineers and lawyers. And at the highest level South Asia also provides key men. The director of the Al-Ain Museum, the commander-in-chief of the UAE air force, the personal pilot and doctor of Sheikh Zayd are all Pakistanis. The Sheikh is quoted as saying that although the Egyptians and Palestinians provide the brains for the UAE – the academics, government advisers – the Pakistanis are its heart, with their uncomplaining stance and identification with Islam. The entire UAE show would collapse if the expatriates were to be withdrawn at short notice.

So important have the Pakistani expatriates become in society that the language of Pakistan, Urdu, has been established as the strongest language after Arabic. In parts of Dubai it is the *lingua franca*. Arabs, familiar with it through Indian films which have soundtracks in Hindi, akin to Urdu, speak it easily. Language thus acts as the main distinguishing feature in the maintenance of ethnic boundaries.

Pakistanis in the UAE may be divided into two groups: the trained professionals – the whole range of bankers, doctors, lawyers – and the manual labourers – construction workers, drivers, domestic servants. Both groups have contributed to the development of the UAE and both have done well in economic terms. The first, reflecting some of the original opulence of their employers, wear Western clothes, use expensive perfumes and live in air-conditioned rooms. They may be seen strutting about in the lobbies of the UAE hotels with the arrogance of those who have made money quickly and sometimes illegitimately. They participate in the *dolce vita* of the Arabs, if not as equal partners at least as junior colleagues. For them the entire family lives, shares and enjoys the UAE dream.

This group is culturally malleable and socially docile, clinging to the money it makes and determined to make the most of it. Well placed Pakistani executives can earn up to 20,000 dirhams monthly, ten times more than they would at home. But their sudden wealth makes them insecure. Blandford found these Pakistanis 'scared stiff'. They will not rock the boat at any cost. Among members of this group are a few who are out to make quick money and therefore cut corners.

In attempting this some Pakistanis get caught up in the rigid code of the Arab tribesman. One such incident involved Pakistanis who were on the personal staff of Sheikh Zayd (*Newsweek*, 7 March 1983). They were discovered to have been quietly siphoning off the Sheikh's money in to their own accounts abroad. They had done this by operating a multi-million-dollar company based in London and registered in Panama. The authorities acted in tribal manner when the code is involved and loyalties betrayed. The accused were swiftly put under arrest and their associates came under a cloud; their assets and their lives were frozen.

The other group, on which the edifice of the *dolce vita* rests, lead harsh lives. These are the hardy Baluch and Pukhtun tribesmen, noted working on the roads by foreigners like Raban: 'These were the people who were keeping the opera afloat.' The working conditions for this category, in the open sun constructing roads or buildings, are difficult. Equally difficult is their relationship with ruthless agents and bosses. They risk deportation at the slightest provocation, which in UAE parlance includes requesting their legitimate rights. Stories of broken lives abound, men put on boats and sent back across the Gulf, agents disappearing, local employers profiteering at the cost of illiterate tribesmen. Their families are in Pakistan. They come from the villages of the Frontier, Baluchistan and Punjab. Tribal and rural life with their particular codes sustain this group. They are expected to return home every year rich with money and laden with gifts such as radios and watches. They live in appalling conditions in rooms knocked together from tin and bits of wood. Lonely men, they work desperately to live up to the *Dubai chalo* myth.

Jarnia Fur, a makeshift shanty-town outside Abu Dhabi, expresses and symbolizes the lives of the labourers in the UAE. It is inhabited by a mixture of South Asian Muslims, Egyptians and Sudanese. Jarnia Fur is not the make-believe world of the Dubai Hyatt. It is reality – an Afro-Asian reality – and here reality festers.

Pools of stagnant water covered in green slime surround the camp. The lanes reek with filthy drainage water; old boots, tyres and garbage lie about in them. The 'homes' are little more than pieces of wood hammered hastily together. Rents, none the less, are exorbitant. A few men usually hire a room, often as small as 40 square feet, for 600–700 dirhams per month. In the midst of this filth and squalor are the symbols of affluence which make the enterprise worthwhile for the labourer: the odd air-conditioner jutting out of a room or a Mercedes taxi parked outside one.

Corrupt local officials and rapacious agents on both sides, and a sense of alienation, haunt the labourer. Horror stories of ethnic discrimination are told in hushed voices: 'The authorities have sharp ears and swift methods.' A recent story was related of an Arab who raped an Indian woman in the camp and got away with it. There are two laws in the land: one for *watani* and the other for foreigners.

Foreigners know that Arab justice is swift and moves mysteriously. Rigidity has become a substitute for human understanding, for compassion. An American, after locating companions in jail, said they make the Turkish ones in *Midnight Express* look like Buckingham Palace. The jails on the Arabian peninsula are little more than holes in the ground. They are also over-crowded, inmates sleeping in rotation. Defiance is punished by hanging from the ceiling, head down. The foreign embassy, already deferential, does not care to be contacted in case of problems. It is rumoured that thousands of non-locals languish in this dark world waiting for release.

Nevertheless, the spirits of the South Asians are high as they stand rooted in their own traditional cultures and civilization. They refer to the Arabs as Bedu – from Bedouin – with contempt. 'The *bedu* has no culture, only sudden money,' they observe (also see chapter 8, section 1). 'We are better Muslims than these people.'

For all the sullen defiance in the camp it is an established fact that Indians, Egyptians and Sudanese are well-behaved and docile. They are in a Muslim country, within their Muslim *ummah*, in pursuit of legitimate earnings. Whatever the reality of ethnic divisions in society they are prepared to turn a blind eye. They are good labour. So, too, are the Pakistanis. But Pakistani society is not uniform.

Ethnic encounters in the UAE

Pakistani society was generally categorized as comprising tribesmen, agriculturalists and city people earlier. The last two are abroad to make money and go about their business diligently and quietly. But the Pukhtun from the North-West Frontier Province is himself too much of a tribesman to make allowances for the sudden wealth and its attendant complexities that afflict the UAE tribesman (chapter 7, section 2). His life revolves around the concept of Pukhtunwali or the code of the Pukhtun. Ethnicity clearly can be ignored in the argument so far and no more.

The Pukhtun will not compromise his own sense of personal honour and wears his Pukhtunness like a badge – knowledge of Pukhto, the language of the Pukhtuns, will ensure a free ride in a taxi driven by a Pukhtun. He retains his customs in language, dress, behaviour and the rites of passage; for birth and marriage, the Pukhtun goes – and for death is sent – home. Pukhtuns are distinctive in their customary dress, the *shalwar kameez*. By contrast many others in this group, including the Baluchis, have taken to wearing the Arab shirt. The boundaries are blurred between them and the Arabs. Pukhtuns are adamant that their dead be buried back in their native land. The Baluch too, perhaps learning from the Pukhtun, have now begun to send their dead back to Baluchistan. Pukhto films are screened. The two popular Pukhto stars, Badar Munir and Yasmin Khan, are seen in Pukhto films regularly.

Pukhtun unity in the face of non-Pukhtun opposition has become proverbial:

a story widely circulated concerned a Pukhtun teacher in the Pakistani school who was reinstated due to their united pressure in spite of opposition by the local authorities. Other well-known recent episodes further illustrate the point.

A young Pukhtun driver was driving his truck along one of the main highways when a Mercedes, driven by an Arab, attempted to overtake him. The truck was heavy and the sand along the road made it difficult to clear the road immediately. So the truck-driver did not give way. The driver of the car made desperate but futile passes to overtake the truck. By now the passengers of the car were yelling and the driver hooting furiously. All to no avail. Then an opening allowed the car to speed forward. Accelerating to gain distance the car stopped, blocking the road for the truck.

The truck-driver was asked by the passengers in the car to step down. Hot words followed between them. The truck-driver was slapped. He immediately hit back. A revolver was pulled out and he was shot dead. The driver of the car sped away. He little realized the complex laws of honour that he had invoked among the Pukhtun community. That he was a prince of the land would simply add to, not detract from, the problem.

The Pukhtuns reacted in their traditional manner, swiftly and boldly. Members of the family of the deceased were outraged. The news spread rapidly and infuriated Pukhtuns were soon demanding revenge. They insisted that the culprit be handed over to them for execution or that his family be prepared for his assassination. If he was not available, they conceded, any adult male member of his family would be acceptable as a substitute. Elaborate plans for ambush were made and rumours circulated of shots fired in the night.

The authorities were as horrified as they were helpless in this case. Their own justice is retributive; it is also swift, sure and condign. Being tribesmen themselves they understood the code of tribesmen, especially the part relating to revenge. They offered up to 3 million dirhams, it is said, if the truck-driver's family would forget the matter, and were refused. They had no idea how to cope with the situation. To treat it with the usual stern administrative measures such as banishment of the victim's family would widen the conflict and scandal. Ignoring it would not work, as the Pukhtuns were mounting an increasingly vociferous campaign. In the end complex and tortuous negotiations succeeded. They involved tribal leaders from both parties, promises, financial deals and substantial concessions to the family of the deceased. The unity of the *ummah* was invoked, as was the special relationship between Pakistan and the UAE. Finally, the strategy of employing both tribal and official channels succeeded. Blood money was paid and accepted; honour was thus satisfied.

Another incident involved the Pukhtun Mahsud tribe, counted among the fiercest fighting men in South Asia with a formidable history of unity in battle (see chapter 7, section 2). The Mahsuds were working as labourers in Al-Ain and lived in a makeshift shanty town just outside it. The hills and terrain resemble that of South Waziristan Agency, in the Frontier Province of Pakistan, the home of the Mahsuds. On being repeatedly provoked by their employers on what they interpreted as unjust grounds the entire tribe gave the battle cry and prepared for a showdown. They clambered up the hills around Al-Ain with guns, the possession of which is illegal, and took up positions at vantage points. The authorities were at their wits' end. A shoot-out would have been costly and also scandalous. It would have made international headlines. Finally members of the Pakistani embassy were rushed from Abu Dhabi to act as mediators. The situation was defused and the Mahsuds were persuaded to come down. No retribution would follow, the authorities promised. The Pukhtuns saw this incident as vindicating their position and their honour.

It is for these reasons that employers often prefer the more docile Indians. Especially popular, particularly as domestic servants, are Muslims from Kerala in south India. The prevalence of their films and posters testify to their numbers. The Kerala Muslims, like the Pukhtuns, but for opposite reasons, have made distinctive marks in UAE society. Only members of the second group of Pakistanis, like labourers, can afford to rock the boat; their illiteracy allows them to maintain some integrity. None the less both groups pay a price.

The Dubai syndrome

The price for working in the UAE has been termed as the 'Dubai syndrome' by Pakistani psychologists. The syndrome is defined as a sense of disorientation resulting from the harsh working conditions, social isolation, culture shock and sudden acquisition of (relative) wealth in the UAE, which together produce psychosomatic disorders. Dr Malik Mubashir, head of the department of psychological diseases at the Rawalpindi General Hospital, talks of the 'Dubai syndrome' which consists of the pre-Dubai, Dubai and post-Dubai stages. The victim feels isolated and guilty for leaving his family and overcompensates with gifts on his return. He 'tries to justify himself by earning more and more money' (*The Muslim*, 4 May 1983).

Dr Malik calculates that about one quarter of the entire population of Pakistan – those working in the UAE and their relatives – is affected by the Dubai syndrome. Its effects will be felt over the coming years in Pakistani society. Pakistanis are concerned about the syndrome. *The Muslim* carried an editorial called 'The Dubai syndrome' on 7 May 1983 (promptly picked up by *The Times of India* under the banner 'Dubai syndrome creates problems for Pakistan' on 10 May).

My own observations confirm that Pakistanis working in the UAE do so under considerable socio-psychological stress. They may ignore it or in some cases convert it to the *dolce vita* lifestyle, though cursing the place in private, as happens among the affluent group. Alternatively, they may re-assert their ethnicity through outward symbols such as dress.

Islam offers an ideological framework within which the two communities meet and interact. Islam is the belief, and its rituals the set of social actions which identify Muslims. Pakistanis in particular identify vigorously with Islamic values and symbols. However, we have noted that in a situation of economic inequality which confirms an employer-employee relationship both groups may experience a revival of ethnicity. The revival serves both groups. It provides the dominant group with a justification for its superior position and the dominated group with a rallying point.

The analysis in the section reveals ethnic rifts within UAE society between local and non-local groups. The concept of *watani* negates that of the *ummah*. But it is also clear that Islam helps to bridge the ethnic and cultural alienation between the groups. It allows a sense of familiarity – through mutually accepted mythologies, rites, customs – to be fostered in spite of difficult conditions. There is always the common ideological frame with the concept of the *ummah* at its centre to provide a focus for Muslims. Therefore social scientists may usefully turn the question of ethnic rifts in society around the other way. That is, not how rifts in society are created by ethnicity but how Islam helps to bring groups together in spite of cleavages based on ethnicity and unequal economic relations.

2 MUSLIM WOMEN

The position of women in Muslim society mirrors the destiny of Islam: when Islam is secure and confident so are its women; when Islam is threatened and under pressure so, too, are they.

Women in the ideal

The ideal Muslim woman is in many important ways like her male counterpart – modest, pious and caring for her family. Islam confers numerous rights: to be educated, to inherit, to divorce. Among those she looks up to as ideal examples are Khadijah, the Prophet's wife, and Fatimah, his daughter.

We have seen the pre-eminent position of women in the early days of Islam. The Prophet's reply to questions on how a person may best locate paradise is at once a comment on the role of women in society and on Islamic ideology, as we noted in chapter 2. Thrice he replied that paradise is to be found 'under the feet of the mother', and only the fourth time did he say 'under the feet of the father'. Indeed the privilege and title of the first Muslim in Islam goes to Khadijah, the Prophet's wife. Older, wealthier, more aristocractic than her husband, and widowed, Khadijah was the ideal wife. Consoling him in loss, encouraging him in despair and believing in his mission when others doubted, she stood by him like a rock in those early unsettled Makkah days. He was to remain inconsolable at her death. He would marry again about a dozen women

– widows and daughters of political allies – but, he would sigh, it was not the same. Their daughter, Fatimah, also plays a key role in early Islam. She was the wife of Ali and mother of Hassan and Hussain, from whom are descended the Sayyeds, the descendants of the Prophet.

In the early socio-historical categories that I have suggested women have led armies (Aishah, in the first category) and earned immortality as artists and writers (in the second and third). In their own right they have been famous Sufi saints (Rabia), and rulers (Razia of India). In each category they have wielded power both in the homes and at court; towns have been named after them (such as Madinah-at-Zahra in Andalusia), and their names, like that of the Mughal Empress Noor Jahan, have appeared on coins alongside that of the ruler. Clearly, wielding power or leading armies may not be usual for Muslim women but it is not uncommon either.

This somewhat stylized picture is far removed from the lowly situation of women in our times. What factor, what catastrophe, took place to alter the status of women so drastically? The answer lies to a large degree in colonialism. The impact of colonialism from the last century onwards affected society externally and internally in the most extreme manner. First and foremost, the already existing sexual divisions of roles and labour were further exaggerated. Colonialism imposed foreign values at the same time as it destroyed or eroded native ones. As a result, society collapsed internally, its destiny unsure, its confidence evaporated. Men retreated into the shell of rigid customs and sterile ritual, finding a form of security there. They also forced their women to hide behind *burkhas* (shuttlecock veils) and remain invisible in the courtyards of their homes. In India, Mughal princesses were reduced to becoming prostitutes (see Ghalib's letter in chapter 7). The stereotype of Oriental females as chattels and playthings was formed. It was a bad time for Islam, a time of retreat. When the European masters began to leave from the middle of the twentieth century Muslim women were to be glimpsed still in various degrees of deprivation and subjugation. They still have to recover.

The answer can no longer be a pious wish to return to early ideal Islam. Too much has been damaged. Deprived of economic and hereditary rights, and everywhere behind men in education, women are formed into an inferior class. The actual situation of women, their social status and privileges, is usually far removed from the Islamic ideal, whether in the tribe, village or the city. This is confirmed by women Muslim social scientists from Morocco to Malaysia (see the work of Professors Fatimah Mernissi for Moroccan, Nawal El Saadawi for Egyptian, Shaila Hariri for Iranian, Sabiha Hafeez for Pakistani and Wazir Jehan for Malay women). The women authors seldom sensationalize their material, nor do they traffic over much in anecdote. It is sober, measured yet, because of the subject, engrossing material. None the less their revelations and analysis will upset many male Muslims because they are so far from the idealized picture carried in their minds (President Sadat threw El Saadawi, a medical doctor, in jail for her writings). Let the skeletons lie in the closet, it will be argued. But there are no solutions in darkness.

But I do not really need to cite the academic research studies and material of these social scientists to support my arguments. The daily newspapers (English and vernacular in Pakistan, for instance) are full of incidents which reveal the situation of women: husbands leaving them penniless for other women or mutilating and killing them on the slightest suspicion, or girls, not yet out of puberty, molested by their religious instructors. Such crimes are dealt with leniently. Both custom and law take a tolerant view; society does not wish its placidity to be disturbed.

Whether in Pakistan, or the Arab world, the position of women is not very different in this regard:

> I remember an incident involving a teacher who sexually assaulted nine female school children whose ages ranged from seven to twelve years. The case appeared before the courts but the judges decided to suspend the proceedings in order to avoid the scandal that would inevitably have involved a number of families. The accused was merely transferred from his profession to a job of a different nature. (Nawal El Saadawi, *The Hidden Face of Eve: Women in the Arab World*, 1982)

The killing of Princess Mishail in Saudi Arabia (chapter 8) confirms that however educated or connected the woman, society will not allow her to disturb its balance and symmetry.

Problems for the girl begin at birth. From her childhood she is made to feel unwanted, an accident, a poor substitute for a boy:

> From the moment she is born and even before she learns to pronounce words, the way people look at her, the expression in their eyes, and their glances somehow indicate that she was born 'incomplete' or 'with something missing'. From the day of her birth to the moment of death, a question will continue to haunt her: 'Why?' Why is it that preference is given to her brother, despite the fact that they are the same, or that she may even be superior to him in many ways, or at least in some aspects? As a child, I saw one of my paternal aunts being submitted to resounding slaps on her face because she had given birth to a third daughter rather than a male child, and I overheard her husband threatening her with divorce if she ever gave birth to a female child again instead of giving him a son. (El Saadawi, *op. cit.*)

The same reactions are equally true of Pakistani society, especially in the rural areas. When my first child, a girl, was born my wife's foster mother was inside the labour room. Anxiously waiting outside my parents and I heard a heart-rending shriek followed by loud wailing. The worst fears assailed us and we rushed into the room. The foster mother was beating her head and chest, crying 'it's a girl'. Over the years as we chided the old lady she would be confused and puzzled. She was merely following custom. It was the manner in which female children were greeted on arrival in her society in Swat, north Pakistan. My wife, she averred, received the same reception.

When she is older and faces the world either to go to school or shopping the girl is constantly reminded of her sexual difference. Venturing outside the house is fraught with anxiety as El Saadawi recounts:

> As a girl I used to be scared of going out into the streets in some of the districts of Cairo during my secondary school days (1943–8). I remember how boys sometimes threw stones at me, or shouted out crude insults as I passed by, such as 'Accursed be the cunt of your mother' or 'Daughter of the bitch fucked by men'. In some Arab countries women have been exposed to physical or moral aggression in the streets simply because their fingers were seen protruding from the sleeves of their dress.

In Iran today a girl not dressed in a black veil runs the risk of having stones or acid thrown at her. Many Pakistani girls recounted similar stories. Boys would walk alongside a girl wearing trousers and ask, 'Why do women wear trousers?' and one of them would answer, 'So that they can air their private parts.' Being pinched on the buttocks or breasts is a common hazard in a Cairo or Karachi bazaar. Humiliated, girls are nervous about leaving their homes; it also creates ambiguity about their sex and role in society.

Afghan and Baluch tribal women

The conditions of women vary from place to place, sect to sect. (Shia women, who appear to be better off than Sunni, are discussed in 'Women in Shiaism', in section 5, chapter 3.) But the discussion below of two groups of women, both Sunni, Afghan and Baluch tribal women and urban Arab women, reveals common themes.

The role of women in tribal ideology among the Afghan and Baluch is a central one. Ideally women are conceptualized in terms of two opposite and polar types. On the one hand is *mor*, the mother, with emotive echoes from the sayings of the Prophet of Islam. On the other hand, where her chastity has been compromised and the honour of her close agnatic kin – father, husband or brothers – is at stake, she is considered in a state of *tor* (Pukhto) or *siah* (Baluch), literally black. Black symbolizes the colour of death, evil and negativity while white symbolizes purity and goodness. Empirically, *tor* cases almost always approximate to the ideal where both actors, but especially the woman, are killed by the closest male kin.

Among certain tribes in Baluchistan suicide is still the swift answer to compromise of honour. The woman has no other option. She will not be provided with food or shelter by the tribe. A woman accused of compromising her honour will quietly, without fuss, tie a rope around her neck and to the low, single beam of her tent and hang herself. Baluch tents are low and she must bend her knees in order to hang. Extraordinary courage and will power are required to face the excruciating ordeal. The act reveals the helplessness of women and the strength of tribal custom.

While *tor* cases approximate to tribal ideology the actual *mor* deviates considerably from the ideal. Women may be idealized as *mor* or mother, implying high status and position in society, but their daily lot is a hard, monotonous and exhausting one. Women cook meals, clean the house, collect water, feed and milk animals, besides performing other normal duties such as caring for children, etc. During the agricultural seasons they help in harvesting and threshing crops.

Chastity and seclusion of women are rigidly observed by society. The penalty for deviance is extreme. They are secluded from social life. They rarely, if ever, go to the market. Men shop and provide household necessities. Women usually visit only their own near relatives. If women frequent a path to a well, it becomes 'private' or 'women's path'. Men are supposed to avoid using it especially during the hours women use it.

The family is acutely conscious that 'a female belongs to another (her husband)' and is therefore a 'temporary visitor' in the home. Patriarchs rarely remember the names or the number of female descendants from married daughters; they simply do not exist or count in the social universe. Even their names are 'lost' and are 'anonymous', they are referred to as 'house' or 'family' or simply 'woman'. Once married they maintain little connection with their natal kin and are tradition-bound to defend and uphold their husband's honour even to the extent of killing their own male relatives.

The position of women is best summed up in the Pukhto proverb 'For a woman either the house (*kor*) or the grave (*gor*).' Many tribesmen admit in private that the life of a woman is hard: 'The lot of women is miserable, they are helpless.' Her main role in life appears to be to serve her husband and is summed up in another proverb: 'Husband is another name for God.' As a Baluch woman put it succinctly: 'You know what rights a woman has among us Marris. She has the right to eat crap. That's all' (R. Pehrson, *The Social Organization of the Marri Baluch*, 1966).

Women are excluded from traditional and central prestige-conferring institutions such as the council of elders, the village guest rooms, the war party or the sectional clan chieftanship. Worse, their legitimate Islamic rights are denied them.

The following customs embody tribal concepts and clash with Islamic ones. They are tacitly maintained although widely condemned. The un-Islamic custom of 'money for the head' (*sar paisey* in Pukhto) or 'bride-price' for the girl is condemned by older and younger men alike, and is slowly but steadily losing hold. Anthropologists working in Africa suggested 'bride-wealth' as an alternative term to 'bride-price' as the latter, crudely put, implies buying and selling. However, in the Pukhtun and Baluch areas the more appropriate term would still be 'bride-price' because daughters are literally bought and sold. The bride's father takes a sum – 20 to 40,000 rupees for an average marriage – for the girl from the groom's family, usually the father. The price depends on a variety of factors such as the girl's beauty, age, lineage, status and whether she was previously married or not. The re-marriage of widows does not involve bride-price. Ideally the father is supposed to re-invest the money as part of the dowry but he rarely does so. Recently there is a tendency to divert some of the 'bride-price' into making clothes, furniture or jewellery for the bride, especially among groups more exposed to education.

Bride-prices were low a century ago. 'A man wanting a hard-working, useful wife could easily procure an Afridi or Orakzai woman for a sum varying from rupees 150 to 200,' noted the Kohat District Gazetteer of 1883–4.

Pukhtun elders relate the following anecdote which illustrates why bride-price is expected and taken. A father married his daughter 'free' and when the bridal party was returning home a stream had to be crossed. The husband made his new bride wade across it. The girl was furious and rebuked the groom, saying he had no respect for her. The husband agreed: 'You were given free to me. You cost me nothing.' So she returned home promptly to her father who then charged a bride-price. This time the husband arranged for her to be carried in a litter over the stream.

Another tribal custom derives from mothers 'booking' a girl at birth. The 'word' is given and accepted as such by the community. The 'booking' by the boy's mother of a new-born girl is tantamount to the formal engagement. Henceforth the girl is considered engaged and as good as married to the boy. She has no say in the matter. Violation of this verbal and informal agreement involves the entire revenge and *tor* sequence as if the girl were actually married.

Contrary to Islamic law the agreed rights of a woman in the event of divorce, *haq mehr*, are not mentioned by either party, let alone claimed. Yet another deviance from Islamic tradition is that the formal marriage ceremony, *nikah*, is performed after the bride is brought from her natal home to the groom's house. Implicit in the custom is the reflection of the lower status of the 'girl-giver' and the general status of women. Once at the groom's house the bride is in no position to refuse consent to the marriage. Most tribesmen are married like this. Although a woman has the right to divorce her husband under Islamic law, this is a social impossibility in tribal society. If she is divorced legally and married to another man she would be considered as having become *tor* and both would run the risk of being killed; the question of rights in divorce cases therefore remains hypothetical.

In theory women stand in low status but in practice many women exert considerable influence on, and even dominate, their men. They are often close and valued companions, directly affecting at all generational levels – mother, wife, daughter – the lives of their men. In one of the tribal settlements where I conducted anthropological fieldwork, among the Mohmand tribe which straddles Afghanistan and Pakistan (*Pukhtun Economy and Society*, 1980), an elder was a broken man when his wife died. He was about 80 years old, otherwise tough and invulnerable. For days on end he would not eat. He would cry like a child at the slightest provocation. Sitting in the *hujra* he would repeat that his life was over, finished. Those around him, representing various lineages and groups, would nod their heads in agreement that his wife was like a mother to all of them. The cause of her death heightened the sense of tragedy. The elder's son had brought pesticides for the sugar-cane crop from the agricultural department. His mother, thinking it was medicine for her as she was ill at the time, drank it and died within an hour. The village elders rushed her to the nearest dispensary. There was no one on duty. They then hoped to save her life by taking her to the hospital in Peshawar, but she died in the bus. The elder was inconsolable. He constantly said, 'I'm ruined', and that until this time, at 80, he could work 'harder and better' than his sons and grandsons, but now no longer had the will power to carry on. He said he had married his wife, who was 15 years younger than himself, some fifty years ago and she was like a friend, adviser and comrade to him. In a similar situation, again during my fieldwork, another elder's wife, an old and trusted companion, died. He suddenly seemed to have lost the will to live and passed away within two weeks of her death.

The answer to why women, a group so obviously suppressed, are among the strongest supporters of tribal ideology lies partly in their insecurity. The stability and continuity of tribal life provides them with a balance, a rhythm, a security in an otherwise harsh and oppressive environment. To maintain this security and respect in society they must live up to the ideal concept of a woman, a concept conceived by and for men. *Tor* and *mor*, the binary and opposing types of tribal womanhood, conceptualize two forms of oppression from which there appears to be no immediate escape.

Arab city women

City life brings with it different kinds of problems for women: expensive living, polluted air, constant noise and over-crowded apartments. Crowded rooms create the conditions for one of the least written about and most complex relationships, incest. El Saadawi deploys her case material to describe how the incestuous relationship develops:

> The only female whom a young boy or man can probably find within easy reach is therefore his young sister. In most homes she will be sleeping in the adjoining bed, or even by his side in the same bed. His hand will start touching her while she is asleep, or even awake. In any case it does not make much difference since, even when awake, she cannot stand up to her elder brother because of fear of his authority which is consecrated by custom and law, or fear of the family, or as a result of a deep-seated feeling of guilt arising from the fact that she may be experiencing some pleasure under the touches of his hand, or because she is only a child, not able to understand exactly what is happening to her.

Saadawi concludes and warns us:

> Most people think that such incidents are rare or unusual. The truth of the matter is that they are frequent, but remain hidden, stored up in the secret recesses of the female child's self, since she dare not tell anyone of what has happened to her; neither will the man ever think of admitting what he has done.

In a chilling case-study the victim of incest talks of her childhood – chilling because the extended family with its central character, the pious bearded grandfather, is so familiar. The chapter is called, appropriately, 'The grandfather with bad manners':

> 'I remember that I was five years old when my mother used to take me to visit her family. They lived in a big rambling house in the district of Zeitoun near Heliopolis [in Cairo]. My mother used to spend the time talking and laughing with her mother and sisters while I played with the children of the family. The house was full with the merry clamour of voices until the moment when the door bell rang, announcing the arrival of my grandfather. Immediately voices became hushed, my mother would speak in low tones, and the children would disappear. My grandmother then tiptoed to my grandfather's room where she would help him to remove his clothes and shoes, standing in front of him silently with lowered head.
>
> Like the rest of the family, whether elders or children, I feared my grandfather and never played or laughed in his presence. But after lunch, while older people were having their siesta, he would call me in a voice that was a little less harsh than usual: "Come, let us pick some flowers from the garden." When we reached the far corner of the garden, his voice would become as gentle as that of my grandmother, and he would ask me to sit by his side on the wooden bench, facing the bed of roses. He would hand me a few red and yellow flowers and when I became engrossed in their petals and colours, seat me on his lap, and start caressing

> me or singing to me until I closed my eyes like one going to sleep. But I never fell asleep, because each time I could feel his hand creeping tenderly and stealthily under my clothes, and his finger disappearing to a hidden spot under my knickers.'

The violation of her privacy by the senior-most member of her family created ambiguous feelings in the child:

> 'I was only five years old, but somehow I realized that what my grandfather was doing was wrong and immoral, and that if my mother found out, she would be angry with me and would scold me. I understood vaguely that I probably should have jumped off my grandfather's knees and refused to go with him into the garden when he called me.
>
> Other ideas occurred to me. Even though only five years old, the feeling that I was not a well-mannered child grew on me, for I used to remain seated on his knees instead of jumping off. Furthermore I derived some pleasure from the movements of his hand beneath my underclothes. When he heard my mother's voice calling me, he would hastily draw away his hand, shake me as though he was waking me up from my sleep and say: "Your mother is calling you." I used to open my eyes as though waking from sleep and run to my mother with the open face that a small child of five is wont to have. She would ask me: "Where were you?" And I would answer with the innocent tones of a child: "With grandfather in the garden."
>
> She would feel relaxed and secure the moment she learned that I had been with my grandfather in the garden. She used to caution me against going down into the garden alone, and never tired of repeating her warning about "that man", the gardener, who wore a flowing robe and used to spray water over the flowers, which led me to fear not only the gardener but even the water drops that used to fill the air from his can.'

The grandfather would slip back into the posture of respectability once he had finished with his granddaughter:

> 'Once my grandfather had climbed the stairs back into the house, he would put on his usual personality once more, the personality that all feared including myself. The yellow prayer beads would start slipping through his fingers. In my imagination I almost came to believe that the grandfather that used to caress me in the garden was not the grandfather who sat at the table, and whom I feared. Sometimes I even used to think I had two grandfathers.'

Incest, precisely because it involves the deepest family secret and cannot be discussed, devastates the victim. Guilt, depression and bitterness remain throughout life. And society has little sympathy or patience with the victim, as El Saadawi discovered in this case from Cairo:

> Among the cases that I examined during my research study on women and neurosis was that of a young female doctor who had just graduated. She had been engaged and then married to one of her colleagues. On the marriage night her husband discovered that she was not a virgin. She explained to him that she had lost her virginity while still a child and that her father was the culprit. But her husband was unable to take the shock in his stride and divorced her. The young woman returned to her parents' home. She was unable to tell her mother the truth out of fear for the father. The good woman accused her of being perverted and the father zealously joined in, heaping blame upon his daughter. The girl, at her wits' end, wept and finally confessed to her mother all that had happened. In turn the poor woman, exposed to the terrible shock of finding out what her husband had done, almost collapsed. The father, however, accused his daughter of lying and beat her savagely. She was seized with a nervous breakdown which the father used to his advantage. He accused the girl of being insane and sent her off to a hospital for mental disease. The psychiatrist in charge of the case put his trust in the father's story and refused to believe the girl. The result was that she ended up by losing not only her integrity and honour, the man who was her husband, and her whole future, but also her reason, since for some people at least she was now considered mentally unbalanced.

Although these cases may be unusual it is obvious that in the city or in the tribe women have a long way to go before they recover the respect and confidence that the Islamic ideal implies.

Thwarted ideal: the dilemma of women in Islam

The problems facing women in Islam are not simply women's issues. They involve both sexes, males feeling most vulnerable through their women. The problem of women must therefore be seen as directly relating to the entire society and not just the concern of women. Together men and women must chart a course for the future.

For Muslim women the answer is not to be found in the aggressive Western Women's Lib stance. Maimuna Quddus reviewing El Saadawi's book *Two Women in One* (1985) wrote: 'Anyone who has read the journals of the so-called women's liberation movement in England, for which Dr Saadawi often writes, will be taken aback by the descriptions of matters once considered sacred, in a style more appropriate to graffiti on a lavatory wall!' (*Muslim World Book Review*, 7, no. 1. 1986). These feminists 'wish to destroy the family, religion and society with their calls for free sex, lesbianism, Marxism and whichever other fashionable lunacies they fancy.' If the answer is not in Western society it is apparently not in the other extreme position of the subjugated, suffering, invisible Muslim wife who faces 'cruelty as assault, unequal pay, forced marriage and the like' (*Ibid.*). The situation is complex; the ideal pointing one way, the actual showing another. Paradoxes and contradictions abound.

The position of women among the very rich (Saudis) and the very poor (Hyderabadis) appears to be weak. They were conspicuous by their absence in discussions of these societies (chapter 8). They are slightly better off in middle-level income countries like Egypt, Iran and Pakistan. Women have helped to shape policy here (Jehan Sadat, Farah Diba, Miss Fatimah Jinnah respectively). In these countries there is some awareness of their problems; all the Muslim women social scientists we cited above are from these countries. In Pakistan women have been governors and ambassadors. In these countries they are also important political challengers to some of the most powerful military dictators of the age. Miss Jinnah led the opposition against Field Marshal Ayub Khan and Miss Benazir Bhutto challenges General Zia-ul-Haq in Pakistan. Mrs Hasina Wajid and Khalida Zia spear-head the campaign against General Ershad in Bangla Desh.

Women, notably the Shia, continue to be in the forefront of Islamic practice and ritual and among its staunchest believers in spite of being deprived of their Islamic rights. Piety and faith are not the preserve of men. Women reformers argue for rights within Islam, not a rejection of Islam. Tribal women, illiterate, deprived of economic rights, often brutally exploited, feel relatively more secure in their known, stable, unchanging tribal ways than the better-off and more educated urban women. Overwhelming arrogance and frequent blatant anti-feminism may characterize Muslim males publicly but at home mothers exert wide-reaching influence and most males are as gentle as kittens to their children.

Another paradox: although Muslim polygamy has been reduced to a caricature and is universally used as a stick with which to beat Islam, its incidence is rather low – 1 to 2 per cent. Concubines and harems are the characteristics of kings and courts, not exclusively Islamic ones. Confronted with a barren wife, or large numbers of widowed women due to war, the Quran made provision – 'marry as many women as you wish, two or three or four.' But this was not a licence for lust. Indeed the conditions were so severe, even improbable, that each wife be treated equally, that many religious scholars argue polygamy is not permissible. 'If you fear not to treat them equally, marry only one. Indeed you will not be able to be just between your wives even if you try,' says the Quran itself.

Few Muslim women outside the urban areas may want to behave like Western women. The sexually exploitative element remains high in the West, however strident the rhetoric of sexual equality. Perhaps this is best illustrated by the well-known cigarette ad depicting a woman smoking: 'You've come a long way, baby.' The message is clear: you too may now die of cancer through smoking. The high rate of divorce and sexual disease are common consequences of the reckless drive to equate the sexes and 'free' sexual relationships. Comparisons may mean little outside the cultural context but it is important to point out that until a hundred years ago Western women had virtually no rights in law or practice. Over a thousand years before the first European woman suffragette Islam gave far-reaching rights and a defined status to women. But the Western campaign has undoubtedly helped to stimulate discussions of the problem in Muslim urban society thereby revealing the gap between the talk of the Islamic ideal and the actual situation of women.

The case of Afghan and Baluch women tells us something of women in other Muslim tribal societies like the Berbers of Morocco or the Bedouin of North Africa and the Middle East. Trapped in local tribal codes and customs they are unable to take advantage of their Islamic rights. The Islamic ideal remains blurred, half-understood and out-of-reach. To simplify: the gap between the Little Tradition of tribal culture and the Great Tradition of Islam is widest in their case. It may be less yawning in the urban areas but the gains are at the cost of the sense of security – however false it may be – that tribal society provides.

We saw the active role of women in early Muslim society (chapters 2 and 3) and during the great Muslim empires (chapter 4). The long colonial period perverted and distorted the role and image of women. Recovery is painfully slow and in many Muslim societies not clear: women are reviled, beaten, divorced and deprived of their Islamic rights with impunity.

The damage caused by the colonial era needs first to be recognized and then repaired. Granting a few seats in Parliament or extra girls' schools is window dressing. It will only marginally improve the lot of women. The fundamental problems will not change. Until the Islamic confidence – which presupposes universal respect for knowledge and human beings of all sexes – is restored in society the plight of women will not improve.

Only with wide-spread education, which must be enthusiastically supported by males in both city and tribe, will Muslim women be able to move meaningfully towards the ideal. Only then will contemporary Muslim women take their rightful place in society – and the Prophet's saying about paradise lying at the feet of the mother assume meaning and relevance.

3 AFGHAN REFUGEES: DISPLACEMENT AND DESPAIR

In December 1986 was the seventh anniversary of the Russians entering Afghanistan. As a result of those events almost 3 million refugees fled to neighbouring Iran and Pakistan. In Pakistan the refugee problem is assuming serious proportions for hosts and guests. Over both hangs the question of the future of the refugees.

Returning to the scene of a great tragedy is not easy; it is more difficult when the tragedy is not over. On a visit to Peshawar, after a year abroad, I talked with Afghans involved in various degrees with the problems of their country.

Waiting for victory

Javed, whom I had last met a year ago as a boy of fourteen, appeared older, more in command of himself. There was a hint of new-found strength in him. Javed talked of his father who had disappeared since his last incursion into Afghanistan as a guerilla fighter. Deep inside Javed was a conviction that perhaps something had gone wrong. His new maturity attempted to hide his unease. He had a mother and three sisters to worry about now. The honour of his women – a cardinal feature of the Afghan moral and social code – was his new anxiety. He was still too young to cope with this responsibility. It was a chilling awareness of a new pain. His pain touched me, but I had nothing to offer. For me he symbolized the Afghan resistance – and the Afghan tragedy.

Exile diminishes anyone. Yet to many Afghan refugees Pakistan is historically a second home. Culturally and ecologically they are in familiar surroundings. Peshawar and Quetta are cities familiar to many Afghans. Their exile is therefore partial and complex.

The refugees feel that they may be in Pakistan for an indefinite period. Mud and brick rooms are replacing tents in the refugee camps. Aza Khel, a few miles from Peshawar, is perhaps the most famous camp because it is on the itinerary for foreign dignitaries. Aza Khel has the appearance of a permanent, well-organized bustling little town. Pakistan, too, appears to have resigned itself to this idea. Opposite Aza Khel, on the other side of the Grand Trunk Road, government has recently built gigantic godowns to hold wheat and other commodities.

It is a paradox of the Afghan situation that the 'Pukhtunistan' problem has been unceremoniously killed, not by political machinations but as a result of the refugee situation. 'Pukhtunistan', Afghan propaganda once claimed, would be a homeland for the Pukhtun tribes of Pakistan and eastern Afghanistan. The idea was rooted in the memory of Afghan conquerors who once ruled the Peshawar valley up to the river Indus before the British came. Now the

Afghans are in Peshawar but not as conquerors, and those Pakistanis who toyed with the 'Pukhtunistan' idea in the Peshawar valley are showing signs of impatience with their guests. As a result of the 300,000 refugees in Peshawar prices have risen sharply. Accommodation is difficult to find and competition for cultivated land heightens local resentment. But this does not detract from the struggle in Afghanistan.

'How is the fighting in Afghanistan?' I asked Javed and his friends. The answer was not simple. Both adversaries are learning from and adapting to each other. The classic Afghan strategy of capturing the heights to stop an enemy, so successful against the British, is proving ineffective. The Russian helicopter gunships simply fly in from behind to attack and dislodge the snipers. The Afghans have learned not to destroy captured Russian equipment as they did in the early days of the conflict. Now they cannibalize tanks, for instance, and use the parts with an ingenuity born of adversity.

The fight in Afghanistan is also linked with a larger global pattern, Javed explained. 'If', he said, 'we are getting weapons we need from Egypt the death of one man there – Sadat – affects our supplies.' Not for the first time in history an Afghan war was becoming part of a Great Game in world politics.

Two inter-linked themes appeared strongly in Javed's talk: the determination to return home and the realization that the path home will not be easy. The realization of his refugee status, the greater convulsions in his life, the struggle for the future, had pushed a bewildered young boy prematurely into adulthood. He was consumed by the desire to return – and the need for restoring honour. 'We have a saying,' he told me, 'an Afghan took revenge after a hundred years and said, "I took it too quickly".' Javed was already filling his father's shoes.

Suspended lives

For Pakistanis the problem really stems from the type of refugees the Afghans are. They are swaggering, armed and aggressive. Their bearing adds to their historical image of themselves as conquering warriors. They are quite unlike the refugees who came to Pakistan from India in 1947 and the Biharis from Bangla Desh in 1971. Those refugees, their lives permanently broken, their destinations unknown, were grateful to accept whatever they could get. In any case the Afghans do not accept their own role as guests passively.

'This land', Afghans aver, 'was conquered by our ancestor Ahmad Shah Abdali.' Indeed, Ahmad Shah the first king of modern Afghanistan, ruled most of what is now Pakistan in the eighteenth century. Never known for their fear of trespassing south of the Khyber Pass – India has been ruled by five or six Afghan dynasties – they do not feel trespassers. Pakistanis, especially those in the Punjab and Sind who are unacquainted with Pukhtun history, find this kind of assertiveness grating. They would like to see more gratitude, perhaps even some humility, on the part of their guests.

On their *hijra* into Pakistan Afghans were received as fellow Muslims and, equally important, fellow tribesmen. The government set up one of the most successful refugee organizations of the world. They were given a tent, subsistence allowances and, most critical of all for refugees, hope. But there was a price of a sort. They became part of an international argument in geo-politics. Their private agony was put on display. They played a part in the circus arranged for VIP visitors to Pakistan, mimicking anger and swearing revenge. From Princess Anne to Kirk Douglas celebrities applauded them and had photographs taken in their camps. One of Pakistan's major foreign policy planks – and strengths – became the presence of the Afghan refugees.

Among the refugees there is a painful survival of the fittest process at work. Afghans have muscled into various enterprises such as trucking and selling cloth from Peshawar down to Karachi. Some have reverted to more customary employment. Their tribal networks, crossing international boundaries, allow them also to traffic in banned weapons and drugs.

The anarchy that is revolution, a world turned inside out, is reflected in the camps. Families are dispossessed, their unity shattered. Young men disappear in turns to fight the holy war, *jihad*, in Afghanistan. Women and children wait. Squalor and despair are evident. More important, the kaleidoscope of traditional patterns has been shaken: leadership, women and even children are affected. New voices are being heard, new values are emerging. Afghan society will never be the same again. Perhaps also affected will be their reputation as invincible warriors, the Jacks who slay giants in the shape of super-powers.

The Afghan are reacting in a traditional manner to the crisis. There is talk of Islam and *jihad*, also of raids, revenge and guns – the stuff of Pukhtunwali. There is a great deal of rhetoric. But it is mimicry. Their mock aggressiveness and mock fanaticism have become a substitute for substance, serious thinking and concerted action. The clarity of their political vision remains obstructed by petty squabbles and personal jealousies. Repeatedly the major half-dozen parties have failed to unite. Recently their mutual animosity has resulted in expulsion orders from Peshawar. Their attempts to blow up rivals with explosives were making Pakistanis in the Frontier Province nervous. These Afghans do not quite fit the romantic mould of the dashing tribesmen in *Kim* or *The Far Pavilions*, created by the novelists of the British Raj.

The romantic image of the Pukthun was that of a fearless, blue-eyed, hawk-nosed warrior silhouetted, with his *jezail*, on a mountain ridge. Heroic deeds from the past littered the barren land. Caroe, one of the last British governors of the Frontier Province, supported the image in his popular book, *The Pathans* (see chapter 7). Some years before his death he confided to me that writers like the two of us, who lived and worked in the Frontier Province, were partly responsible for this image. Indeed, he could only think of one or two examples–Wali Khan, for instance–of those who approximated to the ideal. The actuality did not match the ideal. It needed a test, a jolt, to be exposed. One victim of the Afghan crisis may well be the romantic image of the Pukhtun warrior.

In contrast to the Pukhtuns who were expected to perform well, the performance of non-Pukhtuns has been notable. The best known resistance fighter, Ahmad Shah Massoud of Panjshir valley fame, is not a Pukhtun.

However depleted, the Afghans have extracted a high price from the enemy: three heads of government assassinated, 3 million refugees living outside national borders, and a state of civil war in the country.

The world whose capacity for concentration is infantile has grown indifferent to the sufferings of the Afghan refugees. It seeks its news of tragedy with morbid fickleness elsewhere: a famine in Somalia last year, a religious riot in India in the summer, an ethnic massacre in Sri Lanka in the spring. Had it not been for the efforts of the State Department in Washington in keeping the Afghan issue alive, for the sake of their own Great Game with the Soviets, perhaps this interest would have been further weakened.

Revenge and honour – the core themes of Pukhtun folklore – still sound in the village *hujras* where men sit in discussion. But the Pukhtun code has become a burden. The world has moved swiftly for the Afghans and the tribal code appears bankrupt in dealing with their problems. Behind the vitality which shines in the eyes of young Afghan children in the camps there are flashes of grief. There is a growing neurotic uncertainty about the future for the elders, an uncertainty which is contagious for Pakistanis.

In the trans-Indus provinces of Pakistan, Baluchistan and the Frontier, people wait. They wait for dramatic solutions to seemingly insoluble problems, and in their despair they have nothing but traditions, including proverbs, to cling to. The Afghans still have time – 93 years – to take revenge. This raises a host of questions for apprehensive Pakistanis: will this period be spent in Pakistan and if so will the refugees become permanent residents? and how will the presence of thousands of battle-trained armed Afghans affect life in Pakistan? and will the enemies of Pakistan use the refugees as part of a Trojan Horse strategy? The answers have wide-ranging social and political implications for Central and South Asian Muslim societies.

10

The reconstruction of Muslim thought

The age of the complete Islamic man, the scholar and traveller, was long over in the Muslim world; the age of mediocrity had begun. The *alim*, scholar, would be reduced to the *babu*, the clerk, myopic and self-righteous; a legacy of the European empire. The scholar would become a bigot and the saint an introvert, and this in spite of the central position of *ilm*, knowledge, in the ideal. Muslim society in the twentieth century has still to emerge from the ravages of colonialism. Henceforth, a scholar, saint or ruler would tend to work within his own defined arena reflecting the caste and class system of European imperialism. They would condemn each other with shrill voices employing sterile labels taken from Western scholarship and Orientalists.

1 CONTEMPORARY MUSLIM SCHOLARSHIP

Western Orientalists perceive in Muslim scholarship and their society two distinct, contradictory and exclusive alternatives – 'Westernized modernists' or 'traditional fundamentalists' – a lead followed somewhat uncritically by Muslim scholars themselves. The former are seen as 'liberal', 'humanist', 'progressive', and by implication the 'good guys'. The latter are 'fanatic', 'retrogressive' and the 'bad guys'. The application of these Western labels best suited for political analysis in Western democracies could be misleading in the Muslim world. Both are authentic expressions of their time – not unlike the two opposed forms that emerged in South Asia in the seventeenth century when the crisis was upon Muslim society (chapter 4). But the Western labels do not take into account the complex and dynamic interplay of local religious, cultural and ethnic factors. Such simplistic labels cannot satisfactorily illuminate the complexity of Islam; they may aid in obfuscating it.

The chasm between positions defined by modernist and traditionalist, freely translated as left and right in the Muslim world, is wide. Positions taken are extreme. There is no dialogue, no wish to listen to the other side. The argument is divided into black and white. Debates are not about issues and ideas. They degenerate into a crude exhibition of self-righteousness. The intolerance is brittle. The hysteria in society breaks easily from beneath the surface revealing the bankruptcy of thought in Muslim society.

Missing the side of Islam which is applied to social issues, many Muslim intellectuals are tempted to reject it altogether, There has thus developed a leftist tradition in the social sciences among Muslims. Professors Talal Asad and Hamza Alavi, both living and working in English universities, represent this tradition. On the other hand, Professors Khurshid Ahmad in Pakistan and Ismail al-Faruqi in the USA represent the Islamic tradition in the social sciences. Of note in this tradition, also, are some younger scholars such as Professors Kemal Oke in Istanbul, Anis Ahmad in Islamabad and Kamal Hassan in Kuala Lumpur. Unfortunately there is little interaction or dialogue between the two positions. What is needed is a synthesis. Professor Ali Shariati in Iran showed us one way. Perhaps Shariati, the activist sociologist-anthropologist, best symbolizes Ismail al-Faruqi's contention that today the Muslim social scientist must be included in the *ulema*.

While presenting some ideas from this book in a seminar chaired by Dr M. Afzal, General Zia's Minister for Education, stimulation came from an unexpected quarter. When I cited Hassan al-Banna – Muslims with the Quran in one hand and the *sunna* in the other – the Minister interjected, quite loudly for all to hear, 'And a blank in the middle.' Later, he explained. The holy Quran exhorted Muslims to think, to use their mind, something they had abrogated. 'We complain of freedom of speech but we are ourselves cowards,' he said ('Muslim society as seen by a social scientist,' by M. Yasin, *Pakistan Times*, 28 January 1985).

The poverty of Muslim education

In Muslim society figures for literacy and intellectual activity are not encouraging. The total number of PhDs in Pakistan, one of the largest Muslim nations – 100 million people – is about 400. Leading the Muslim world in Islamization, Pakistan's educational statistics are appalling: 8 per cent of its population are educated up to primary, 2 per cent secondary and 0.02 per cent university level, according to Dr M. Afzal (official statistics are 'padded' and inflated). 'O My Lord! Advance me in Knowledge,' the Quran had appealed.

The following little gem tells us of Islam and education at one of Pakistan's leading schools from a letter written in 1985 by a young boy to his father:

> All the periods were boring except maths. It was our last period, ten minutes were left for holiday, and suddenly a boy stood and quickly said, 'Sir, earthquake.' As he said this I stood and was about to run when our

> teacher said, 'Sit and don't move, God will help,' because he was an Islamyat teacher. I protested and said, 'Sir, please take us out.' The Sir said, 'Why?' I said, 'Because the building might fall.' The Sir said, 'No, if the time has come for death then we will die.' I did not listen to him but ran out of class, after one second the whole school ran out. It was quite a long earthquake. One of our teachers ran as fast as he could when he heard about the earthquake.

The Islamyat teacher had forgotten the Prophet's saying 'have faith in Allah but tie the feet of your camel.' Fortunately there are still students – and teachers – of sense left in spite of the devastation wrought in education in the name of Islam.

An entire generation has come of age since independence from the European masters. We may ask how many academics of world stature have we produced in Pakistan? The answer is almost none. Professor Abdus Salam on his return from England as a young scientist was offered about twenty dollars a month to work in Pakistan. He was pointedly encouraged to seek employment abroad. Later, after he won the Nobel Prize, Pakistan claimed him. One can only conjecture as to how many Abdus Salams the education system in Pakistan has suffocated or expelled.

A barren, stifling mediocrity hangs over intellectual endeavour. The endeavour is monopolized by the professor and the bureaucrat, and the two are often interchangeable. Platitudes, clichés and plagiarism mark their work. Their problems are genuine. No incentives for innovative work, bureaucratic interference, low salaries, political pressure and departmental jealousies discourage movement toward excellence. The absence of research facilities retards scholarship. Trade journals are hard to come by. The number of copies of *MAN*, anthropology's foremost academic journal, could be counted on the fingers of one hand in Pakistan. Furthermore, strikes, the closure of universities for indefinite periods, and the general air of apathy discourage scholarship. Language presents peculiar difficulties: a Pakistani may speak a provincial language at home, use Urdu for his official work, English – of the Pakistani variety – on his files and a smattering of Arabic for religious purposes. The mix discourages innovative or even standard work. The bright sparks are spotted early and either chased or snuffed out. Abdus Salam, it can be easily argued, is a product not of Pakistan but of Western universities.

Blaming world conspiracies – the Jewish lobby or the Hindu conspiracy – is the easy way out. The fact remains that there is little status accorded to academic work. While corrupt business tycoons and government servants live a life of ease and even luxury, a glance at the appearance of writers and poets and the way they live is instructive. They die by the dozen in the most degrading conditions of poverty. Their payments are ludicrous: ten dollars for an article, five for a poem. And this is not a recent development. The letters of Mirza Ghalib and Muhammad Iqbal, one begging the Nawab of Rampur for 50 rupees and the other the Nawab of Bhopal for 500 to pay for his wife's illness, make sad reading. *Ilm*, so highly placed in Islam, has been relegated by society and by government to a low place.

The expenditure on education compared to that set aside for buying tanks and fighter planes in most Muslim countries would be revealing. Two things would become apparent: the priorities within the country and the general paranoia of the rulers in relation to often imagined threats.

Some of the complexes engendered by colonialism return when confronting European or American academics; it is the lingering influence of Macaulay's Minute. *The Muslim*, in its editorial of 24 November 1983, noted:

> At the launching ceremony of Dr Akbar Ahmed's book titled *Religion and Politics in Muslim Society* held in Islamabad on Saturday, observations made by speakers on the occasion had been thought provoking. It is a sad commentary on our response to literary activities of our own countrymen that little official recognition is accorded to them.

The editors concluded:

> With perhaps a lingering hang-over of our colonial past, it appears that most of us have yet not been able to grow out of the illusion that British or American authors are intellectually far superior to our own countrymen howsoever accomplished. After more than three decades of our independence, we are still inclined to extend VIP treatment to men of letters from the West, welcome them to write on our country, and provide them with all facilities to travel around at state cost and hob-nob with the highest in the land. While Pakistanis can seldom venture to write about such areas as the country's Armed Forces, or produce books on provinces plagued with a sense of deprivation, even these sensitive subjects are not taboo for foreign writers.

There are other, perhaps more serious problems, than grappling with theoretical academic issues which face the Muslim scholar. Once Muslim scholars could escape uncomfortable political situations by moving from one country to another. Language, Arabic, was universal and the notion of the *ummah* well developed. A Muslim could be honoured away from his birth place. Our two social scientists, Al Beruni and Ibn Khaldun, were honoured far from their homes. During the Muslim empires people of talent flocked to Istanbul or Delhi from distant homes irrespective of sect and kinship. In contemporary Muslim society the treatment meted out to artists and writers can be shabby and ungenerous.

It is no coincidence that three of the most influential Muslim reformer-scholars of this century – Hassan al-Banna, Imam Khomeini and Maulana Mawdoodi – worked under extreme pressure from other Muslims in their own societies. Attempts were made to frustrate their efforts with every means possible including assassination. Al-Banna was actually killed, Khomeini escaped assassination and Mawdoodi survived a death sentence. Representing three distinct Muslim geographical and cultural zones – the Arab, Iranian and the South Asian – the examples serve to support the point generally for Muslim society.

Escape to the West

The intellectual or writer who is not appreciated in society today finds his avenues of escape and expression blocked. He may face a blanket silence at home. A notable example was the official indifference in Pakistan to Faiz Ahmed Faiz – the most famous Urdu poet after Iqbal and winner of the Lenin Prize – during the last years of his life. In Iran the intellectual may face extinction. Persecuted at home, scholars have found refuge in the West, the USA and UK. Muslim scholars comfortably absorbed abroad include Hamza Alavi, Khalid bin Sayeed and Fazlur Rahman, to take Pakistani examples. A loss for Muslim society is a gain for the Western world.

It is not surprising to find, therefore, the most prolific Muslim scholar-activists living in the West. A combination of being pushed out from their countries and pulled in by the West is responsible. Among these are Professors (the late) Ismail al-Faruqi (Palestinian) at Temple University, Muhsin Mahdi (Iraqi) and Nur Yalman (Turk) at Harvard, Dr Z. Bedawi (Egyptian) in London, and Dr Hameedullah (of Hyderabad; see chapter 8, section 2) in Paris.

Western societies are more stimulating and attractive for Muslim scholars to live in, Dr Hameedullah explained to me. Ascetic and active, although about eighty, with his *karakuli* (fur hat), and beard he looks unmistakably Muslim. Yet he has never faced racial or religious discrimination in Europe. In Turkey, on the other hand, the *karakuli* was snatched from his head and thrown on the ground. The angry Turk saw it as a symbol of traditional Islam, associating it perhaps with the fez, once the hat of the Turks. In another incident, again in Turkey, he walked out of a hotel because the management made adverse comments about his appearance. Turkey's central obsession – the struggle between its Islamic and European identities – is clearly apparent (chapter 4) in Dr Hameedullah's encounters.

Western and Muslim society were compared by Dr Hameedullah in another story – to the detriment of the latter. He has a passion for collecting translations of the holy Quran. His collection includes 150 languages. Wishing for a translation of a Surah in Welsh he wrote to the two Imams of Cardiff. Repeated requests went unanswered. In desperation he wrote to the Lord Mayor of

Cardiff. An answer, with the translation, dated the same day as the receipt of the letter, arrived promptly.

This is not to say that there are no examples of extraordinary devotion to scholarship in the Muslim world. Professors Ba-Yunus and Farid Ahmad – critical of Ibn Khaldun (chapter 5) – rate Basharat Ali highly in *Islamic Sociology: An Introduction* (1985). Professor Ali has spent his life struggling to establish Islamic sociology in the indifferent milieu of Karachi. In 1983 I met him at the National Institute of Public Administration there. The Institute had organized a special course in social sciences for senior government officials in which I delivered three lectures. After hearing me Professor Ali, too old and frail to walk by himself, asked to be brought to the podium. 'I can now die in peace as I see the flame of Islam is burning brightly in my discipline,' he said, presenting me with his books on Islamic sociology. The unexpected and generous public gesture left me wordless.

As a response to the challenge for Islamic knowledge and an expression of the Islamic revivalism, Islamic academies and institutes have proliferated in the West. The ones in Pennsylvania, London, Cambridge (England), and Leicester are most active. Unfortunately they are centred around one man of learning and dedication. In spite of a general ideological and intellectual sympathy for each other they remain somewhat isolated from one another. There are, therefore, no schools or theoretical frames which are being developed; nor are young intellectuals, working under learned scholars, being groomed for scholarship. It is still too much of a hit or miss method.

It is interesting to note that the work of the centres is in English. These include the Islamic Cultural Centre, Regent's Park, London, The Islamic Academy, Cambridge, the International Institute of Islamic Thought, Pennsylvania, the Islamic Institute of Advanced Studies, Washington, and the Islamic Foundation in Leicester like its sister organization, the Institute of Policy Studies in Islamabad. In international conferences on Islam, whether in London or Kuala Lumpur, English is the main language of communication. Arabic is spoken almost exclusively by the Arabs. This is significant.

It is significant because it indicates that Muslim scholars are overcoming their fear of European languages created by the colonial period. Whatever its imperial connections English has emerged as the *lingua franca* of the world, and the position is not likely to change in the near future. English permits a vital connection with the world through university, media and government networks. We may talk of the Islamic world as an abstract unit; perhaps it does exist as an ideological entity. But there are barriers of culture, history and politics within this entity, as we saw in the last two chapters.

A question confronting these Islamic centres is: must Muslim scholarship reject non-Muslim works? for instance, the Greeks – in particular Socrates and Plato, from whom Muslims a thousand years ago gained so much? writers

– Shakespeare, Milton, Goethe, Tolstoy, Turgenev and Tagore? the Eastern philosophers – Kalidasa, Confucius and the Zen masters? The question is fundamental and needs an answer from the Islamic centres. These writers belong to humanity. They are not addressing a particular group or race. Their work enriches the human experience and celebrates its genius. The human expression of literature cannot be a threat to faith. It is a weak faith that is so easily swayed.

In whichever manner Muslims reject or deride the West certain facts have to be faced: the inventors of the modern age – Edison, Bell, Pasteur – and the scientists – Einstein, Von Neumann – are Western. The inventions which have revolutionized modern life – starting with the steam engine, electricity, the telephone, the motor car and going on to telecommunications and micro-chips – are all Western. The simplistic rejection of two of the important qualities in the West, liberal values (democracy, arts) and technology (science, medicine) is tragic for Muslims. It also ensures the increasing imbalance in the equation between an advanced West and Muslim society. Humanism and scientific knowledge are not exclusive properties of the West. Indeed they are to be found clearly embedded in the ideal of Islam. Understandably in the capitals of the West, among non-Muslims, Muslims, like the Egyptian scholar Muhammad Abduh, saw many of the Islamic virtues – piety, cleanliness, compassion, knowledge – 'I saw no Islam but many Muslims.' At home he despaired – 'I saw Islam but no Muslims.'

The death of a Muslim scholar

Ilm – knowledge – is at the core of Islam. The ideal Muslim spends his life in pursuit of *ilm*, even, as the Prophet suggested, going to China to seek it. Professor Ismail al-Faruqi went in the opposite direction, to the USA, in pursuit of *ilm*.

In his active life and intellectual output, Professor Faruqi combined the ingredients making for the ideal Muslim scholar. Man of action and ideas, he was in the tradition of Ibn Khaldun and Al Beruni. Perhaps he was numbered among the world's best known half-dozen Muslim scholars. *Arabia* (London) had him on its cover in July 1986 with the question 'Who killed the Faruqis?' and observed he 'had become a living symbol of Islamic resurgence in the United States'.

Professor Faruqi's life followed an interesting and, at one stage, almost Buddhist pattern of renunciation: he moved from a full and successful worldly life – he was the last Palestinian Governor of Galilee (1945–8) – to search for *ilm* at Al-Azhar, one of the oldest universities of the world, in Cairo. Later from his base in Temple University, where he headed the Islamic Studies Department, he embarked on the serious and gigantic task of re-thinking the fundamental concepts of modern social sciences within an Islamic framework.

He called it the 'Islamization of Knowledge'. This was his vision and it became his passion. Towards this end he helped set up the International Institute of Islamic Thought, and, recently, the Islamic Institute of Advanced Studies, both in the USA. (My name was placed on the faculty of the two Institutes thanks to him.) He organized various international conferences to assist further in the task. The fourth was scheduled for this year. His wife, also killed with him, was an indefatigable and loyal assistant. The last major book of the Faruqis, published by the Macmillan company shortly after their deaths, *The Cultural Atlas of Islam*, is a lavish, visual feast, with a substantial text.

Articles, books and editorials poured forth from his pen. His prodigious learning and industry spanned the Muslim world. He was a passionate advocate of his people, the Palestinians, and a powerful champion of Islam. Kings and commoners were among his friends.

I first met him when I was invited to the Institute for Advanced Study in Princeton in 1980–1. At our first meeting his warmth, sense of humour and moral earnestness impressed me. At dinner in his large and comfortable house, full of books and papers, where he was to be killed, we argued for hours, he wishing to persuade me to join him in the 'Islamization of Knowledge' by writing on Islamic anthropology for the Institute, I arguing that I was not yet equipped for it. In the early hours of the morning, in spite of fever, he insisted on driving me to Princeton. For the next few years our arguments would continue. In the end he prevailed. My book, *Toward Islamic Anthropology*, one of the first in the series, was published about the time of his death (the following section contains some of the ideas in it). For me the death assumed added poignancy. The book, to which he had contributed a foreword, was advertised in Western journals along with news of his death. He must have also received the manuscript of the present book just a few days before his death. Did he approve of its main arguments? What were his comments? I shall never know.

On hearing the news of his death I remained awake for many nights pondering on a number of urgent questions: is death by dagger the final destiny of a good Muslim – a destiny going back to the roots of Islam and established with the death of Umar, an ancestor of Faruqi? will Faruqi's task of 'Islamization of Knowledge' – 'the most important collective intellectual project in the contemporary Muslim world' (R. Abdul Wahab Boase, review of *Toward Islamic Anthropology*, in *Arabia*, January 1987) – now collapse? was the death premeditated? what is the extent of the loss to the Muslim world? The answers concern Muslims everywhere.

Reflecting the central importance of *ilm* in Islam the Prophet had said '*mawt al-alim, mawt al-alam*' – 'the death of a scholar is the death of the universe'. In memory of Professor Ismail al-Faruqi I offered the following lines (*Dawn* Magazine, 25 July 1986, Karachi):

On the death of Ismail Faruqi

There are many ways
to kill an Arab

you can shoot them down
in public places
or torture
them to insanity
in closed rooms
and call them terrorists

you can surround their villages –
making sure their women and children
are inside –
and use machine guns
until no one moves
and call the villages
Sabra and Shatilla

you can even enter
their safe university homes in the USA
with long, serrated – Rambo – knives,
pass the books written by the victim
pass the symbols of honour,
and stab until death occurs,
for good measure stab the family too
and call it the act of a black burglar.

As I said
there are many ways
to kill an Arab.

The problem is
ideas of freedom and revenge
do not die so easily,
they live on in these deaths –
and we call them martyrs

2 CREATING ISLAMIC SOCIAL SCIENCES

The Islamic urge for learning is strong and defined but Muslim scholarship is in a shambles. The bleakness of the academic situation demands the recreation of Muslim thought. With the scholars of Islam – the Al Berunis and Ibn Khalduns – went the lively Muslim mind interested in every aspect of the environment in which human beings lived. Ossified texts and ritualistic formulae now pass for Muslim scholarship. In particular the social sciences suffer. With their interest in social disorder they are either seen – erroneously – as Western or as an attempt to denigrate and criticize the *ummah*. The vacuum which has developed in the social sciences ensured what it set out to prevent: their domination by non-Muslim sources.

For contemporary Muslim scholars ideal Islamic scholarship rests on the following assumptions made by Professor S. A. Ashraf:

> Firstly, the Islamic concept of Man has the width and range no other concept of Man has. As Man can become Khalifatullah by cultivating or realizing within himself the attributes of God and as these attributes have a limitless dimension, Man's moral, spiritual and intellectual progress is potentially limitless. Secondly, as knowledge is the source of this progress and development, Islam does not put any bar to the acquisition of knowledge. Thirdly, the range of this acquisition must be all by acquiring an intellectual expertise; in isolation a person cannot maintain a balanced growth. Fourthly, the spiritual, moral, intellectual, imaginative, emotional and physical aspects of a man's personality are kept in view in establishing the interrelationship among the disciplines. Fifthly, the development of personality is seen in the context of Man's relationship with God, Man and Nature. Therefore the organization of disciplines and arrangement of subjects are planned with reference to Man as an individual, Man as a social being and Man as a being who has to live in harmony with Nature. (S. A. Ashraf, *New Horizons in Muslim Education*, 1985)

This is all very well as a charter of intent but what does it mean? There are certain structural faults in the edifice of contemporary Muslim scholarship which must be remedied by its architects. Islamic scholars must watch out for: too many generalizations of the 'Western scholarship is bad, Islamic is good' variety; too little critical self-analysis; charges of sexual chauvinism – no women scholars contribute to the recent Islamic volumes published by the Islamic Institutes and Academies referred to in this chapter; blurred thinking: Ibn Khaldun is singled out for criticism because he falls short of Islamic scholarship by Ba-Yunus and Farid Ahmad in the series edited by Ashraf, and as the ideal Islamic scholar by Hossein Nasr in his Foreword to Ashraf's book; the dangers of academic ethnocentricity; and creating one-man intellectual shows, which most of the contemporary Islamic centres are in danger of becoming.

Muslim social scientists suggest a revolutionary role for themselves as modern-day Islamic scholars – *faqih* and *ulema* (Ismail al-Faruqi, Ba-Yunus and Farid Ahmad). They wish to expand their role to include the religious domain. But their knowledge of society *as it is* rather than the nebulous concepts of society *as it ought to be* imagined by theologians will determine how Muslims see themselves. They must learn to be clinically accurate; they must not fall into the trap of Islamic chauvinism.

Islamic economics

Is there such a thing as Islamic economics? Muslims argue that if there is a Marxist or a Keynesian economics why not an Islamic economics? Muslim thinkers, starting with Ibn Khaldun, known to the world as a sociologist, are cited to support the point. Islamic economics, as viewed by its protagonists, and there are a growing number, is distinct from the capitalist and socialist economic systems. The major difference lies in the application of Islamic morality to economic systems.

The starting point is the central concept of *tauhid* (God's unity and sovereignty). That Allah has made the earth for man – hence the good things it produces are his to enjoy – is made explicit in the holy Quran. Also explicit is man's central role in the universe as *khalifa*, God's viceregent on earth. From this follows the strong moral imperative to care for one another. 'Basic needs' – the current development jargon – are the right of every human being. Basic needs in the Islamic framework include the right to education, transport, founding of a family and ensuring self-reliance. Conspicuous consumption is strongly discouraged. Both the Quran and the life of the Prophet – the two major sources of Islamic life – support austerity. The Prophet's saying aptly sums up the position, 'my poverty is my pride'.

The Islamic concepts of *al-adl* or equilibrium and *al-ahsan* or compassion are keys to understanding Islamic economics and society. Islam sets out to create 'balance' in society and 'balanced' people.

Islamic economics is thus embedded in Islam. In Islam, Professor Khurshid Ahmad writes, 'Human life is looked upon as an organic whole and its problems are approached, not in a purely mechanistic way, but in the light of the moral values and social ideals that Islam expounds' (in *Studies in Islamic Economics*, 1981. Also see Introduction to N. Naqvi, *Ethics and Economics: An Islamic Synthesis*, 1981). For the Muslim ' "progress" and "prayer" do not represent two water-tight compartments but two sides of the same coin.' Recent development in Muslim countries has created confusion as it is 'Islam-neutral', argues the Professor.

As Western capitalist and socialist theories – such as those of Professors Paul Samuelson and Otto Eckstein – are no longer viable universal models there is an urgent need to work at developing an Islamic system for the Muslim countries.

This urgency was reflected in the Second International Conference on Islamic economics held in March 1983 in Islamabad and inaugurated by the

President of Pakistan. The main champions of Islamic economics were prominent at the conference. A few words on the conference, which I attended as a delegate, may throw further light on Islamic economics and its practitioners.

About 300 delegates attended the conference and 25 papers, 14 in English and 11 in Arabic, were read. The sessions were well attended, the discussion serious and the time-table strenuous. When Professor Khurshid Ahmad suggested a small 'nap' in the afternoon to break the gruelling pace a younger economist over-ruled him, saying, 'Muslims have been napping for centuries, it is time to wake up.'

Rarely did the rhetoric assume stridency. The economists argued for 'academic vigour and scholarly detachment'. The tone was that of a serious international university seminar. Indeed, some participants were unsparing of Muslim society in their comments. Sadiq al-Mahdi, past and future Prime Minister of Sudan and great-grandson of the Mahdi, made two major points: women were conspicuous in the conference by their absence, and self-criticism should be even sharper.

One positive effect of such exercises has been to force traditionally Westernized Muslim economists – notably from Turkey which was well represented – back to the Quran. Every major argument is backed by references to the Book and examples of the life of the Prophet. The earnestness of the exercise underscores the need to think out issues seriously and dispassionately by Muslim economists and demarcate areas of interest.

There is a certain undergraduate exuberance about Islamic economists. Like Wordsworth during the French Revolution Muslim economists feel bliss to be alive in today's world of Islamic revolution and resurgence. But are they better Muslims than economists? Is Islamic economics only fizz and pop? There is a great deal of serious work to be done. Conceptual fuzziness remains. Bertrand Russell, a self-confessed atheist, is cited without a trace of self-consciousness (by N. Naqvi in *Ethics and Economics: An Islamic Synthesis*, 1981). Iqbal is constantly invoked to attack Marx, his verses in praise of Lenin discreetly overlooked. Some of the welfare programmes look as though they have been lifted without changing a comma from a Western liberal manifesto.

As a social scientist my major complaint could be applied to economists generally not just the Islamic ones. Too much of the argument is ethereal and macro. We confront 'models' and statistics but rarely people. I would like to see economic theories related to actual social structures, real societies.

At the forefront of Islamic economics are, again, South Asians: Pakistanis like Professors Khurshid Ahmad, N. Naqvi, and Indians like N. Siddiqui. They dominated the conference as they dominate the International Centre for Islamic Economics at the King Abd-al-Aziz University, Jeddah. However nebulous Islamic economics in its present form, the attempts to define it are of interest not only to economists but to all those interested in Muslim society. And if Islamic economics why not Islamic anthropology?

Islamic anthropology

Anthropology is well placed to define the Muslim ideal and assist in its construction; therefore many of the arguments in this book will be reflected in the discussion on Islamic anthropology. The method of anthropology allows it special insights into the way people behave and live; its scope covers the entire gamut of daily life.

The subject of Islamic anthropology as distinct from Western anthropology raises serious questions in the discipline. These are of a philosophic as well as an anthropological nature. For better or worse the issue of Islamic anthropology has been raised by Muslim anthropologists. In particular, those studying Muslim societies are faced with questions of a fundamental nature. Let us explore some of the possible problems – and there are as many for Muslims as there are for non-Muslims – that must follow in its wake, with no pretensions at solving them in this section. Three basic problems may be identified, first, that of definition.

What is Islamic anthropology? The answer lies in the rejection of Western anthropology by Islamic anthropologists because, as Professor A. Elkholy observes, 'The field attracted two types of people: missionaries and colonial administrators' ('Towards an Islamic Anthropology' in *Muslim Education Quarterly*, vol. 1, no. 2, 1984). Western anthropology is acceptable only 'if purified from the subversive material, methods, and terminology of the missionaries and colonial administrators.' Elkholy asks, 'Can the Muslim accept the assumptions of the discipline?' The answer, clearly, is in the negative.

Islamic anthropology is therefore linked to Islam by these Muslim anthropologists. Does this mean that only Muslims can be Islamic anthropologists? And if Muslims, of what sect? If the 'right' sect, how 'good' must they be as Muslims? And who will determine their worthiness?

An attempt to answer the last question is made by another practitioner of Islamic anthropology, Professor M. Mauroof. He warns: 'The Muslim anthropologist stands under the terrible charge of prostituting his mind and betraying his tradition if he continues to ignore the Islamic anthropological legacy and to think, write and teach as if he were a Westerner' ('Elements for an Islamic Anthropology' in al-Faruqi and Naseef, 1981). For these anthropologists Muslim society is ideal. No cleavages cause tension in it, no blemishes mar it. Even ethnicity is absent. Muslims in 'any Muslim city . . . parade on the streets in total un-consciousness of one another's ethnic differences.' But we are dealing with actual, empirically observed reality, not an abstract ideal.

Ethnicity, as we know, often plays an important role in the politics of Muslim society. In Pakistan ethnicity dominates social and political life, in spite of the majority belonging to one religion. For example: in 1971 Bengalis, rejecting Punjabi-dominated West Pakistan, created Bangla Desh; in 1973 riots in Karachi between Sindhis and non-Sindhis cost many lives; and again, in the last couple of years, in the interior of Sind lives were lost as Sindhis battled a Punjabi-dominated administration supported by the army. In the winter of 1986 ethnic riots paralysed Karachi and Quetta, taking a heavy toll in human lives.

Anthropologists like Clifford Geertz have argued that race and language, the main components of ethnicity, play a major role in the new states generally and in South Asia particularly. Mauroof's statement is remarkable for a South Asian, more so as he is from Sri Lanka where ethnic riots have recently torn the fabric of society. His Islamic anthropology, critics would be tempted to say, is too much Islam, too little anthropology.

Elsewhere regional passions break through the surface of Islam. Elkholy, an Arab, having begun his paper cited above with a universalistic Islamic position unconsciously – perhaps inevitably – veers to a parochial one. He equates Islam with Arabism by asking 'How can the Arab society achieve social justice?' This is followed by a discussion – again inevitable – of Zionism and Palestine.

Not only are the younger Islamic anthropologists disenchanted with the West. More serious, perhaps, is the rejection out of hand of Western scholarship by older, more established, Muslim intellectuals like Khurshid Ahmad and Altaf Gauhar (who edited, respectively, *Islam: Its Meaning and Message*, 1976, and *The Challenge of Islam*, 1978). Even Professor Fazlur Rahman, himself once under attack from religious conservatives, doubts the impartiality of Western scholarship ('The Academic Study of Islam', in *Islam and the History of Religions*, ed. R. C. Martin, 1982). Serious charges, indeed, from serious scholars.

The set of questions raised above may be counter-posed by an important, logical riposte: are there, then, to be Jewish, Hindu, Buddhist anthropologies? Are we not thereby restricting a universal science to particularistic groups in the face of opposite trends in the discipline? The above complex questions may be met by simple answers. Western anthropology, it has been argued, is embedded in recent Western colonial history. It is, thus, tainted and its claims to be neutral or fair are weak. Furthermore, it may be argued that there are already existing, fairly well-defined 'schools' in the discipline. Some of these are – albeit loosely – based on nationality such as a Soviet or British anthropology. There are others rooted in ideological ground, notably Marxist anthropology. So why does the concept of an Islamic anthropology raise so many hackles?

A second fundamental problem concerns the role of Islamic anthropology as an applied science. It cannot be a passive or neutral science. It would attempt solutions to the major social problems facing humanity in the late twentieth century. The Islamic use of the word *jihad*, striving – popularly seen as religious war – to better the world, is apt.

The argument to apply anthropology to practical problems is not necessarily a popular one in mainstream Western anthropology. But my argument is based on the assumption that the discipline, by adding a key dimension to human knowledge, has much to offer practically. The assumption touches a raw nerve in the discipline. Is anthropology to be restricted to a handful of students who work sometimes for as long as a decade with a remote group on an exotic aspect of their lives, or is it to have wider, more general, more practical application? Such questions reflect a deeper crisis in Western anthropology itself, a crisis which has not been resolved. The emergence of an Islamic anthropology will benefit the crisis. If nothing else, it will act as a corrective to the notorious ethnocentricity of much of Western anthropology.

The third fundamental problem facing Islamic anthropology concerns the nature of Islam. Islam not only encourages commitment, it demands it; it not only strives for moral consensus, it insists on emotional loyalty as well. Islamic ideology has, as we know, much to say about an entire range of social issues, behaviour and organization. There is an important social side to Islam. From birth to death, through the rites of passage, how a Muslim eats, walks and speaks is suggested in text and tradition. Muslim sociology for Islam is the manifestation of its theology.

Certain characteristics of Islam are also important in relating it to our subject. Islam is a universal religion speaking to humanity. The Prophet in his last great address at Arafat summed up his philosophy by decrying barriers between people. Islam, for him, transcended divisions of caste, colour and race.

Islam also places gaining of *ilm*, knowledge, at the highest level of human endeavour. Text ('Say: Travel through the earth and see now how God originated creation', Surah 29, *Al Ankabut*, the spider) and tradition ('seek knowledge, even unto China', the Prophet) strongly support learning whether through travel to other lands or interaction with other groups. People are exhorted to contemplate, to think of and marvel at, the multitude of variety in the heavens and on earth: 'And among His signs are the creation of the heavens and earth, and the variations in your languages and your colours', Surah 30, *Ar-rum*, the Romans. Islamic anthropology is thus ideally placed to fulfil Islamic endeavour.

Islam is, above all, the middle way according to the Quran; in its geographical and historical position it became literally so. The ideal Muslim balances *din*, religion, with *dunya*, the world. Islam's intellectual triumphs were recorded when Muslims interacted with Greek, Hindu and Christian thought. From Al

Ghazzali to Iqbal the greatest Muslim thinkers have responded to non-Muslim thinking. Traditionally Islam has ideally acted as a bridge between different systems.

It is this permanent and dynamic link between religion and society that many people in the West find difficult to appreciate. To them after a struggle of centuries religion was first controlled in and then ejected from social ideology. Marvellous technical and scientific achievements followed. Along this linear progress were signposts to the rational and scientific man. The word religion to them, understandably, smacks of priests, Inquisitions and the middle or dark ages.

Non-Muslims may see more Islam than anthropology in Islamic anthropology, Muslims more anthropology than Islam. When introducing a seminar on Islamic anthropology at the École des Hautes Études en Sciences Sociales in Paris in June 1984 I said, half in earnest, I may appear as if I have just flown in from Tehran. But, I added, I would deliver the same lecture at Kuala Lumpur to the Third International Conference on the 'Islamization of Knowledge'. For some colleagues there I would appear as if I have just arrived from Moscow. Professor Imtiaz Ahmad, the Indian anthropologist, who attended the seminar, later said he was thinking of the same thing.

The problem for the concerned anthropologist is to bridge the gap between different theoretical positions. My own efforts in this direction are speculatory and far from satisfactory (*Toward Islamic Anthropology*, 1986.) The anathema attached to Western anthropology as a child of Western imperialism by Muslim anthropologists like Elkholy and Mauroof is a false one, I suggest. The first professional and practising anthropologist is probably the eleventh-century scholar Al Beruni (see chapter 5, section 2). He is a small but important link between Western and Islamic anthropology. I see the need for a holistic analysis of Muslim groups within the frames of Islamic history and theology. We must also not lose sight of the continuing impact on Western anthropology of Orientalism, as defined by Edward Said. Sometimes these influences are as seductive as they are subtle. Professor Dale Eickelman's book, *The Middle East: An Anthropological Approach* (1981), has a chapter on Orientalists called 'Intellectual Predecessors'. Eickelman was, I am sure, innocent of the Saidian implications. Certain suggestions for a meaningful synthesis between Western anthropology and Islamic anthropology have been made in my book. In concluding I have underlined the universalistic and humanistic philosophy of Islam. The charter of an Islamic anthropology is thus humankind.

The label of Islam is not sufficient to produce good anthropologists or anthropology. Indeed, according to our definition, some of the finest material in Islamic anthropology is being produced by non-Muslims of diverse backgrounds. This includes the work of Professors Ernest Gellner in Cambridge, Clifford Geertz at Princeton, Marc Gaborieau in Paris and Mitsuo Nakamura in Tokyo. To my mind such anthropologists have provided the most meaningful analytic methods of studying Muslim society. Ernest Gellner, who worked in Morocco, suggests a 'pendulum swing theory'. Muslim social groups oscillate between P – urban, puritan, literate society and C – rural, informal, illiterate society. Adding data to the Moroccan material from the other end of the Muslim world, Indonesia, Clifford Geertz distinguishes *santri* groups (orthodox, traders) in opposition to *abangan* and *prijaji* ones (animistic, peasant), the former seeing the latter as idol-worshippers.

The idea behind Islamic anthropology is thus not to belittle Western anthropology and its achievements, or to annul its past, but to create an additional body of knowledge based on scientific and unbiased information which adds to our understanding of it. Anthropology to me has helped in understanding, and therefore making sense of, seemingly strange, exotic customs practised by alien people in far-away places. The contrast between different peoples and their customs and my own environment has helped me to understand myself and my society better. Anthropology for me plays a key role in bridging the gaps that divide people. It can help us to appreciate that we are a global community.

Socrates' statement, 'I am not an Athenian or a Greek, but a citizen of the world', is today better understood literally not philosophically. People all over the world are irreversibly interlocked through the power of high technology – computers, video-cassette recorders and satellite television. In this complex world of ours anthropology can assist, in its own low-key but meaningful way, in understanding the major contemporary problems such as those of population, refugees, poverty, drugs, pollution, famine and hanging over it all the threat of nuclear doom (see next chapter). This application to me is the relevance of anthropology in today's world and its special destiny in making sense of it. To validate the assertion that Islamic anthropology is a universal science it would be necessary for Muslim anthropologists to examine some of the problems of non-Muslim societies from an Islamic perspective. What does Islam have to say about them and what remedies are available through the application of Islamic anthropology? Have Muslims themselves solved these problems? The relevance of the answers would determine the fate of Islamic anthropology for non-Muslims; their quality, its future.

11

Only connect

To me certain basic values are universally held by human beings regardless of religion, race or caste. These include hospitality, friendship and kindness. Such values connect people. 'Invite others towards good, establish good deeds and prohibit what is bad' (Surah 3, *Al Imran*, the family of Imran). Although embedded in the Muslim ideal they are not the exclusive property of the Muslims, as this chapter will illustrate. This will be made clear when we see how and where different groups belonging to different religions and races come together or collide with each other. In both actions lies the assumption of a larger relationship linking groups to a common humanity, transcending race and religion.

Muslims, turning a blind eye to their own societies, see sybaritic systems, political intolerance and senseless violence as some of the characteristics of Western societies. Of these the USA appears to bewitch Muslims – whether as friends (Egypt, Saudi Arabia, Pakistan) or foe (Libya). In Iran the relationship underwent a complete roundabout within a short space of time. From being the nearest thing to paradise on earth, the USA became the Great Satan. Whichever, friend or foe, the relationship is complex, one of love-hate. It holds Muslim society in thrall.

1 AMERICAN SOCIETY: GREAT SATAN OR PARADISE ON EARTH?

The USA projects conflicting images of its undeniable strengths and weaknesses. It therefore rouses conflicting emotions. It has made two major contributions to the modern world: the nearest thing to a working democracy which includes rights to hitherto neglected groups and the greatest technical advances and scientific achievements known to humanity culminating with the walk on the moon. But while it excels in high technology, micro-chips, communications and space exploration, it cannot hold families together, dispel depression and drugs. Strong on science, the USA appears weak on society. American contradictions affect its foreign dealings and abroad they appear farouche one moment, eupeptic another and imperious the next.

Once, a long generation ago, the USA emerged from the Second World War, seeing itself as the champion of what it termed as the free world, a knight in shining armour. It was an idyllic picture drawn by Norman Rockwell. Sanity had been suspended in the most devastating war in history; a new order was to follow, one promising hope and glory. The USA was the society of the future. It stood for universal education, democracy and freedom. There was a spirit of challenge in the land, of adventure and enquiry. The USA had come close to achieving these ideals.

In an age devastated by a global war, America produced approximately half of the world's manufactures. It was a nation of awesome power and energy. While the other major powers – Russia, Britain, France, Germany, Japan – were heading down, the victorious USA towered as the pre-eminent economic and military power. The hubris of Americans like Henry Luce, founder of *Time* magazine, was understandable: 'American experience is the key to the future. . . . America must be the older brother of the nations in the brotherhood of man.'

The USA still remains a paradise for people seeking to escape from poverty or persecution, including Muslim scholars (chapter 10). For them, like earlier arrivals, it is literally a 'new world', a world promising the individual dignity and hope. It remains a land of plenty, with the supermarkets full to bursting. Individuals are friendly and the land vast. The standards of living are high, the universities excellent, the parks magnificent and the capacity for individual expression unlimited. The myths of Horatio Alger and Abraham Lincoln are embedded in this perception. There is 'room at the top' for those with talent or prepared to work. The 'green card', the passport to staying on in the USA, is still the dream of immigrants from all over the world. But the times are changing for the Americans.

For Muslims claims of American heroism or supremacy would appear absurd, confirming its empty arrogance. Much has changed since the last world war. The Soviets have achieved nuclear and Europe and Japan economic parity. And through the vicissitudes of recent history Muslims see one consistent feature in American foreign policy – its support of Israel. When Israel annexed Muslim lands and tortured and terrorized their inhabitants, American commitment did not waver. At Sabra and Shatilla its armed forces killed Arabs in the same way its historians accuse Nazis of killing Jews: by unrestrained genocide. The American posture explains why many Muslims – particularly the Arabs – prefer the godless Soviets to Christian America. Uncle Sam's image is tarnished for them. The knight is ailing; and – like John Keats' knight – in danger of finding itself 'alone and palely loitering'.

American history seems to be marked by a steady and irrevocable decline. The assassination of the Kennedys, Martin Luther King and Malcolm X snuffed out political dreams. Watergate exposed the myth of democracy and fair play in government. The deaths of the American idols Marilyn Monroe, Elvis Presley and Janis Joplin, and the random violence – Hinckley shooting at the President, John Lennon being shot dead by a stranger in the street – speak of an irrational, lunatic streak in American life. Insecure, everyone is armed, which is both cause and effect of the violence.

In May 1986 the random violence came home to me in a personal and tragic manner when my friends Professor Ismail al-Faruqi and his wife were stabbed to death by an unknown assailant in their university home in Pennsylvania (previous chapter).

Where Muslims are stimulated by some of the most brilliant minds and discoveries of the modern world in the USA – which can boast 121 Nobel Prize winners – they are also uncomfortable with the American obsession to compete: first on the moon, the fastest on earth, the biggest, the latest. In turn, the ethos of competition creates neurosis in society; people are no longer satisfied. More is better – more money, more sex, more property. It is a society with too much freedom, too many expectations. Suicide, drug abuse, depression, divorce, incest, rape and hysteria regarding venereal diseases – herpes last year, AIDS this year – are the indices, signs, of insatiable self-indulgence. People appear to live only to enjoy sex and gorge food. In this direction a vital civilization has gone astray, its exuberance dissipated, its social life a parody of its phallus and palate obsessions.

The very core of society, the nuclear family, appears to be disintegrating. Frequent divorces (1 in 3 or is it 2 now?), residence transfers and job changes of the parents leave a permanent sense of insecurity in the child. Parental neglect has become a way of life – only one of three children under the age of eighteen lives with both natural parents. The insecurity is further heightened by the cardinal principle of the American way, once so suited to frontier life, the need to be independent and assertive. From an early age the child is taught to fend for itself. American television daily beams the jingle 'the most important person in the whole wide world is you'. 'I' and 'me' are the most important words in the child's vocabulary. Groups in the Mid-West, as remote as on another planet, await the inevitable nuclear war in comfortable bunkers, frightening away visitors with guns. Only 'I' and 'me' matter. The spirit of the jungle, creatures snarling and snapping at each other, pervades the big cities. The jails are bursting with unrepentant and disorderly inmates, the streets of the cities unsafe. The old and weak, black or white, are vulnerable to muggings and violence. By the time the citizen is retired, old and perhaps sick and feeble, he faces numerous problems: where will he live? who will care for him? His nuclear family has crumbled; his prospects are bleak. Perhaps the worst ailment in American society is loneliness, especially in the aged. The plight of these Americans is summed up by Oscar Wilde, the master of the epigram:

> Something was dead in each of us,
> And what was dead was Hope.

In contrast Islam emphasizes the group and community. Three of the five injunctions of Islam – prayers, fasting and *haj* – are directly related to group activity and participation. The Muslim is rarely alone. Because of the emphasis on the group the Muslim family is still relatively cohesive and not broken down. Children are secure and sons pampered. Muslims can boast that their societies may need a RSPCA but not a society for the prevention of cruelty to children.

The USA has indeed marvellous achievements in science and technology to its credit but all is not well with *Homo sapiens*. The collective images conjure a futuristic world of the astronauts, space shuttles and shining technology, but also that of the anthropologists, mumbo-jumbo and magic.

A random selection of some popular films, box-office hits, will confirm this, although they are not to be taken as a yardstick of American artistic excellence. The themes are either cataclysmic disasters (*Avalanche*, *The Towering Inferno*, *Earthquake*), senseless violence (*Amityville*, *Halloween* – so popular that two sequels followed of both) or goblins and fantasy (*E.T.*, *Superman*, *Star Wars*, *Poltergeist* and their sequels). Another theme is the helplessness of the individual in the face of an arrogant and insensitive society. The lone individual challenges authority successfully (*Rambo* I and II, *Death Wish* I, II and III) and unsuccessfully (in a prison situation, *Cool Hand Luke*, and in hospital, *One Flew Over the Cuckoo's Nest*). The effort to make sense of modern life appears to have exhausted an entire civilization. It appears to be reverting to more traditional ways – ritual murder, witchcraft and senseless violence. We were back to square one, back to the jungle, voodoo and mumbo-jumbo.

Muslims who feel that these trends reflect a malaise in American society have no right to be smug. The same films are out every night in the video centres of Muslim cities, from Casablanca to Kuala Lumpur. And they are not restricted to urban groups. The deepest, most isolated recesses of the Muslim world have been penetrated (as we saw in chapter 8 when considering Saudi society). At this point the two civilizations feed each other, each other's neurosis.

The concept of individualism

It is the relationship between individualism and equality which differentiates the Muslim and Western, especially American, systems. The relationship inspires political scientists and leaders as much as it frustrates them. It is still to be discussed in the context of Western culture. The industrial and the American revolutions, technical advance, growth of democracy, etc. in the West are justifiably linked to each other by the notions of the supremacy of the individual and that of equality.

Islam presents an interesting if somewhat contradictory picture: although there is minimum premium to the individual the highest value is placed on equality. The individual is clearly subordinate to the *ummah*. God is the focus, the pivot, of creation and everything else takes its cue from this reality. But before God human beings are equal. The egalitarianism in Islam is genuine and pronounced. The daily prayers, and the very formation in which they are said, confirm this. Similarly, during the *haj* to Makkah Muslim status and race signs are removed as pilgrims tie around them the prescribed two-piece cloth.

It is of course the Muslim tribesman, across the Muslim world from the Berber in Morocco to the Pukhtun in Pakistan, whose society symbolizes egalitarianism. But bear in mind the Ibn Khaldunian thesis: maximum *asabyah*, when the tribe is at its most vigorous, is precisely the point when individualism is at its lowest. Once settled and in urban areas individualism supersedes, as it destroys, *asabyah*. So we confront a different situation to the West: one that suggests equality but discourages individualism – this is, of course, in theory.

In practice the data depict a depressing picture of inequality: royalty, holy lineages and strong chiefs lord it in society; women, children and the poor universally suffer. Politically, too, almost without exception the forty-four Muslim nations – keeping the fusion and fission between states constant for a moment – are run by different varieties of dictatorship. These exploit the holy Quran, often misquoting and misapplying it, in support of their rule. Many constitutions purport to be Islamic. In this post-Khomeini era not even the token bow to the British or American models is felt necessary.

To Tocqueville's categories of aristocratic and democratic societies we need to add another, a 'religious' society, one already suggested by Dumont. Agricultural, rural, still illiterate societies dominated by a major religion qualify. Islam or Hinduism are powerful social systems either blotting out or negating alien concepts. Western notions of individualism and equality do not feature in the indigenous normative context; what filters down is parody. An example is the Indian Civil Service, which, critics said, was neither Indian, nor civil nor a service. But there are points and values which connect peoples irrespective of different political and religious systems.

2 CONNECTING

Kindness to the distressed and generosity to the wayfarer are advised by the holy Quran – providing a main theme of the Islamic ideal. But these values are not exclusive to Islam; they are universal. Let me cite random examples, drawn from different parts of the world, to illustrate my contention. The first is from the remote tribal areas of the North-West Frontier Province of Pakistan (see chapter 7, section 2).

A young man drives late at night alone through the tribal areas on his way to Peshawar. These areas are still considered administratively unsettled, and traffic comes to a standstill in the afternoon. The young man has to hurry home. He speeds through the winding narrow roads of the mountains near Kohat, the home of the famed Afridi warriors. The jonquil lights of his car pierce the darkening mists of the winter night. Not a soul is stirring. On either side of the road the mountains loom large and dark.

He is thinking of the incident in 1923 when the Afridis kidnapped Miss Ellis from the Kohat military cantonment. It was an act of revenge against the British, and the empire responded with fire and thunder. Honour was at stake on both sides. When she was finally recovered from the tribal areas, Miss Ellis told the world she had been honourably treated by her captors. She became an instant international celebrity. She still recounts her story when the British empire has long vanished, and there is no malice towards her captors.

The young man is lulled into half slumber and suddenly he cannot take a curve fast enough. He skids off the road and into a ditch. The car lies helplessly on its side and he is miles from home late at night in one of the most ferocious areas of the world. A short time later, without warning, he sees ominous figures, armed with guns, looming around the car.

A voice speaks to him enquiring if he is injured. Fortunately he is not. But he is shaken. He is asked to follow his nocturnal companions. He becomes apprehensive. He has heard recent stories of kidnapping and murder in the tribal areas. But he has no choice and follows them home.

The Afridi patriarch, a big man with a heavy, red beard and shaven skull, greets him. He sets his mind at rest and orders his own sons to make the car road-worthy. There is, he observes solemnly, one condition. The traveller becomes tense. The condition is that the traveller must have dinner before leaving. Pleasant hours of companionship follow.

When the patriarch walks to the car to see off his guest, he has a suggestion. When the young man returns home, perhaps his father will be annoyed because of the damaged bumper, so may he offer money for repairs? The young man, already deep in the elder's debt, refuses. He drives away slowly to Peshawar, and the mountains no longer threaten.

Was it the well-known Pukhtun code of hospitality, so valued in Pukhtun society, which motivated the Afridis? Or was it a more universal desire in people to help strangers in distress? The answer may be gleaned from the next example.

A young Pakistani, eighteen years old, and his younger sister, barely in her teens, arrived in London for schooling. This was their first trip to the West, and both were bewildered and unsure. The money, streets, names and language appeared forbidding. The young man entered his sister in a boarding convent school just outside London and left for Cambridge. Feeling claustrophobic and alone in the strange atmosphere, the girl panicked. She hastily packed some clothes in a suitcase and ran away to find her brother in Cambridge. She managed to board a train which would bring her to her destination, but she did not know where to find him.

The flush of excitement passed and she confronted her journey with growing fear. Just then an old lady boarded the train and sat by her. When the ticket collector asked the girl for her ticket it became clear she had little idea of where she was going. The old lady intervened. She, too, it appeared, was headed for Cambridge, where she lived. Once they got talking the lady realized that the girl had no idea what kind of place she was going to nor where she would stay. She chided her for behaving in such an impetuous manner and then insisted that she stay with her. At Cambridge the old lady not only kept her guest for the next couple of days – spoiling her thoroughly – but helped her to locate her brother. They made an unlikely pair, the stern Victorian lady and the impetuous young Pakistani girl, but their affection was real.

What then, did the frail old lady in Cambridge and the hardy tribal patriarch on the Frontier have in common? If the explanation rests on the assumption of civilized behaviour at Cambridge, how do we explain that of the tribesman, purportedly wild and unruly? Conversely, if we explain the behaviour of the tribal warrior in terms of his code of honour, how do we explain that of the old lady? The answer is that both were moved at the moment of the encounter by a humanity transcending race, age and sex. By their actions they illustrated that however mankind is divided by passions generated on the basis of colour, caste and religion, no one people has a monopoly on goodness.

Only connect

Connecting broken lives in India and Pakistan, especially in the aftermath of the religious slaughter at Partition is an insurmountable task. But it is possible, as the following encounters illustrate.

'My father taught me if you see a Muslim and a snake kill the Muslim first,' the Indian, a Sikh, said to me in London with the candour of class-fellows in a distant land neutral to our passions. I was taken aback by the intensity of the emotion. The speaker was talking of the Partition of India in 1947 and claimed to come from Hazara where I spent my childhood. One day, I promised myself, I would explore the reasons behind the intensity of the emotion; I feared it would be a journey into my own past. Many years later, and after we had become fast friends, I found myself in Delhi visiting the family of my class-fellow for dinner.

There was something terminally melancholy about that hot, stifling night.

The senior ladies of the family and I were trying to weave something meaningful from the broken fabric of our lives, and we were not succeeding.

They came to Delhi in 1947 from Abbottabad, in Hazara; and my father, a serviceman who opted for Pakistan, boarding the train from Delhi, sent me to Abbottabad for schooling. In a sense our lives accurately reflected the trauma of Partition from the two opposite positions. We were refugees who had escaped to new lives and new lands. But like refugees everywhere the pain remained, the pain of a shattered life, of attempts to create a new one, of memories of past places and faces.

So much in the neat flat was familiar; the father was a serviceman and had recently passed away. Familiar were the books of Ghalib, Iqbal and even the holy Quran, the warm spontaneous hospitality, the food, the talk of Hazara, and the Urdu. The elder member of the family talked of their home and life in Hazara with tears dancing in her eyes. At first shy, like a swimmer testing the water, she soon spoke unreservedly. Her enthusiasm affected the younger members of her family, who had not known her land and who were sceptical and yet half-believing. The climate ('that perfect Hazara climate, cool in summer, snow in winter'), the hills, the dales, the lakes, the people, yes, indeed, the people, were described with increasing warmth. The 1907 District Gazetteer, written by Britishers and still the best account of Hazara, speaks of it as the District made by nature for the British.

Theirs was a large thriving Sikh family owning businesses and lands. It was strange to hear these modern liberated Sikh women – now reverted to their childhood – talking with enthusiasm of Muslim customs in Hazara such as the *purdah*. 'Of course, we had to cover ourselves as everyone knew our family. Our servants, *chokidars*, would escort us to the bazaar saying "out of the way, ladies are coming." ' In describing their happy childhood the pain had slipped and was replaced by a child-like joy, and they asked a hundred questions: how has Hazara changed? its people? its women? its schools? Names returned with fluency. Then the events of Partition intervened, unexpectedly, finally, like death, and the mood changed.

There was talk of Sikhs and Hindus being raped and killed in the villages of Hazara. One family of women and children was burnt alive in their house, it was said. In Abbottabad the girls felt terrorized. Fear and terror stalked the land. The family was escorted to Kashmir with assurances that they would be back shortly, and left Srinagar by air with a suitcase each. They were never to return. Bitterness replaced the sweetness of their memories as they contemplated the broken parts of their lives.

Old friends had betrayed each other; loyalties had collapsed and treachery was common. Even the loyal family *chokidars* had gone on the rampage. The family perceived Muslims as maddened with religious fanaticism; they saw them clearly as villains in the drama.

The unfolding of their lives in their new land was difficult and permanently embittered by Partition. The prospects of finding employment and accommodation were daunting. So was the problem of being a refugee. The local people in Delhi, after first emotions cooled, resented the competition from the outsiders and their social airs. Property claims, a mere pittance of the total, were paid fifteen to twenty years later by a sluggish bureaucracy. Perhaps the major problem was that the memories of the past did not completely die out. Indeed they remained to disturb the present. The male elder of the family did not attend the dinner that evening. The past was too painful for him and he did not wish to revive it.

I, also a victim of those events, now attempted to recount my story, to show how we were mirrored in each other's images and minds. I was a child – four years old – at Partition but the horror remains through the re-telling. My tale was almost the same as theirs. My parents had chosen to migrate to a land that promised them the safety of their religion (see 'You, my father' in chapter 7). Migration or *hijra* is crucial in Islam. We know that the Islamic calendar dates from the Prophet's *hijra* from Makkah to Madinah.

In 1947 established homes and families living in villages for generations were uprooted on an unprecedented scale. For us there was sudden flight with a few suitcases on the train to Pakistan. We missed our train at Lahore in spite of earlier bookings. Later we were to learn that all the passengers on it were killed between Lahore and Multan by Sikhs. Stories were circulating of passengers being raped and tortured to death. The only difference in my story was the religion of the villains. They were Sikhs and Hindus; maddened religious fanatics.

At one stroke my parents lost everything. Arriving in Pakistan as refugees, suspended in a rapidly changing and chaotic world, they were forced to redefine themselves. I, born in the plains of the Ganges, where the waves of the Sayyed saints and Pukhtun warriors – my ancestors – coming from the north had spent themselves, grew up in the beautiful valleys and mountains of Hazara which I learned to love.

Memories of those months in 1947 were bitter. I recounted a story of an uncle. He was a feudal lord, a *nawab*, who left his estate in the care of his Sikh friend, a class-fellow from Doon school in the hills. Only a few miles from the estate his confused wife thought she had left a jewellery box behind. The *nawab* told the group to keep moving, he would join them down the road, and returned to his home to fetch the box. He was never seen again. He had been hacked to death and the pieces were thrown into the family well. The jewellery box was found amidst the luggage when it was opened in Pakistan. On arrival in Pakistan his wife refused to believe he would not come. Every evening she stood by the door of her home looking out and repeating, 'I know *nawab sahib* will arrive any minute and I must welcome him.' She had lost her mind. Even after a generation my mother finds it difficult to mention her relative without tears.

In London I tried to coax another uncle to talk of those days by broaching the topic circumspectly. But his mind closed abruptly and he would not be drawn. His tension was plain to see; and it was compounded by happy memories of his youth, which he often mentioned, of tiger shoots and schooling in the Indian hills.

My hosts found it difficult to accept that the Sikh would have killed his best friend, just as I had found it difficult to believe that the Hazara villagers, whom I came to know, would run amuck killing Sikh women and children. So much information was based on rumour, and horror stories fed communal hate. When pressed they could not confirm names of Sikhs actually killed by Muslims; I, in turn, could only repeat the story of my uncle without hard evidence of his murderer.

Accompanying us to Pakistan was a Hindu couple. Lalo – from Lal – had long served my father. His wife, who looked after me like her own child, was my *ayah*, a native nanny. 'Where my sahib goes there will I serve,' said Lalo. 'I would die rather than leave my son,' said his wife. So they accompanied us to our new land. Lalo and his wife had expressed faith in my father, and my father had reflected confidence in the Islamic ideal. Pakistan was good to us, and with us Lalo and his wife prospered.

Looking back now I am struck by their example. They were leaving their home in India – a land devastated by Hindu-Muslim rioting – and arriving in one where Hindus were fleeing Muslims. Like ours their journey was one of faith; unlike ours their faith lay not in a religion but in human relationships. At the core of the universal Indian upheaval individual faith had survived.

Perhaps my hosts in Delhi and I were expressing a simplistic faith in our co-religionists, reflecting prejudices which are part of the myths of 1947. But in our pain we had become one.

For me that evening in Delhi summed up the relationship between Muslim and non-Muslim in South Asia. The tears were real, the bitter memories lingered, and the warmth was genuine. In the old ladies I saw my mother, in the younger people, my siblings, and the memories that lingered converted the relationship to a real one. 'We have just enough religion to make us hate, but not enough to make us love one another,' Swift had written. Perhaps now given a choice between a snake and a Muslim my class-fellow would have difficulty in deciding which to kill first. It is a comment on our times that this statement is in itself an advancement.

3 CONCLUSION: THE DISCOVERY OF ISLAM

In drawing in the main strands of this book it is apparent that we live in harsh, cruel times, on the edge of violence. The need for sympathetic understanding, of building bridges to, of knowing, other peoples, is all the greater. We have not lost sight of the Islamic ideals of piety, devotion, austerity and gentleness. Faisal's piety, Zia-ul-Haq's humility, Khomeini's austerity are recognized. But sceptics would point out, kindness and magnanimity are less conspicuous. Observe the treatment of political opponents, the indifference to the poor and dispossessed. Compare the final return of the Prophet to Makkah and his declaration of general amnesty to the unending bloodshed after Imam Khomeini's arrival in Tehran. Little *al-adl*, equilibrium, and less *al-ahsan*, compassion, in evidence here, the critics would aver.

We may find the gentler qualities elsewhere, in the behaviour of Sufis, in the company of scholars – Professor Faruqi, Dr Hameedullah, Sheikh Bin Baz – with their motto *sulh-i-kul*, peace with all, which guides them. Love, tolerance and peace are their message; one easily found in places like Ajmer, Makkah and Madinah.

Muslims are fond of stating that Islam is a complete way of life, a total ideology. In an important sense they are right. Islam, as we saw, carries the process for renewal and revolution within it. Although most revolutions contain similar central ideas of equality, fraternity and egalitarianism, the Iranian revolution is entirely an Islamic one. Symbols, allusions, references are Iranian; it is as native as the revolution of 1789 in France, 1917 in Russia and 1949 in China.

The revolutions in Russia and China brought down corrupt, inefficient, decaying social orders. But they were one-shot experiments. In turn the revolution solidified and congealed. China has come full cycle – there Marx is publicly pilloried.

In Islam renewal and revolution continue to give it dynamism and life. Islamic fervour knows no national boundaries, no class differences, no racial barriers. Throughout history it has transcended these. Islam emphasizes belief and behaviour over race, practice not blood. It is important how people behave, how their customs, culture and society are organized, not who their ancestors were. Islam in the ideal believes in 'nurture' not 'nature'; it transcends class and nation. It is notable that Marxism, the most seductive ideological force of modern times, has not been successful in Muslim societies although succeeding for short periods in certain areas. The reason is clear. Islam carries its own revolutionary charter within it; and this may be read as a prognosis for the future, too.

The past in the present

It is also incorrect to view Muslim society today as if the past did not exist. The Muslim views the world through the filter of the socio-historical categories we created in our theory of Islamic history. The past explains, as it relates to, the present. Not too deep down in Muslim society the pain of Andalusia still lingers; it is an old wound that flares up to remind Muslims that history can repeat itself. In another instance we see how certain central obsessions engaged the energies of the Muslim empires – the Ottoman, the Saffavid and the Mughal. The obsessions still haunt the successors of these empires. Turkey is still not rid of its obsession with Christian Europe; Iran once again recreates Shia society through revolution; and Pakistan is always facing, watching, what it sees as the minatory moods of India and responding with energetic attempts to maintain its Islamic identity. We are thus able to make sense of Turkey's generals, Iran's Ayatullahs and Pakistan's Islamization programme. An understanding of the past helps us to appreciate the present.

The notion of the Mahdi and the expression of millenarian populist movements in their push toward the ideal have provided a promise of hope, but also uncertainty, to Muslim society. Economic, political and ethnic discontent are thus channelled into these movements of which the leader is a Mahdi or Mahdi-like figure. The movements continue to create the dynamics of society and disturb the sleep of the wayward and corrupt ruler.

It is also abundantly clear that Islam's days of glory were created not by the sinews of its warriors but the vitality of its scholars and Sufis. More than the soldiers they were struggling *fi sabil Allah*, in the path of Allah. The scholars – jurists, historians, ethnographers and astronomers – expanded the frontiers of knowledge through study; the Sufis the frontiers of human relationships through compassion and understanding. Both, in their own ways, aimed for the Islamic ideal. Both would remain independent of the kings and courts. Many would feel the lash on their backs. But they would rarely falter. The end of Muslim scholarship and Sufi commitment was the cause and effect of European colonization. In the post-colonial era Muslims have yet to repair the damaged fabric of Islamic scholarship and Sufi thought.

The nineteenth-century European concepts of nationhood created ambiguity and tension among Muslims; nationalism was opposed to the notion of the *ummah*. The two were seen as contradictory (look, for example, at the life and thought of Jamaludin Afghani). Every generation would produce a movement for pan-Islamism which would stand in opposition, at least conceptually, to nationalism. But in the main by the late twentieth century the problem was, if not solved, at least accommodated. Nationalism absorbed and channelled Islamic fervour (as in Saudi Arabia, Iran and Pakistan, three nations discussed in this book). Islam was equated with nationalism. Different and interesting interpretations of Islamic nationalism, still with the ideal at the centre, would thus be available.

One result is obvious. There are too many directions, too many experiments. It may take another few generations before the *ummah* fully recovers from the damage of the colonial period. It will also have overcome its obsessive hatred of the West, its suspicion of non-Muslim nations – a logical consequence of the colonial encounter. In spite of the warp introduced by the colonial experience it is not easy to sustain the charge that Islam encourages bigotry. Once whole, secure again, the Islamic values of compassion and kindness will characterize it; Muslim civilization will be able to glow and ring with vitality again.

The threat to humanity

The problems that face humanity concern both Muslims and non-Muslims. Unchecked they could drastically affect the human race, even terminate it. The major contemporary problems – of ecology and environment, poverty, famine, drugs – mar but do not destroy social life. Those singled out threaten to destroy its fabric – as in the cases of refugees and population – or with nuclear war annihilate it altogether.

First, is the problem of refugees, including those of Palestine, South East Asia, or more recently, Afghanistan. It is not generally realized that about 75 per cent of the world refugee population is Muslim. Muslim history encourages migration in the face of persecution, as we have noted above. Frustrated, these refugees create instability in the region where they live. Finding an indifferent world they resort to hijacking and terrorism. They are dispossessed people, whose past is shattered, and whose future is suspended.

Second, is the population problem. Pakistan, created in 1947 with about 30 million people, has within forty years more than trebled the total to 100 million. The Muslim world maintains the highest rate of reproduction, 3 per cent, and altogether 150 children a minute, 80 million a year, are born round the world. World population doubles every 35 years: 2 billion in 1930; 4.6 billion in 1985 and it is estimated 9 billion by the second decade of the next century.

Third, hanging over everything, dwarfing all problems, feeding on the contradictions, on the edge of our consciousness like some horrific but inevitable nightmare, is the threat of universal nuclear doom (children playing with razors, Gandhi wrote of Western science).

Ours is a century disposed to battle: more people have been killed in war in this century than in wars in the rest of human history; lives lost through ignorant armies clashing by night. Without the use of nuclear bombs since the Second World War there have been 20 million civilian and military deaths in Third World conflict alone. Of these the bigger losses include: 3 million in the Korean war (1950–3), 2 million in Vietnam (1965–75), 2 million in the Nigerian civil war (1967–70), 1 million during the Partition of India (1946–8), half a million in the Iran-Iraq war begun in 1980 (R.L. Sivard, *World Military and Social Expenditures*, 1985; Keesing's *Contemporary Archives*). The recent world trend is not encouraging either. Since 1960 there have been 65 major wars resulting in 6.2 million civilian deaths (*American Annual World Military and Social Expenditures*, 1982). America caused 750,000 civilian deaths in South East Asia and the USSR 90,000 in Afghanistan (so far). In this frame of violence the bomb becomes the final argument, the final solution, threatening the very existence of the species.

The destruction caused by nuclear energy is not restricted to times of war, its use not determined by the compulsions and passions of battle. The recent accidents in the USA (Three Mile Island) and USSR (Chernobyl) prove this. They also prove the urgency of the threat and its universal nature.

More than the chariot and gunpowder in their day, the presence of the bomb influences behaviour in our times. The anxiety and uncertainty it creates generate a universal sense of imminent doom. Islam's confidence in the destiny of the human race is a corrective, its movements towards the ideal a stabilizing force.

The function of the ideal in history and society

We have seen how the ideal assists in explaining Muslim behaviour and historical sequences, how its functioning helps us to answer the questions raised at the beginning of the book. The ideal provides rulers with legitimacy and a rallying point for those who oppose them; for wayward sultans it is a pressure, for mindful saints a stimulus; for the learned it is a source of wonder, for the illiterate a part of mythology. All sections of society are affected by its presence, their actions to an extent determined by their understanding of it.

We saw how the Islamic ideal influenced Muslim history over the centuries and across the continents. How in the difficult colonial days it provided inspiration and hope to Muslims; how in more recent times it made a frame for them to organize their lives, whether as tribes, in villages or in cities; how it restrains Muslims when they are dominant and affluent (as in Saudi Arabia); how it sustains them in adverse situations as Afghan refugees or in India, the USSR and China; how it forges bonds that override ethnic divisions (as in the UAE); how it emphasizes the protection of the weak and exploited in society – such as women; how it points to the direction of learning and knowledge in societies with little time for either.

We have heard authentic Muslim voices across the world and from the earliest Islamic times. These are disparate, varied voices. From the past come Abu Bakr's accession speech, Khalid ibn Walid's challenge to Persian chiefs, the complaint of an Abbasid caliph helpless, a prisoner, in the splendour of his palace, and the disgust of an ordinary citizen with the state of affairs under the Arab caliphs; we hear the comments of Al Beruni on Hindu society in

India, Rumi on the mystery of Sufi mysticism, Aurangzeb at the end of his long life questioning the rigidity and blindness of a system he helped to create and came to symbolize; and with the emergence of European colonization, Ghalib speaks of his damaged Muslimness, Imam Shamyl valiantly fights against impossible odds to maintain an Islamic order, Sir Sayyed strives to salvage Muslim society in a period of transition and crisis. We hear from the present Dr Hameedullah, the gentle Islamic scholar in Paris, contrasting the intolerance of Muslim society with that of the West, Imam Khomeini on society and politics, a labourer from south India whose heart was broken, the anguished voices of the Baluch woman and the Arab girl, and more personal voices – that of my father who was born when the British ruled India, and that of my son who is being educated in Islamic Pakistan.

We have seen the rise and fall of empires – their eventual destiny symbolized by their deserted capitals built with grandeur and affection: Madinah-at-Zahra of the Umayyads in Spain, Samarra of the Abbasids in Iraq, and Fatehpur Sikri of the Mughals. The ruins are a testimony to the Quran: nothing remains except the name of God. Flux and reflux, we note the pattern, the rhythm, of history; we view the panorama of Muslim history and appreciate the complexity of Muslim society.

For Muslims the exercise illuminates the vitality and richness of their inheritance, for those outside Islam it provides a better understanding of it; an understanding which will exorcize the Islamic ghosts of those whose sleep is disturbed by them.

Ours has been a sociological exercise, not a theological explanation of Islam. We may sum it up by enunciating a simplified formula. The nearer to the ideal the minimum tension in society, the further from the ideal the maximum tension. The conjunction of ideal and actual is what Muslims strive for; the failure to achieve it creates stress in society. The formula can help us to interpret Muslim history and society. Rising and falling and rising again, there is rhythm in Muslim history. At its core, providing a constant measure, a powerful stimulus, is the ideal of Islam; Muslims living up to it, sometimes partly, sometimes fully. Because of the universal message of the ideal, transcending race and colour, and because of its rationality, it may help to connect, to build bridges between peoples and thereby provide answers to contemporary problems.

APPENDIX: Muslim chronology

BC	
853	First mention of Arabs, in an inscription of Shalmaneser III
25–24	Expedition of Aelius Gallus to southern Arabia
AD	
105–6	Fall of the Nabatean kingdom, part of which becomes a Roman province
c. 250	Rise of 'kingdom' of Palmyra
273	Aurelian suppresses Palmyra
525	Fall of Himyar – the Ethiopians occupy southern Arabia
570	Birth of Muhammad, the Prophet
575	Persian occupation of southern Arabia, which for a few years becomes a satrapy
602	End of Arab principality of Hira, on Iraq-Arabian borderlands
610	Prophet receives call to Islam
622	*Hijra* of Prophet from Makkah to Madinah – beginning of Islamic era
624	Battle of Badr, first major Muslim victory
630	Prophet conquers Makkah
632	Death of Prophet. Abu Bakr becomes the first caliph
633–7	Arabs conquer Syria and Iraq. At Qadsya in 635 Arabs defeat Persians
639–42	Conquest of Egypt
644	Umar assassinated after being caliph for ten years
656	Murder of Uthman – beginning of first civil war in Islam
657–9	Battle of Siffin
661	Murder of Ali – beginning of Umayyad dynasty
680	Massacre of Hussain and supporters at Karbala
683–90	Second civil war
685–7	Revolt of Mukhtar in Iraq – beginning of extremist Shia
696	Abdul Malik introduces Arab coinage, as part of reorganization of imperial administration

710	Muslims land in Spain
712	Muslims conquer Sind
750	Fall of Umayyads, accession of Abbasids
751	Arabs capture Chinese paper-makers in Central Asia; use of paper begins to spread westward across Islamic empire
756	Umayyad prince Abdur Rahman becomes independent Amir of Cordova
762–3	Foundation of Baghdad by Mansur
767	Imam Hanifa dies
788	Independent Idrisid dynasty in Morocco
795	Imam Anas dies
803	Haroon-ur-Rashid deposes Barmecides
809–13	Civil war of Al Amin and Al Mamun follows Haroon's death
813–33	Reign of Al Mamun – development of Arabic science and letters
820	Imam Shafi dies
825	Aghlabids of Tunisia begin conquest of Sicily
833–42	Reign of Mutasim – beginning of Turkish domination
836	Foundation of Samarra
855	Imam Hanbal dies
868	Ahmad b. Tulun, a Turkish general, founds a dynasty in Egypt and later Syria
869–83	Revolt of negro slaves in southern Iraq
871	Rise of Saffavids in Persia
877	Death of Hunain b. Ishaq, translator of Greek scientific works into Arabic
890	First appearance of Carmathians in Iraq
901–6	Carmathian bands active in Syria, Palestine, Mesopotamia
910	Establishment of Fatimid caliphate in North Africa
922	Al Hallaj executed
923	Al Tabari dies
925	Death of physician Razi (Rhazes)
929	Abdur Rahman III of Cordova adopts title of caliph
932	Persian Buwayhid dynasty established in West Persia
935	Creation of office of *Amir al-Umara*, commander in chief of Turkish guards in the capital, and effective ruler
945	Buwayhids occupy Baghdad
956	Al Masudi dies
969	Fatimids conquer Egypt – found Cairo
c. 970	Saljuq Turks enter territories of caliphate from east. Mahmud of Ghazni invades India. Al Beruni visits and writes of India
1020	Firdausi dies
1030	Umayyad caliphate of Spain breaks up into 'Party Kingdoms'
1037	Death of Ibn Sina (Avicenna)
1048	Death of Al Beruni
1055	Saljuqs take Baghdad

1056–7	Hilali Arab invaders sack Qairawan
1061	Normans take Messina – begin conquest of Sicily
1070–80	Saljuqs occupy Syria and Palestine
1085	Christians capture Toledo
1086	Almoravid victory at Sagrajas
1090	Hassan-i-Sabbah seizes Alamut
1094	Death of Fatimid Caliph Mustansir; split in Ismaili movement, Hassan-i-Sabbah leads extremist (assassin) wing
1096	Crusaders arrive in Near East
1099	Crusaders take Jerusalem
1111	Death of Al Ghazzali
1127	Zangi, a Saljuq officer, seizes Mosul – Muslim regrouping against Crusaders
1171	Saladin declares Fatimid caliphate at an end – founds Ayyubid dynasty in Syria and Egypt
1187	Battle of Hattin. Saladin defeats Crusaders and captures Jerusalem
1220	Mongols conquer eastern territories of the caliphate
1236	Christians capture Cordova
1250–60	Emergence of Mamluk Sultanate in Egypt and Syria, from the decay of the Ayyubid kingdoms
1254	Alfonso X establishes a school of Latin and Arabic studies in Seville
1258	Mongols under Halagu Khan capture Baghdad and end the caliphate
1260	Mamluks defeat Mongols at Ain Jalut in Palestine
1273	Death of Rumi
1300	First Osmanli – hence Ottoman – the dynasty would last until 1922
1348	Construction of the Gate of Justice at the Alhambra, Granada
1400–1	Taimur ravages Syria
1406	Death of Ibn Khaldun
1453	Constantinople captured, renamed Istanbul, city of Islam
1492	Christians capture Granada
1498	Vasco da Gama sails to India via Cape of Good Hope
1501	Shah Ismail, first ruler of the Saffavid dynasty in Persia
1517	Ottomans conquer Syria and Egypt – destroy Mamluk Sultanate
1526	Babar captures Delhi at the first battle of Panipat
1529	Sulayman comes close to taking Vienna
1535	First Capitulations granted by Ottoman Sultan to France
1639	Ottomans finally wrest Iraq from Persia
1707	Aurangzeb, the last great Mughal Emperor, dies
1792	Death of Muhammad Wahab in Arabia
1798–1801	French occupation of Egypt
1801	Followers of Wahab sack Karbala
1803–4	Followers of Wahab sack Makkah and Madinah
1803	General Lake enters Delhi, Mughal Emperor reduced to a puppet
1804	Usman Dan Fodio defeats Hausa tribes
1805	Muhammad Ali becomes effective ruler of Egypt

1809	Beginning of regular shipping service from India to Suez
1820	British pact with Arab sheikhs on the Persian Gulf coast – beginning of British supremacy in the area
1822	Muhammad Ali establishes printing-press in Egypt
1830	French invade Algeria
1831–40	Egyptian occupation of Syria
1835	Macaulay's Minute on Education in India
1836	British steamboat service established on Iraqi inland waterways. Beginning of regular British steamship service to Egypt and Syria
1839	British occupation of Aden
1850s	'The time of the *Shariah*' in the Caucasus. Imam Shamyl
1851–7	Alexandria-Cairo-Suez railway built
1857	Revolt against British in India. End of Mughal dynasty
1861	Creation of autonomous Lebanon
1869	Suez Canal opened
1875	Founding of Muhammadan Anglo-Oriental College at Aligarh
1880s	onwards. Extraordinary Sufi activity in Africa – Tijani, Sanusi, Mahdist – and in Asia – Naqshbandi
1881	French occupy Tunisia
1882	British occupy Egypt
1901	Ibn Saud begins the restoration of the Saudi emirate of Najd
1902	Ibn Saud captures Masmak, the fort of Riyadh
1906	Muslim League established in India
1908	Young Turk revolution
1911–12	Italians seize Libya
1916	Arab revolt in Hijaz. Sharif Hussain assumes title of king
1918	End of Ottoman rule in Arab lands
1920	Mandates established for Syria and Lebanon (French), Palestine, Transjordan and Iraq (British)
1924–5	Ibn Saud conquers Hijaz
1932	End of Mandate in Iraq Ibn Saud proclaims Saudi Arabian kingdom
1934	Ibn Saud defeats the Yemen in short war. Peace treaty of Taif
1936	Anglo-Egyptian treaty, recognizing independence of Egypt
1940	Muslim League in Lahore passes Pakistan Resolution. Struggle for Pakistan under Muhammad Ali Jinnah begins
1941	End of Mandate for Syria and Lebanon, which become independent republics
1945	League of Arab States formed
1946	Britain recognizes independence of Transjordan, which becomes a monarchy
1947	Pakistan created
1948	End of Mandate for Palestine – establishment of state of Israel – Arab-Jewish war. Hyderabad and parts of Kashmir States occupied and merged with India by Indian troops

1951	Libya becomes an independent kingdom
1953	Egypt becomes a republic Ibn Saud dies
1954	Colonel Jamal Abd al-Nasir becomes leader in Egypt
1955	British evacuation of Suez Canal zone – signature of Baghdad Pact
1956	Sudan, Tunisia and Morocco become independent – Egypt nationalizes Suez Canal – Israeli campaign in Sinai – Anglo-French expedition to Suez
1957	Tunisia becomes a republic
1958	Formation of United Arab Republic – Iraq becomes a republic. First Martial Law in Pakistan under General Ayub Khan
1960	Mauritania becomes independent
1961	Kuwait becomes independent – Syria withdraws from the United Arab Republic– 'Arab socialism' adopted in Egypt
1962	Algeria becomes independent. Republican revolution in the Yemen
1963	Revolution in Syria and Iraq
1965	Revolution in Algeria. India and Pakistan war
1967	Israel-Arab war. South Yemen becomes independent
1969	Muslim heads of state meet in Rabat
1971	India and Pakistan war. Pakistan's defeat creates BanglaDesh from East Pakistan.
1973	Ramadan war – Israel-Arabs
1975	King Faisal assassinated
1977	General Zia-ul-Haq deposes Bhutto; Third Martial Law; the Islamization of Pakistan begins
1979	Khomeini overthrows Shah of Iran. Islamic government. Soviet troops enter Afghanistan. Juhaiman attempts to seize the Kaaba
1981	Anwar Sadat assassinated
1986	Martial Law lifted in Pakistan Professor Ismail Faruqi and wife murdered in the USA

GLOSSARY
of Islamic terminology

adab manners, proper behaviour
al-adl equilibrium (Quranic concept)
al-ahsan compassion (Quranic concept)
bida innovation
caliph from *Khalifat*, successor. Ruler of Islam
din religion, life of piety – see *dunya*
dunya world, life of the world; the here and now – see *din*
fana annihilation, Sufi concept, merger with God
hadith sayings – and doings – of the Prophet, his traditions
haj the annual pilgrimage; it is obligatory for every Muslim once in a lifetime
hijra departure, emigration; from the Prophet's *hijra* to Madinah
ijma consensus
ijtihad independent judgment
ilm knowledge. Hence *alim*, scholar, *ulema*, scholars
Jahiliyya age of ignorance; time before coming of Islam
jihad striving spiritually or physically against evil; colloquial: religious war
nasab ancestry, lineage
qiyas analogical reasoning
Rahman, Rahim Beneficent, Merciful – names of Allah
salaam peace, colloquial: greetings. Hence Islam, religion of peace
salat prayer
Shariah law based on the Quran and the *sunna*; literally: the path to be followed
al-Shura consultation; colloquial: consultative body
sulh-i-kul peace with all; Sufi saying and motto
sunna custom, of the Prophet; hence *ahle-sunna* or followers of the *sunna* and Sunnis
tauhid unity of God
ummah Islamic community, brotherhood

BIBLIOGRAPHY: suggested readings

Ahmad, K. (ed.) (1976), *Islam: Its Meaning and Message*, Islamic Council of Europe, London. A collection by well-known Muslim scholars, statesmen and activists.

Ahmad, K. and Z. I. Ansari (1979), *Islamic Perspectives: Studies in Honour of Mawlana Sayyid Abul A'la Mawdudi*, The Islamic Foundation, UK. A wide-ranging collection of papers on Islam by Muslim scholars.

Ahmed, A. S. (1983), *Religion and Politics in Muslim Society: Order and Conflict in Pakistan*, Cambridge University Press, USA. Sociological analysis of the interaction between central authority, traditional and religious leadership at the district level in Pakistan; also applied to other Muslim societies outside Pakistan.

Ahmed, A. S. (1986), *Toward Islamic Anthropology: Definition, Dogma and Directions*, International Institute of Islamic Thought, USA. An attempt to frame an Islamic anthropology in relation to Western anthropology. Foreword by I. al-Faruqi.

Ahmed, A. S. and D. M. Hart (eds) (1984), *Islam in Tribal Societies: From the Atlas to the Indus*, Routledge & Kegan Paul, London. A collection covering North African, Middle Eastern, Central Asian and South Asian tribes by distinguished anthropologists.

Arberry, A. J. (1978), *Aspects of Islamic Civilization*, The University of Michigan Press, USA. An old classic. It remains full of delights containing a selection of poems, Sufi sayings and stories.

Asad, M. (trans.) (1980), *The Message of the Quran*, Dar al-Andalus Ltd, Gibraltar. Translation by Muhammad Asad, living in Morocco, with extensive contemporaneous notes.

Azzam, Abd-al-Rahman (trans.) (1979), *The Eternal Message of Muhammad*, Quartet Books, London. An Egyptian statesman's life of the Prophet handled with reverence and dignity.

al-Faruqi, I. and A. O. Naseef (eds) (1981), *Social and Natural Sciences: The Islamic Perspective*, Hodder & Stoughton and King Abd-al-Aziz University, Jeddah. Muslim scholars writing on social and natural sciences within an Islamic methodological and theoretical framework.

al-Faruqi, I. and L. L. al-Faruqi (1986), *The Cultural Atlas of Islam*, Macmillan. A richly illustrated coffee-table book with a substantial text.

Gellner, E. (1981), *Muslim Society*, Cambridge University Press, Cambridge. A collection – articles, reviews – written over a distinguished academic career by one of the most interesting Western social scientists, now at Cambridge.

Haykal, M. H. (trans. I. al-Faruqi) (1976), *The Life of Muhammad*, Trust Publications, North America. A sympathetic and authoritative study translated from the Arabic by a leading Muslim scholar.

Hitti, P. K. (1937; 1961, 1970), *History of the Arabs*, Macmillan, London. Standard textbook with extensive index.

Irving, T. B., K. Ahmad and M. M. Ahsan (1979), *The Quran: Basic Teachings*, The Islamic Foundation, UK. A collection by three Islamic scholars working in association with the Islamic Foundation in England.

Khomeini, Imam (trans. H. Algar) (1981), *Islam and Revolution: Writings and Declarations of Imam Khomeini*, Mizan Press, Berkeley. Faithful translation by Professor H. Algar, a European Muslim teaching at Berkeley, of wide range of topics.

Lings, M. (1983), *Muhammad: His Life Based on the Earliest Sources*, Allen & Unwin, London. Exhaustive study by one of the leading European Muslim scholars.

Rahman, F. (1979), *Islam*, University of Chicago Press, Chicago. A standard introduction after a life-time of Islamic studies. A Pakistani, Professor Rahman lives and works in Chicago.

Robinson, F. (1982), *Atlas of the Islamic World Since 1500*, Phaidon Press, Oxford. Delightfully illustrated and supported by clear text.

Said, E. W. (1981), *Covering Islam: How the Media and the Experts Determine how We See the Rest of the World*, Pantheon Books, New York. The follow-up to his earlier widely read *Orientalism*. Said's work reflects Arab passion and commitment.

Schacht, J. and C. E. Bosworth (eds) (1974), *The Legacy of Islam*, Clarendon Press, Oxford. Indicates the debt of the West to the Muslim world in all branches of learning.

Schimmel, A. M. (1981), *Mystical Dimensions of Islam*, University of North Carolina Press, Chapel Hill, USA. A scholar with a wide command of Muslim languages, Professor Schimmel divides her time between Germany and Harvard. This is Professor Schimmel's best known introduction to Sufism.

Shariati, A. (trans. H. Algar) (1979), *On the Sociology of Islam*, Mizan Press, Berkeley. Modern sociology and anthropology within an Islamic frame as worked out by one of the main intellectual leaders of Iran's revolution.

Index